Men in the middle

To Sally and our children,
my parents, Ogwiji,
and the Idoma

Men in the middle

Leadership and role conflict in a Nigerian society

—————

ALVIN MAGID

Manchester
University Press

Africana Publishing Company

© 1976 Alvin Magid

Published by
Manchester University Press
Oxford Road
Manchester M13 9PL

ISBN 0 7190 0583 3

Published in the United States of America by
Africana Publishing Company, A DIVISION OF
Holmes & Meier Publishers, Inc.
101 Fifth Avenue
New York, New York 10003

Library of Congress Cataloging in Publication Data

Magid, Alvin, 1937–
    Men in the middle.

    Bibliography: p. 270
    Includes index.
    1. Local officials and employees – Nigeria.
2. Leadership – Case studies. 3. Role conflict – Case
studies. 4. Social perception – Case studies. I. Title.

JS7656.4.A4 1976   301.15'53'09669   75–42145
ISBN 0–8419–0254–2

Design / computer composition / print in Great Britain
by Eyre & Spottiswoode Ltd at Grosvenor Press

Contents

Tables, figures, and maps

Figures

Maps

Abbreviations

AG   Action Group
IHRU   Idoma Hope Rising Union
MLG   Ministry for Local Government
NCNC   National Convention of Nigerian Citizens (prior to 1960,
National Council of Nigeria and the Cameroons)
NEPU   Northern Elements Progressive Union
NPC   Northern Peoples' Congress
UMBC   United Middle Belt Congress
UPP   United People's Party

Here we stand
infants overblown,
poised between two civilizations,
finding the balance irksome,
itching for something to happen,
to tip us one way or the other,
groping in the dark for a helping hand
and finding none.
I'm tired, O my God, I'm tired,
I'm tired of hanging in the middle way—
but where can I go?

Mabel Segun, 'Conflict', in
Frances Ademola, ed.,
Reflections: Nigerian Prose and
Verse (Lagos, Nigeria: African
Universities, 1962), p. 65.

Preface

For some time now my interests as a political scientist have centred on role conflict and on the Idoma, a people in Nigeria's lower 'Middle Belt' sector. *Men in the Middle* is an attempt to wed the two interests. During that time, many have encouraged and assisted me in the enterprise. I acknowledge them here.

Lewis Edinger first stimulated my interest in 'role theory' and, by extension, in role conflict as well, and it was he who directed my attention to Nigeria as a country where fieldwork might usefully be undertaken. William Hanna carried on from there, spending many hours with me discussing my research. My appreciation for their efforts, and for the camaraderie which I have long shared with both men, cannot be adequately conveyed in these few words. Some years ago Eugene Jacobson and Joseph Roberts asked probing questions about role conflict which have stuck with me. *Men in the Middle* is a partial and, I am certain, not wholly satisfactory response to them. Anthony Kirk-Greene set me to thinking seriously about the Idoma in a chance meeting more than a decade ago at Michigan State University. Within Nigeria's academic community, it was Robert Armstrong who encouraged me to plan well for the field investigation among that people.

Many hundreds of creditors in Idoma are simply too numerous to list individually. I am indebted to the district councillors and the district heads in Boju, Ochekwu, Oglewu, Oturkpo, and Yangedde – among whom I spent many hours listening, probing, and learning. The Chief of Idoma, the Honourable Ajene Ukpabi, assisted me in numerous ways, along with officials at all levels in the central administration of the Idoma Native Authority in Oturkpo Town. The Methodist Mission and the Roman Catholic Mission were generous in providing encouragement and ancillary support, as were two District Officers and their staff in the headquarters town. Clement Uwemedino was a loyal friend. Patrick Unoogwu taught me much about his people. Ogwiji Ikongbeh, friend and companion, stands out even in this list of notables. I also acknowledge my debt to the Idoma people, whose hospitality, generosity, and compassion helped me to learn and to understand. To them I was *iticha* (the teacher), the man from the 'higher high school', the university, in America. I prefer to think of myself as their student.

I have benefited greatly from comments made on an earlier draft of the manuscript by the late Max Gluckman, and from his scholarship over many years. Martin Spencer and John Banks at the Manchester University Press were encouraging of my efforts to prepare the manuscript for publication.

The field investigation was supported by a Michigan State University International Programs Fellowship. An archival investigation was carried out some years later in London and at Oxford University with grants received from the American Philosophical Society and the State University of New York Research Foundation. I also gratefully acknowledge the assistance which I received on various occasions from staff at the Nigerian National Archives branches in Enugu and Kaduna; at the Public Record Office and the International African Institute, London; and at the Colonial Records Project and Rhodes House Library, Oxford. For permitting me to use in this book portions of several of my articles, I express appreciation to the Editors of the *Administrative Science Quarterly* and the *African Studies Review*; the Cambridge University Press, which publishes the *Journal of African History*; the International African Institute, London, which publishes the journal *Africa*; and the Michigan State University Press, publisher of an anthology on communal politics and modernisation in Nigeria (see references on p. 278). The reprinted portions appear in Chapters Two, Three, Four, Six, Seven, Eight, Ten and Eleven of *Men in the Middle*.

I have capitalised on the typing skills of Ann Wright, Kathy Stutsrim, Betty Jones, Laura Strauss, Blanche Hermalyn, and Elizabeth Figueroa.

And finally, there is my family – Brooke, Dawn, Glenn, and my wife, Sally. They have shared my frustrations and my hopes all the while I have grappled with *Men in the Middle*. I cannot begin to estimate my debt to them.

To be aided in one's scholarship is not to have responsibility for it shared. I alone am responsible for what is written in these pages.

ALBANY, NEW YORK   ALVIN MAGID

SUMMER 1975

Part I Introduction

Chapter One Men in the middle: role conflict in African local administration

Chiefs, village headmen, and other local officials have long been recognised as vital links between different social strata in African tribal societies; and between those societies and the higher institutions of government which are a legacy of colonial rule. At the same time, there has been recognition of the cross-pressures which frequently surround the individuals who occupy linkage positions; and of the relationship between such pressures and the integration and stability of the social units in which those individuals participate. The personal plight of Africa's 'men in the middle', as well as the implications of their situation for social unity and stability (and *vice versa*), have attracted great interest in many quarters, most notably in academic circles. Thus during the past four decades social scientists have been increasingly mindful of role conflict,[1] a phenomenon which

[1]Role conflict involves contradictory expectations which cannot be fulfilled together. The concept is explicated on pp. 119-20.

Role conflict has been widely reported in Subsaharan Africa, particularly with regard to chiefs, village headmen, and other local officials in tribal societies. Its occurrence has been noted in these societies, among others: in West Africa, Ashanti (Apter 1955: 155–6; Busia 1951: 1ff.; Fortes 1948: 23ff.), Hausa (Whitaker 1970: 462–3), and Yoruba (Lloyd 1956: 57–65); in East Africa, Buganda (Apter 1961: 137–8, 141; Southwold 1964: 211–55), Bunyoro (Beattie 1960: 1 ff.), Busoga (Fallers 1955: 290–305; 1965: 155–203), and Lugbara (Middleton 1971: 37–40); in Central and Southern Africa, Luapula (Cunnison 1959: 184ff.), Mambwe (Watson 1958: 218–9), Ngoni (Barnes 1967: 136–64; Gluckman *et al.* 1949: 100–6), Swazi (Kuper 1947: 98), Tonga (Colson 1948: 97–8; 1960: 189–90; 1962: 203–31; 1971: 178ff.; Van Velsen 1964: 271–311), Yao (Gluckman *et al.* 1949: 94–100; Mitchell 1949: 154–9; 1956: *passim*), and Zulu (Gluckman 1961: 46–55; 1964: 34–7; 1968a: *passim*). Individual papers in Richards, ed. (1960: 13ff.) analyse role conflict surrounding chieftaincy and local officials in thirteen societies in East Africa, including the four listed above.

More general references to role conflict involving the occupants of authoritative positions in tribal societies can be found in Burke (1964: 15–6); Brown (1959: 55–6); Cowan (1958: 27, 124–5, 127); Crowder and Ikime, eds. (1970: *passim*); Fleming (1966: 386–404); Gluckman (1965: 165–6).

There have also been scattered reports of role conflict in Africa involving white administrators (Fallers 1965: 204–24; Gluckman 1968b: 72–85); community influentials (Epstein 1958: 65; Hanna and Hanna 1967: 168–9; Southall 1967: 330–1); ordinary citizens in multiracial societies (Wilson and Wilson 1945: 152); and child-rearing practices (Clignet 1967: 277, 279, 286, 291).

in its social psychological and sociological aspects draws attention simultaneously to individuals caught in the middle and to the state of the social unit(s) in which they are participants. I shall have occasion to amplify on these two aspects of role conflict, and on their relevance to this study, after locating various roots of such conflict in Africa.

The roots of role conflict

Endogenous role conflict and exogenous role conflict

Two main sources of role conflict have been identified by investigators. The first of these involves conflicting principles of social relations which are intrinsic in many African societies. (I shall refer to role conflict which derives from this source as *endogenous role conflict*.) As a case in point, Gluckman *et al.* (1949: 92–106) note the difficulties traditionally experienced by the village headman in Central Africa as he sought to maintain harmony among kinship groups inhabiting the village. The headman's deep personal involvement in the kinship network strained his ability to assume the role of a neutral arbiter in village affairs. But his difficulties did not arise solely from the fact that simultaneously he symbolised the village's corporate life and participated in its day-to-day conflicts. As a subordinate of the chief or of some other individual outside the village from whom he derived his political authority, the headman was also the personality in whom the domestic-kinship and the political systems intersected. Predictably, the village headman was the focus, too, of conflict between the village and political authorities in the wider society.

The second source of role conflict involves conflicting principles of social relations which are associated with the superimposition on indigenous political structures of European colonial administrations. (I shall refer to role conflict which derives from this source as *exogenous role conflict*.) Usually such conflict has been observed at the point(s) where administrative positions in two hierarchies, each with its own pattern of social relations, intersect. Gluckman (1968b: 71) has described these intersections as 'inter-hierarchical positions or roles'. In colonial times the nexus could often be discerned where a chief who held office at or near the apex of his own tribal hierarchy was also a salaried civil servant at or near the base of the European administrative hierarchy. As the personality in whom the two hierarchies became enmeshed, he was apt to be caught between the conflicting interests and expectations of white superiors and fellow tribes-

3

men. The situation of chiefs, village headmen, and other local officials was rendered especially difficult where the role conflict with which they had to cope derived simultaneously from exogenous and endogenous sources.

Studies of exogenous role conflict may be distinguished by the analytic perspectives which they variously adopt (*ibid*.: 72). There are, on the one hand, those which concentrate on the dilemma of the African subordinate of a European hierarchy who is pressured by the demands and values of his white superiors in the administration and the demands and values of his own people which are seen by them as conflicting with the former. On the other hand, there are studies which view the problem somewhat more narrowly as a conflict between two ethics affecting the occupants of inter-hierarchical positions. This latter group of studies, generally executed in societies in East Africa (Richards, ed. 1960: *passim*), draws attention to an indigenous personal particularistic ethic which stresses kinship and often also patron–client relationships; and to its contradictory, an alien conception of public administration (the civil service) which in its essential details mirrors the values in the Weberian model of bureaucracy (Henderson and Parsons, eds. and trans. 1947: 329–40; Gerth and Mills, eds. and trans. 1958: 196–240). Endogenous role conflict is seen by these investigators as an expression traditionally of strains inherent in the personal particularistic ethic. Exogenous role conflict is seen as resulting from the superimposition on that base of the civil-service ethic. Several cases from colonial Uganda are presented here to illustrate this perspective.

Fallers (1955: 295–305) reports that in Busoga role conflict had traditionally derived from the operation of a secular hierarchy of chiefs alongside of and in competition with the sacral–familial institutions of patrilineal kinship; and from the fact that relations between superiors and subordinates at all levels of the hierarchy had been governed by the principle of clientship or personal fealty. Even after 1936, when tribute was officially abolished and all chiefs – except village headmen – became salaried civil servants, clientship continued to flourish, albeit clandestinely.

The decision to infuse the traditional kinship and chieftaincy institutions with civil-service norms worked to exacerbate the problem of role conflict. For example, kinsman *A* would pressure chief *B* for preferential treatment; simultaneously he would insist that chief *B* ignore the pressure of a competitor, kinsman *C*. Similarly, sub-county chief X would invoke the client relationship in order to gain the support of county chief Y at promotion time; simultaneously he would condemn chief Y for honouring the same relationship with another aspirant, sub-county chief Z. Operating in a milieu in which kin, client, and civil-service relationships intermeshed, chiefs were apt to experience the following dilemma: while agreeing to the particularistic demands of a kinsman could result in dismissal for nepotism, refusal to agree could be interpreted as a violation of traditional kin obligations. Similarly, while agreement to the particularistic demands of a superior could be interpreted as a violation of civil-service norms, refusal to honour the client relationship could be grounds for dismissal on a contrived charge of corruption.

An analogue to the Busoga case may be found among the Banyoro of Uganda. According to Beattie (1960: 36–47), European officials serving in Bunyoro expected civil-service chiefs to act bureaucratically – that is, chiefs were expected to handle administration, court affairs, and fiscal matters in an efficient and disinterested manner. At the same time, the value orientation of traditionalist Banyoro was essentially different: they expected dignified relations between chiefs and subjects, including frequent visits and generosity (referring to the traditional practice of chiefs preparing feasts for villagers; most chiefs could no longer afford this activity). Failure to conform to expectations which reflected conflicting value orientations gave rise to the following pattern of criticism: European officials condemned deviations from Western standards of administration; older Banyoro deplored the impersonality of civil-service chiefs; and younger Banyoro educated in the European tradition exacerbated the problem of role conflict by assailing chiefs who did not conform to both the efficiency norm and the standards of modern democratic leadership.

Exogenous role conflict and bureaucratisation–debureaucratisation

With some qualifications, the present study draws on (1) the distinction between endogenous role conflict and exogenous role conflict, and (2) a synthesis of the two perspectives (conflicting demands and values versus conflicting ethics) which investigators have previously adopted in analysing exogenous role conflict.

Exogenous role conflict. Broadly speaking, *Men in the Middle* is a study of exogenous role conflict. But unlike many such studies, this

one does not centre on the superimposition on an indigenous structure of a European hierarchy as such. Rather, it examines in one
West African society the strains between its indigenous political system and a local government organisation constructed out of elements
eclectically drawn from that system; from the political system of yet
another society in the same colonial territory; and from the political
system of the British metropole. Nor does the study centre on 'inter-
hierarchical positions or roles' as such – that is, it is not concerned
primarily with administrative positions in which indigenous and
superimposed hierarchies *formally intersect*. Rather, *Men in the
Middle* deals with role conflict surrounding a position – that of the
district councillor in Idoma, a society in the lower 'Middle Belt' of
Nigeria (see Map 1)[2] – which was created a decade after World War
II and which has neither formal status in the indigenous political
system nor a counterpart therein.[3]

Nevertheless, as we shall see, various developments in Idoma did
cause the district councillorship to resemble an inter-hierarchical position beset by role conflict. First, the office was formally created in
that society (and elsewhere in the Northern Region of which Idoma
was then a part) as a new linkage position in local affairs. The District
Councils were mandated to act as agents of the Native Authority or
local government organisation which had been painstakingly constructed by European administrative officers, and as representatives
of the people in their districts.[4] Second, after a half-century of colonial rule, most Idoma were still imbued with the idea of resurrecting a
constitutional system whose main principle – power and authority

[2]The Federation of Nigeria was reorganised in 1967. Twelve states replaced the old
Northern, Eastern, Western, and Mid-West Regions as follows: North-Western,
North-Central, Kano, North-Eastern, West-Central, and Benue-Plateau States were
carved out of the Northern Region; East-Central, South-Eastern, and Rivers States
were created in the Eastern Region; Western and Lagos States (the latter including the
Federal Territory of Lagos) were carved out of the Western Region; and the Mid-West
Region was renamed Mid-West State.

[3]The inter-hierarchical position is encountered in Idoma when the district head, who is
the district councillor's immediate superior in the Native Authority, is also a traditional
clan head. In that event, he is the person in whom the indigenous and local government
hierarchies formally intersect. See pp 59, note 22, 260–5.

[4]The position of the district councillor as agent of government and representative of his
people has many parallels in Africa. See, for example, Mitchell's discussion (1956:
57–8) of the chief's role among the Yao in Central Africa.

divided among the clan head, the elders, and the adult men in a democratic assembly – was incompatible with those around which the Native Authority had been constituted. As a result, role conflict intensified for the district councillors who were caught between their

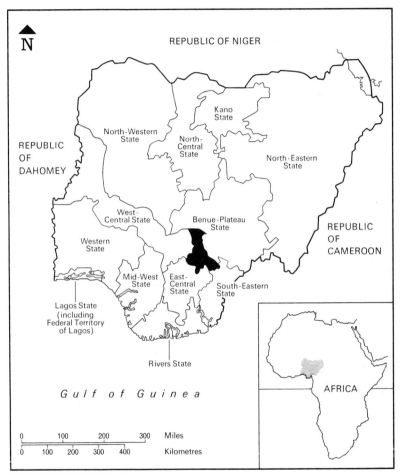

Map 1. The Federal Republic of Nigeria. Idoma Division in Benue-Plateau State is shaded

village supporters and those compatriots who were their superiors in the local government organisation. Finally, although the district councillorship was a new office created in the last phase of colonial rule, it experienced very rapid 'traditionalisation' in Idoma.

7

That process was encouraged by:
(1) a tendency in rural Idoma to regard the councils as representatives of the democratic assembly which traditionally convened to deal with affairs, in the following ways:
   (a) a popular preference for electing councillors in accordance with traditional political norms and procedures;
   (b) a preference for electing men who were influential members of traditional associations (secret societies and dance groups);
   (c) a preference for traditional norms and procedures in deliberations of councils and in the day-to-day activities of the individual councillors; and
   (d) the practice of bestowing old titles of office on the councillors as a way of affirming their 'neo-traditional' status;[5]
and at the same time:
(2) a tendency to regard the councils as a vanguard in the struggle to restore the traditional constitutional system.

Without ascribing to the district councillors as such a formal status in the indigenous political system, the Idoma did succeed in getting a great majority of those officials to act in accordance with traditional norms, principles, and procedures. The measure of their success were the facts that most councillors came to regard their office as an extension of the indigenous political system intersecting with the local government organisation (rather than *vice versa*)[6] and, correlatively, the District Councils were regarded as a vanguard in the struggle to undo the Native Authority *status quo* in favour of the traditional constitutional system.

[5] The Idoma can be quite flexible in the matter of 'traditionalising' the district councillorship. For example, fearing that the Native Authority leadership might try through the district councillors to extend its control over traditional chieftaincy affairs, the elders in particular were wont to argue that as statutory agents of the Native Authority the councillors as such had no right to participate in proceedings over succession to the clan headship. See pp. 171–82.

[6] Every district councillor *perceived* his office as one in which the local government organisation and the indigenous political system intersected. Those who perceived the office as an extension of the indigenous system had usually been elected to serve on the District Council. A minority of the councillors had been appointed by the Native Authority organisation; this group perceived the office rather as an extension of the local government organisation intersecting with the indigenous political system. See pp 110–11.

Bureaucratisation–debureaucratisation. Whatever their analytic perspective (whether they emphasise generally the dilemma of conflicting demands and values faced by African personalities in whom two hierarchies intersect or, alternatively, conflicting personal particularistic and civil-service ethics assimilated by those personalities), studies of exogenous role conflict all point up the bureaucratisation of non-white societies under European rule and popular resistance thereto. Sharing this common ground, both perspectives underscore two elements in exogenous role conflict: *structural intersection* (the gearing together of hierarchies in individual personalities) and *behavioural tension* (the cross-pressures surrounding those personalities which derive from conflicts over the bureaucratising impulse of the superimposed hierarchy).

A caveat ought to be noted here with regard to the concept of bureaucratisation. It has been observed above that many investigators in Africa have operated with that concept narrowly in terms of the civil-service ethic and the Weberian model of bureaucracy on which it draws. I find this construction problematical, as it seems to me to confuse theory and fact. Too much stress is laid in it on a theory of administration which is formed of abstract principles in the civil-service ethic, the model of bureaucracy, and, for anglophone Africa particularly, the basic texts on Indirect Rule (Lugard 1923: 1ff.; Cameron 1934: 1ff.). Viewing administration essentially as the acting out of general principles, these investigators often seem to miss what probably lay closer to the motivational core of bureaucratic life in Africa.

European rule on that continent was a system of power in which conformity to abstract principles was far less important than the push and pull between governor and governed that was daily reflected in their mutual accommodation and adjustment (Heussler 1968: *passim*; Gluckman 1968a: 2ff.; 1968b: 73ff.; Kuper 1947: 92–6). To the extent that they were acted upon by white officials and their African subordinates, administrative imperatives such as 'efficiency', 'economy', and 'impersonality' probably had far more to do with political and other exigencies than with the civil-service ethic and the model of bureaucracy with which those principles are so closely identified.

Viewing European rule as a system of power, we become more sensitive to the bureaucratising impulse of administration, viz. to its efforts to expand and consolidate its power over those whose lives it

9

would regulate. As with institutions generally, European administration in Africa was destined to value its own survival along with the tasks it performed (Selznick 1957: 17, 21). Men who would acquire power and then try to hold on to it often have need to pursue their interests in the cloak of high principle and disinterested service – a truism which appears to have eluded those investigators in Africa who lay stress upon the clash of universalistic and particularistic ethics in exogenous role conflict. Reduced to its essentials, European administration on that continent is more accurately seen as an institution in and around which diverse interests collected; all of them particularistic at the core and all (by their actions or their tacit consent) in varying degrees lending support to, or opposing, the bureaucratising impulse that was European rule.

Adopting a similar view, Eisenstadt (1958: 123; 1959: 302–20) has described as 'bureaucratisation–debureaucratisation' the tension which is engendered by the bureaucratising impulse. 'Bureaucratisation,' according to Eisenstadt (1959: 312), is 'the extension of bureaucracy's sphere of activities and power either in its own interest or those of some elite . . . tend[ing] toward growing regimentation of different areas of social life . . .' Conversely, 'debureaucratisation' denotes 'the subversion of the goals and activities of the bureaucracy in the interest of different groups with which it is in close interaction [e.g., clients, patrons, kinsmen, and so forth]' (ibid.: 312).

This conceptualisation is useful for several reasons. First, it draws attention specifically to administrative behaviour and its consequences, rather than to abstract principles or an overriding ethic which may or may not motivate behaviour. Second, it does not require as a condition of analysis the establishment of any threshold of administrative development. 'Debureaucratisation' does not presuppose a given level of 'bureaucratisation' in administrative life. Rather, as Bidwell (1965: 991) has observed, 'it denotes a set of countervailing forces to bureaucratic operations, under the specified conditions'. Finally, Eisenstadt's conception increases sensitivity to similar tension in a wide range of social contexts, including colonial and independent territories, feudal and modern political systems, and diverse racial and cultural areas (Turner 1947: 342–8; Burke 1958: 153–60; Uganda 1961; Katz and Eisenstadt 1960–1: 113–33; Riggs 1964) – that is, wherever there is, in some degree, support for, and opposition to, those values and interests of the bureaucracy which favour the expansion of its power in social life.

The condition which has been described here as 'bureaucratisation–debureaucratisatron' could be found in Idoma in the aftermath of independence. Led by a strong-willed paramount chief in the decade preceding Nigeria's independence in 1960, and fortified by its political alignment with the governing party in the Northern Region, the Idoma Native Authority had managed to extend greatly the sphere of its activities and power. All but a few Idoma saw this development as affirming the main legacy of colonial rule: the dominance of two principles in local government, strong chieftaincy and centralised political authority. Among the great majority who were averse to the strong bureaucratising impulse of the Native Authority – this group included many Idoma who supported the governing party at the ballot box – most preferred to see a restoration in some form of a constitutional system which was recalled for having inhibited the centralisation of authority under autocratic chiefs. The ideational element in the debureaucratising impulse was thus formed of nostalgia for a constitutional system which colonial rule had broken up.

The idea of constitutional renascence became linked in the popular mind to the idea of 'struggle', around which subject there developed intense discussion in the early independence period and, as a vent to personal frustration with the state of local government affairs, often charges and countercharges of cowardice and betrayal. Practically speaking, debureaucratisation mainly consisted of: (1) the rural population resisting as best it could interference by a powerful local government organisation in village and kinship affairs; (2) the elders and others exhorting the district councillors to assume leadership of the 'struggle' over Idoma constitutionalism and the organisational character of the Native Authority; and (3) the opposition political parties in Idoma trying to block efforts by the Native Authority and its party ally to reduce or punish their following.

As statutory agents of the Native Authority and representatives of their people, the district councillors were subjected to role conflict which mirrored the society's countervailing forces to bureaucratisation. Sensitive to the relationship between their own position as 'men in the middle' and the tension surrounding the bureaucratising impulse, those officials (and indeed most Idoma) could easily distinguish between role-expectations for the councillors' behaviour which reflected either support for or opposition to Native Authority power and the two principles (strong chieftaincy and centralised political authority) around which that power was organised. Drawing

11

for purposes of analysis on the distinction between role-expectations which I have just noted, I shall refer in the study to *bureaucratic–debureaucratic role conflict*, viz. to conflicting bureaucratic and debureaucratic expectations for the behaviour of the councillors in various situations.

Social psychological and sociological aspects of role conflict

Role conflict may be seen as having essentially two aspects, one social psychological, the other sociological (Neiman and Hughes 1951: 141–9; Sarbin 1959: 223–58; Gross *et al.* 1958: 3ff.; Biddle and Thomas, eds. 1966: 3ff.). In the former, the major concern is with the psychic conflicts and anxieties which may be produced in the individual (1) as a result of contradictory expectations which are held for his behaviour either by persons with whom he interacts or by groups in which he is a member and to which he owes loyalty; or (2) as a result of contradictions inherent in a single role-expectation or role pattern (see p 120). Such questions as these are likely to be posed when analysing role conflict from a social psychological perspective: What are the role-expectations which the individual perceives others as holding for his behaviour in particular situations? How accurate are his perceptions? What assessment does he make of the legitimacy of particular role-expectations and of his obligation to conform to them? What sanctions does the individual perceive others as attaching to those role-expectations? How accurate are his perceptions with regard to sanctions? To what extent, if any, does the individual have difficulty coping with role conflict? And by what calculation does he resolve conflict?

Whereas the social psychological aspect has to do mainly with the psychic problems of the individual who must bear the impact of role conflict, the sociological aspect has to do rather with its consequences for the society as a whole. The central question which is posed when analysing role conflict from the latter perspective is this: Has it functional and/or dysfunctional significance for the society, e.g., for its unity and stability?

By and large, empirical studies of role confict lay stress upon its social psychological aspect, particularly with regard to 'men in the middle' in diverse institutional settings in the United States (Coser 1966: 78); and upon the negative consequences for their positions.

Role conflict in African local administration

Those who emphasise the sociological aspect deal for the most part with matters of theory. Within this group, for example, Coser (*ibid.*: 78–9) proposes that the multiple group affiliations of individuals can produce '. . . a multiplicity of conflicts criss-crossing society . . . [and] result[ing] in a kind of balancing mechanism . . . [which prevents] deep cleavages along one axis'. Among the relatively few empirical studies which attend to the sociological aspect of role conflict are several by anthropologists whose observations are of social and institutional life in Africa. Influenced (along with Coser) by the seminal work of early conflict theorists,[7] these investigators see their own work as affirming the functionality for particular societies of role conflict which results from the multiple group affiliations of individuals. As a case in point, Gluckman (1968a: 74–5) notes that such conflict surrounding Zulu chiefs in multiracial South Africa helped to resolve conflicting group interests and to promote cultural diffusion:

. . . two or more sets of group interests may intersect in a single social personality, and this partially resolves the conflicts of those interests, though this personality is caught in strong personal conflicts. Thus, Zulu chiefs, bureaucrats in Government administration at the same time as they are the heads of their tribes opposed to that administration, introduce culture from the White group to the Zulu.
. . . Under the processes described . . . individuals appear to be faced with an absolute conflict between their own behaviour and the values they hold as members of a group. However, generally a social system is full of contradiction and has not consistency in itself, but the conflicts are solved since individuals can act by different values in different situations. Therefore the individual solves many conflicts by what Evans-Pritchard [in *Witchcraft Among the Azande*] has admirably termed situational selection and secondary elaboration of belief.

Fallers (1955: 303) reports an analogue to the Zulu case in Busoga, a society in Uganda:

. . . from the point of view of the chief acting in his role, the discontinuities in the Soga social system impose severe burdens. It is possible to view these discontinuities also from the standpoint of their consequences for the system as a whole. From this point of view, it would appear that some of the conflicts . . . act to stabilise the system in a period of radical institutional change . . . these conflicts do not consist primarily in discrete groups of persons holding opposed systems of value and belief; they consist rather in the *same persons*, to a great extent throughout the society, holding two incompatible systems of

[7]These include Cooley (1909: 199; 1918: 39), Park (1941: 551–70), and Simmel (1964: 13–123), among others.

13

belief and value. They appear *in action* in the form of conflicts between persons. A chief acts in terms of the civil service norm of disinterestedness and he is punished by others who wish him to act in terms of particularistic obligations. The *persons* in such situations, however, are interchangeable; on another occasion, the same chief may act to fulfil particularistic obligations and may have sanctions brought to bear upon him by the same persons who now, however, wish him to act disinterestedly. This *taking into* the social personalities of individuals of conflicts which might otherwise express themselves in conflicts between discrete groups of persons acts, I suggest, to maintain unity and stability in the system. Very often – perhaps most often – in societies undergoing rapid change, the latter situation has developed. The society has divided into intransigently opposed factions or parties with the result that consensus can be re-established only through the defeat, often by violence, of one group by the other. Of course, which of these alternatives one considers 'better' depends entirely upon one's value position.[8]

Idoma and the two aspects of role conflict

Men in the Middle deals mainly with the social psychological aspect of role conflict. The study is set against the background of political developments in Idoma (and in Nigeria generally) during the period 1908–63; and it focuses on the interaction in that society between the district councillors and individuals and groups (audiences) in the local government organisation and their own localities. Role interaction is analysed within the framework of various social situations which were constructed from actual events in Idoma (see pp 132–3) and which reflected the tension between bureaucratisation and debureaucratisation. For each situation, a sample of councillors was questioned about: (1) the bureaucratic and debureaucratic role-expectations they perceived audiences as likely to hold for their behaviour; (2) the evaluations they themselves were likely to make of the legitimacy of these role-expectations and of their own obligation to conform to them; (3) the sanctions they perceived audiences as attaching to the role-expectations; (4) the difficulty they would have coping with role conflict; and (5) the way they would ultimately resolve conflict.

A science is cumulative. This study builds on the work of previous investigators in Africa by attempting to develop techniques for refining and measuring the attitudes (1) of 'men in the middle' (as actors and occasionally as audiences themselves); and (2) of audiences of various kinds who respond to the 'men in the middle'. I give

[8]Also see Fallers (1965: 248).

14

the problem of the conflict in roles a somewhat wider base than others before me by analysing it quantitatively against the general background of political life in the sóciety. The overall difference in approach can be illustrated with reference to the actions which 'men in the middle' take to resolve such conflict. Others have usually dealt with this aspect of the problem essentially by cataloguing the responses of individuals to role conflict. As a case in point, Southwold (1964:235) observes generally that parish chiefs in Buganda, a society in Uganda, would respond by trying to avoid their superiors; by acting rudely; or by lying. Fallers (1965:176–9) reports that village headmen in neighbouring Busoga would resolve role conflict somewhat differently: by adopting the role of a conformist, i.e., by trying to fulfil conflicting expectations; by adopting the role of rebel, i.e., by behaving illegally or antisocially themselves; or by withdrawing, i.e., by refusing to co-operate with superiors and by failing to assume their traditional rights and responsibilities in the village. In contrast, *Men in the Middle* attempts to relate the district councillors' resolutions in particular situations to their role perceptions; to the evaluations they make of the legitimacy and obligatoriness of expectations; and finally, to political conditions in Idoma.

Because role conflict links the individual and society, its consequences at interrelated personal and societal levels merit particular consideration (see pp 225–8). To that end, attention is also drawn here to the sociological aspect of role conflict in Idoma, viz. to its effects on the society as well as on the district councillors as individuals.

Examining that interrelationship, we are led back to the central question which is posed in the sociological perspective: Has role conflict functional and/or dysfunctional significance for the society as a whole? As we have seen, various writers stress its functionality, theorising (1) that the multiple group affiliations of individuals can prevent social cleavage along a single axis; and (2) that the conflict of group interests is partially resolved by its being taken into the personalities of 'men in the middle' (and by situational selection, i.e., by those individuals acting out different values in different situations).

Some warrant for this postulate was encountered in Idoma. In the aftermath of independence there was low consensus in that society on political values and goals – a condition which was reflected in the struggle over traditional constitutionalism and the organisational character of the Native Authority, and in its corollary, the persistent tension between bureaucratisation and debureaucratisation.[9] At the root of bureaucratic–debureaucratic role conflict surrounding the district councillors was the major cleavage over basic values and goals.

Withal the society retained its viability. Possessing a much higher degree of structural cohesion than of consensus – this can be taken as an indicator of low social integration (Gluckman 1968b: 88–90; 1969: 388–9; 1971: 132–4) – Idoma could still absorb the pressures which might have destroyed or crippled another society. Dependence on local government services (especially in the fields of education and public health); economic interdependence; personal and family ties cutting across both the major cleavage and political party lines; fear that violent rebellion would be met by official repression – all of these helped to prevent the destruction of Idoma as a political society or, alternatively, its division into armed camps.

Yet another factor which contributed to social cohesion was the impact of role conflict on the district councillors. This could be seen in the following:

(1) Whereas the elected members who constituted the majority on each District Council could usually be counted on by their own people to resolve role conflict debureaucratically, i.e., by opposing the bureaucratising impulse of the local government organisation on particular issues, they did not act this way on every occasion. Indeed, in some situations those officials were even pressed by the very people who chose them to lead the struggle against the Native Authority (as it was then constituted) to support specific bureaucratic interests, e.g., by agreeing to campaign for its ally, the governing party, in regional and federal elections (see pp 149–53). Similarly, whereas the appointed members who constituted the minority on each council could usually be relied upon by their superiors in the Native Authority to resolve role conflict bureaucratically, there were occasions when they acted otherwise. Resolving role conflict bureaucratically in some situations, and debureaucratically in others, the councillors contributed to social cohesion by symbolising the need to avoid having alienation from the established order harden into a

---

[9] 'Low consensus' refers here to the cleavage between (1) the great majority in Idoma who hoped ultimately to thwart the bureaucratising impulse of the Native Authority by reconstituting it along the lines of the old constitutional system; and (2) the Native Authority leadership, its subordinates, and others in the society who wanted to retain the organisation intact. Each group having established its own consensus on this issue, the cleavage was widely seen in Idoma as involving irreconcilable values and goals.

self-defeating determination never to co-operate with it. (Co-operation did not mean reconciliation, however; the elected councillors and most Idoma were intransigent in their opposition to the principles of strong chieftaincy and centralised political authority. See pp 245–6.)

(2) The district councillors did little to alter the balance of values and goals in the society. Recognising the futility of trying to do so, most elected councillors did not attempt to persuade the proponents of strong chieftaincy and centralised political authority to abandon those values and the bureaucratising goals which were their corollaries. Nor did the appointed councillors often attempt to gain converts among the great majority in Idoma who still preferred to see a restoration in some form of the old constitutional system. But since they were not confident that their respective values and goals would never be fully displaced, opposing elements in the society continued to vent their mutual antagonisms and fears through contradictory expectations channelled to the councillors. From the vantage point of those officials, their own victimisation as 'men in the middle' was a mirror of deep division in the society. That assessment was substantially accurate. However, unbeknownst to the councillors, they were also contributing to social cohesion in Idoma by taking into themselves conflicting group-interests which embodied the ideational struggle over the local government *status quo*. By absorbing role conflict in particular situations, they were acting to some extent as a lightning-rod for inter-group conflict in the wider society.

But as with social conflict generally (Wolff 1967: 137–69), the effects of role conflict are apt to be ambivalent. This could be observed in Idoma, where, on balance, the dysfunctional significance of role conflict for the society as a whole appeared to outweigh what positive contribution it made to social cohesion.

Idoma was straining toward polarisation in the aftermath of independence. As the power of the local government organisation continued to grow, the rural population more and more often expressed its frustration and restiveness by exhorting the district councillors to take up the cudgels against the Native Authority, and by scaling down its own day-to-day co-operation with it (for example, attempts to draft unpaid communal labour for Native Authority works projects met with stiffened resistance). Contributing to this mood, and to polarisation, was bureaucratic–debureaucratic role conflict surrounding the councillors.

17

Social cohesion was being greatly strained by role conflict even as it was deriving some benefit from it. The root of this paradox lay mainly in the way the district councillors resolved conflict, viz. in their preference for the major role procedure (see pp 123–4, 225–8). Faced with conflicting role-expectations, they ordinarily selected one expectation as the major role to be fulfilled. The councillors' decision to fulfil a role-expectation which seemed to them to promote bureaucratisation involved their rejection of one which favoured debureaucratisation, and *vice versa*. Resolving role conflict on the basis of acceptance–rejection had the effect of encouraging the movement of different social elements in opposite directions: most subordinate officials in the local government organisation and a small minority of the rural population were drawn to the Native Authority leadership which remained steadfast in its advocacy of strong chieftaincy within a centralised framework; and the elected councillors were pulled to audiences in their localities who preferred more democratic, decentralised rule along the lines of the traditional system.

More accommodative behaviour by the district councillors might have helped to lessen the intensity of role conflict and of social conflict generally. But an accommodating outlook (especially willingness to compromise when resolving role conflict) was often lacking in an atmosphere where social conflict was widely seen as rooted in irreconcilable values, goals, and interests. The effect was circular: social conflict gave rise to role conflict; reliance by the councillors on the major role procedure when resolving role conflict contributed to the polarising of political and administrative interests; and polarisation, in turn, exacerbated role conflict.

The benefits which accrued to social cohesion from the occasional willingness of the elected district councillors to resolve role conflict bureaucratically, and their appointed colleagues to resolve it debureaucratically, were more than offset by the polarising effects of the councillors' resolving behaviour. Reliance on the major role procedure in a charged political atmosphere virtually ensured that in most, if not all, situations of role conflict, resolution would, in Merton's words (1955:118), not 'prove sufficient to reduce the conflict of expectations below the level required for the social structure to operate with substantial effectiveness'.[10] Residual conflict in each situation intensified conflict within the councillors' network of role

[10]Also see Goode (1960: 494).

relationships. Cumulatively, residual conflict placed great strain on the cohesiveness of a society which was already burdened by low consensus on basic political values and goals. This augured ill for social stability in Idoma.

Having dealt with various matters pertaining to the distinction between endogenous role conflict and exogenous role conflict, and between their social psychological and sociological aspects, I have in this chapter only to highlight what follows in the study.

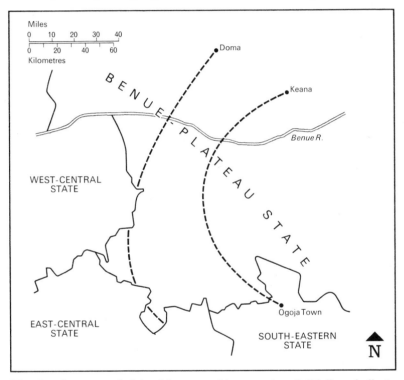

Map 2. Area occupied by Idoma-speaking peoples. Solid lines indicate boundaries of Nigeria States; broken lines indicate crescent-shaped area occupied by Idoma-speaking peoples

Organisation of the study

The Idoma-speaking peoples of Nigeria occupy a crescent-shaped area between the towns of Keana and Doma in Benue-Plateau State and a point just north of Ogoja Town in South-Eastern State (see

Map 2). Despite linguistic unity and certain cultural similarities, it appears that they have never constituted a political unit (Armstrong 1955:94–5).

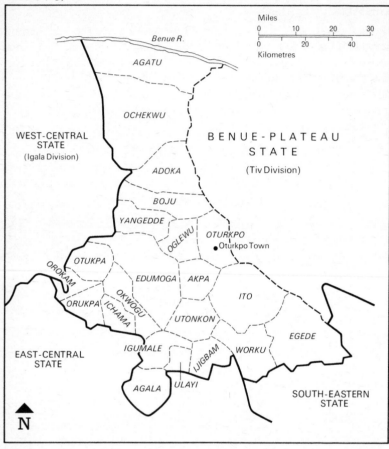

Map 3. Administrative districts in Idoma Division, showing the administrative centre of Idoma Division at Oturkpo Town (after Armstrong (1955))

Within the crescent area are the so-called 'Idoma proper' (*ibid.*: 100–102). Numbering approximately 225,000[11] at the time of the

---

[11]This figure was obtained by subtracting the population of the seven largely non-Idoma districts – Akpa, Ito, Utonkon, Ulayi, Egede, Ijigbam, and Worku (see Map 3) – from the official total for the division: 327,000 (Idoma Native Authority 1962–3).

study, they inhabit Idoma Division in Benue-Plateau State.[12] *Men in
the Middle* focuses on the institution of district councillorship in five
administrative districts in Idoma Division: Oglewu, Oturkpo,
Yangedde, Boju, and Ochekwu (see Map 3, and p 267).

Idoma is an acephalous society, with political authority traditionally vested in clan heads or land chiefs, the elders, and a democratic
assembly comprising the adult men in the community. Unable to
reconcile administrative needs with the democratic and gerontocratic
norms in Idoma constitutionalism, colonial officials turned instead to
the institution of chieftaincy. Thus, during the inter-war period they
sought to establish an efficient Native Authority organisation by
strengthening chieftaincy at the district level in the office of the
district head. Following World War II, the colonial Administration
decided to reform the Native Authority, ostensibly along democratic
lines. Elected councils were introduced at several levels in Idoma
Division. Concomitantly, a powerful Idoma Chieftaincy was established at the apex of the local government structure in emulation of
the Fulani emirship in Northern Nigeria. In the aftermath of these
developments, council democracy combined with strong chieftaincy
and Native Authority centralisation to produce cross-pressures
throughout the society. Among local officials, the district councillors
were especially vulnerable to role conflict which reflected the tension
between bureaucratisation and debureaucratisation. As Native
Authority operatives, the councillors were expected by their
superiors to support bureaucratic values and interests. As popular
representatives, however, they were widely expected to oppose
bureaucratic centralism by spearheading a move to restore the constitutional system as a basis for local government in the division, and
by protecting the villagers against day-to-day interference from
administrative superiors.[13]

The organisation of the study broadly reflects the sequence of
observations made in the preceding paragraph. Thus, Chapter Two
presents a cultural overview of pre-colonial Idoma, emphasising the
relationship between cosmology and political authority. Changes
wrought in colonial Idoma and their implications for bureaucratic–debureaucratic role conflict are surveyed in Chapter Three.

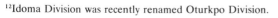

[12]Idoma Division was recently renamed Oturkpo Division.

[13]Local officials are expected to assume the 'protector role' in many societies. See, for
example, the Pacific Islands studies by Rowley (1965: 85) and West (1961: 175–6).

B

Subsequently, the focus shifts to the 'men in the middle' – to the district councillors who have been exposed to role conflict. Aggregate data and personal profiles are employed in Chapter Four to illuminate the backgrounds of a sample of seventy-one councillors (see pp 268–9). Chapter Five examines the process by which they came to hold office. The examination reveals both the interplay of modern and traditional elements in Idoma political life and the intense hostility of most councillors to strong chieftaincy and centralised political authority – key factors in the problem of the conflict of roles confronting those officials.

Five chapters deal with different aspects of the problem. A conceptual language for the analysis of role conflict is outlined in Chapter Six. Chapter Seven and Chapter Eight present data on the bureaucratic and debureaucratic role-expectations which the district councillors perceived various audiences as likely to hold for their behaviour in different situations. The analysis in Chapter Nine deals, among other things, with the relationship between the difficulty councillors would have coping with role conflict and the way they would finally resolve it. Chapter Ten examines various factors (the councillors' evaluations of role legitimacy, obligation, and sanction) which bore upon their ability to cope with role conflict, and their selection of particular expectations as the major role with which to resolve conflict. The concept of 'role buffering' is introduced there to illuminate (1) the scapegoating of councillors by audiences frustrated with the local government *status quo*, and (2) the dilemma which those officials faced as a result of their disposition to rely on the major role procedure when resolving bureaucratic–debureaucratic role conflict.

Chapter Eleven summarises various findings in the study which pertain to the district councillors' position as 'men in the middle'; it also examines several aspects of role conflict analysis in Idoma with a view to undertaking cognate research cross-culturally at a later date.

The study concludes with several appendices. Appendix A summarises the interview schedule; B examines the social backgrounds of the district heads (the district councillors' immediate superiors in the Native Authority) and their perspectives on role conflict; and C discusses various aspects of the field investigation in Idoma.

A brief comment on the utility of the case-study approach in role conflict analysis is presently in order. Clearly a case-study cannot be used as the basis for generalising about role conflict in Africa. Nor can it provide answers to more general questions regarding leadership and conflict in changing African societies. Those objectives can only be pursued by accumulating and analysing a rich variety of data drawn from numerous societies. A case-study executed in Idoma can, however, serve four important purposes. By adding to the meagre literature now available on that society, it can underscore the great need for research on politics and administration in the 'Middle Belt' – an ethnically heterogeneous area whose impact on Nigerian political life can be neither ignored in the aftermath of a tragic civil war nor overestimated (Agboola 1961: 40–6; Sklar 1971: 55). It can also provide sorely needed data on a problem – role conflict – which is reportedly widespread among local officials in independent Africa. Moreover, it can generate insights and hypotheses which, when tested elsewhere on that continent, should deepen our understanding of the problem and stimulate inquiry into the more general questions alluded to above. Finally, it can help strengthen the link between African studies and the nomothetic social sciences (Magid 1969: 89–90). *Men in the Middle* is intended to serve all four purposes.

Part II
Anthro-history

Chapter Two The Idoma: a cultural overview

To understand Idoma culture, we need to know something about the historical context within which it evolved. The story, in so far as it can be traced, begins with the tribal wars of the fifteenth century, in what is now northern Nigeria.

From the late fifteenth to the early seventeenth century, the Jukun (or Kororofa) Empire was at the height of its power, reaching north to Bornu, west to the Igala kingdom on the Niger, and east to the Cameroons.[1] (See Map 4.) But Kororofa was doomed by its annexation of unassimilable peoples. Vulnerable to both internal erosion and external assaults upon a virtually autonomous periphery, the Empire was disintegrating by the end of the eighteenth century (Kirk-Greene, ed. 1962: 111–2; Barth 1857: 659; Mockler-Ferryman n.d.: 166). Tributary states were defecting to its enemies and many of its peoples were in flight. Kororofa was soon unable to withstand the shock produced by recurrent famine and pestilence, the loss of lucrative slave markets in England and America, Chamba aggression along the Cameroons border, and the Fulani *jihad* throughout northern Nigeria (Meek 1931: 29, 45–6; Kirk-Greene 1958: chs. 9–11). More tributary states defected and migration accelerated. The defectors included Keana and Doma, two Arago kingdoms at the upper end of the Idoma-speaking crescent. Despite a long history of administrative autonomy within the Empire and strong cultural ties with the Jukun – the Arago and the Jukun had similar notions of divine chieftaincy and cultship – Keana became a tributary of Bauchi and Sokoto in the mid-nineteenth century and Doma a vassal of Zaria (Baikie 1856: 112; Crowther 1855: 73–4). Among the refugees from the Empire were the 'Idoma proper' (henceforth referred to as the Idoma).

Because there is only fragmentary data on the origin of the Idoma, any effort to reconstruct their pre-colonial past is necessarily incom-

[1] Meek (1931: 23) contends that Igala was founded by Kororofa elements who defeated the previous Yoruba rulers, Talbot (1926: 157–8) that Benin created the office of Attah (king) of Igala.

66746

plete and tentative. Both documentary sources and the testimony of informants indicate that that people migrated from Apa (i.e., Wukari) in Jukun territory (Armstrong 1955: 96ff.; Elliott 1937b; Leslie 1936; Mathews 1933a, 1933b, 1933c; Meek 1925; Money 1935b; Shaw 1934; Wright 1936). Nothing is known about them prior to the migration, not even whether they constituted a distinctive group within the Jukun Empire. What data are available suggest that Idoma history and mythology as such have their genesis in the departure from Apa.

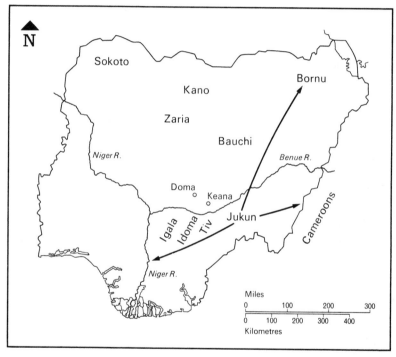

Map 4. The Jukun (or Kororofa) Empire, late fifteenth to early seventeenth century. Centres of Kororofa power were at Wukari and Kororofa Town in Jukun territory. The arrows indicate the extent of the Empire at the height of its power

The Idoma migration from Jukun territory was probably caused by instability within the Empire at some time before the commencement of the Fulani *jihad* in 1805. Theorising that internecine warfare precipitated the migration from Apa, Armstrong (1955: 97) concludes that 'the movement probably took place some considerable time before the big Fulani push against the Benue in 1853 . . . '. Drawing upon tribal traditions and genealogies, Meek (1925) places the migration of the Oturkpo people around 1585, that of Boju at 1675, and of Igumale some time later. European commentators generally attribute the failure of the Fulani to conquer the Idoma and other 'pagan' peoples south of the Benue to such factors as the diminution of the slave trade, crippling the ability of the Fulani to exchange slaves for arms; the inability of raiding cavalry to penetrate dense forest and orchard bush plagued by the tsetse fly; and the steady imposition of the *pax britannica* throughout the area (Abraham 1940: 11; Denham *et al.* 1831: 189; Burns 1955: chs. 13, 15, 16; Meek 1931: 60).

These findings do not accord with the testimony of Idoma informants. In their view, the migration from Apa was a relatively recent occurrence, caused by the murderous raids of their traditional enemies, the Moslem Fulani. Evidence adduced to support this claim includes many tales of heroic deeds performed against enemy cavalry – some obviously embellished; references to totemic animals (e.g., the red monkey in Oturkpo) which supposedly saved the fleeing Idoma by erasing incriminating footprints;[2] and the remains of fortifications throughout northern Idoma Division, allegedly constructed to defend against Fulani raids south of the Benue. In sum, generalised notions of descent from Apa and migration induced by Fulani aggression in the twilight of the Jukun Empire form the basis for Idoma traditions of origin.

But there is general agreement both as to the routes traversed by the migrants from Jukun territory and the implications for Idoma culture. One group came to their present habitat after sojourning in Tivland, another after residing among the Igala. Evidence of sustained contact with different peoples can be found in various Idoma institutions. For example: Idoma notions of chieftaincy and cultship resemble those held by the Jukun and the Igala (Monckton 1927–8: 155–6, 165–6; Meek 1931: 511 note 2; Young 1966: 135–52); some Idoma clans use traditional Igala titles (Mathews 1933a; Leslie 1936); similar headhunting rituals are found among the Idoma and the Tiv (Abraham 1940: ch. 3); there is a resemblance between the *ojira*

[2]Many clans have what Meek (1925) terms a 'degenerate totemism' associated with assistance in critical times. The totemic animals include crocodiles, black monkeys, red monkeys, and pythons. The Boju clan will not cook with wood from the copaiba tree, claiming that it fell between them and their pursuing enemies.

assembly in Idoma and the Tiv moot (Bohannan 1957: 1ff.).[3] While Apa is esteemed as the place from which their ancestors journeyed, the Idoma attach little significance to their connection with the Jukun. As a case in point, this appeal addressed by a Jukun tribal union to an Idoma counterpart failed to evoke a sympathetic response:

... brothers from the same origin (who had raided and devastated northern Nigeria before the advent of the British) . . . [ought] to revive [their] pᵣᵥᵗ heritage and come together irrespective of language and settlement . . . (to form a) confederated union . . . (IHRU 15 August 1957)[4]

Despite conflicting theories of migration from Apa, it is clear that the Idoma have occupied their present habitat for some time. Even before the imposition of the *pax britannica*, European travellers were affirming that Idoma culture had already established deep roots in the area (Barth 1857: 478ff.; Crowther 1855: 53ff.; Mockler-Ferryman 1892: 72ff.; Laird and Oldfield 1837: 442ff.; Burdo 1880: 239ff.). In the remainder of this chapter, I shall consider various aspects of that culture.

Language

Idoma and Igala are closely related languages in the Kwa language family. As such, the two are related to Yoruba. It should be noted, however, that there is not a uniform relationship between the latter and individual languages in the Kwa family. For example, Igala is much closer to Yoruba than is Idoma (Armstrong 1955: 91).

According to Armstrong (*ibid.*: 92), Idoma 'is so deeply divided by dialects that it is probably best considered a "dialect cluster" '. Eight and perhaps nine dialects, varying in mutual intelligibility, are distinguishable within the Idoma-speaking crescent area. They include the two Arago dialects – Doma and Keana – at the upper end of the crescent; Iyala and Nkum at the lower end; and four or five dialects in Idoma Division. As with Yoruba *vis-à-vis* individual languages in the Kwa family, there is not a uniform relationship between the Idoma dialects and either Yoruba or Igala. Doma is probably closer to Yoruba than are the other dialects; Iyala is probably closest to Igala.

---

[3] Aspects of other cultures have also been adopted by the Idoma. Secret societies and dance groups in southern Idoma resemble those found in Iboland. Hausa apparel and Yoruba-style edifices can be seen in the northern districts, the latter built by Idoma who had worked in Western Nigeria.

[4] While the IHRU was preoccupied with internecine conflict, it is doubtful that a similar appeal would have evoked a sympathetic response even in different circumstances (Magid 1971: 349–73).

Natural environment and economy

The ecology of the Idoma-speaking crescent is nearly homogeneous. Most of the area is covered with orchard bush. It is only at the lower end of the crescent that we encounter a different pattern. Rain forest begins to appear along the southern boundary of Idoma Division. Approaching Ogoja Town to the south-east, orchard bush gradually gives way to open grassland.

Agriculture is the mainstay of the economy.[5] Following an annual cycle, farmers cultivate yams, guinea corn, maize, cotton, and other crops during the rainy season; during the dry season, they hunt and clear land by burning the bush. Today the quarry is small game; elephants and lions, which once roamed parts of present-day Idoma Division, were killed off some time ago.

Secondary economic activities include ironwork (e.g., the production of dane guns and farm implements for local use) and weaving of cotton cloth, mats, and baskets.

Markets of all sizes abound in Idoma Division. Generally convened on a four-day rotation basis, they serve as the venue for social intercourse and economic exchange.

Social structure

The essential units of Idoma social organisation are the compound family (*ole*), consisting of a man, his wives, their children, and their sons' wives and children; the sublineage (*ipooma*, 'those of one birth'); the lineage (*ipoopu*, 'those of one *ojira* or council area'); and the land or clan (*aje* or *ipaaje*).

The compound family

Traditionally, the compound family was a compact, virtually self-sufficient unit located around a clearing in the bush. On the periphery of the clearing were round mud huts with cone-shaped thatch roofs. One of these dwellings was occupied by the head of the compound, others by the various wives. Each wife was provided with her own hut. Storehouses, sheltered work-sites, and meeting-rooms were also constructed to serve the economic and social needs of the unit. Users of the surrounding farmland owned only the usufruct. The compound family unit resembled Redfield's (1963: 4) 'little community'.

In contemporary Idoma, demographic and attitudinal changes have

---

[5]Economic life will undoubtedly be affected by the recent discovery of oil in northern Idoma.

conspired against this arrangement. Population pressure on the land and a desire for greater independence[6] have led many married sons to settle in small, outlying farm communities. As a result, the solidarity of the traditional compound family has diminished somewhat.

The sublineage and the lineage

The sublineage or *ipooma* is comprised of several compound families related through the male line. By linking smaller sublineages which have proliferated in recent times, the Idoma have created a level of social organisation which resembles the major lineage; both the major lineage and its constituent units retain the name *ipooma*. Several *ipooma* related through the male line form an even wider lineage, the *ipoopu*.

The sublineage and the lineage both constitute political units. The members of each of these units claim descent from a common male ancestor and also identify with a particular parcel of land. Related sublineages generally reside around a common *ojira* or council area which serves as the venue for lineage ceremonies and deliberations. While colonial officials called these well-defined, densely populated sites 'villages' (Armstrong 1955: 95), this concept is alien to Idoma thinking. The Idoma language has no word which means 'village' as such.

A senior elder of the lineage serves for life as the 'owner' or 'father' of both the ancestral cult (*alekwu*) and the earth shrine *(aje)*. His appointment generally rotates between the constituent sublineages. In theory, the eligible sublineage nominates its most senior member. In fact, however, the principle of seniority is often honoured in the breach. Because the adult Idoma cannot cite his age exactly (see pp 63–4), this factor has only limited utility in establishing seniority. To the Idoma, seniority is primarily a matter of genealogical status. Social conflict usually arises when rival candidates for an office claim closer proximity to the founding ancestor. In the interest of restoring social harmony, it is often necessary to abandon the principle of seniority.

While the Idoma encourage marriage outside the sublineage, neither that unit nor the lineage is strictly exogamous. The sole requirement is that persons with the same mother's father or father's father should not marry.

[6]This reflects both the tradition of inter-generational discord in Idoma and the feeling that young men should be encouraged to strike out on their own (Magid 1971: 354–9, 365).

The land (the clan)

The highest level of traditional social organisation is the land (henceforth referred to as the 'clan', a term employed for administrative purposes since the early days of colonial rule). The clan is formed by the unity of several lineages around a common earth shrine. While clan members often claim blood relationship, they are only able to assert a putative common ancestor – that is, they are unable to trace the actual genealogical relationships or demonstrate that the common ancestor actually existed.[7]

Nearly a third of the twenty-two districts in Idoma Division have more than one clan. Ochekwu district alone has more than a dozen.

Each clan appoints its own chief – the clan head – to serve for life. The clan headship normally rotates between the constituent lineages. Where feasible, the eligible lineage nominates its most senior member. In the central and northern clans the office combines secular and spiritual authority. In the south, clan headship is exclusively secular; spiritual authority is vested in a senior elder. In most clans throughout Idoma, a hierarchy of titled elders (*aiigabo*) assists the clan head in the performance of his duties.

Many clans have ties with collateral uterine groups – that is, with groups descended from the marriages of female clan members to outsiders.[8] An example is the relationship between the Yangedde clan and the uterine *AiArobi*. According to tradition, an itinerant Hausa married Arobi, the great granddaughter of the Attah of Igala and a member of the Yangedde clan. The descendants of that marriage – the *AiArobi* ('sons of Arobi') – have since resided on clan land near the Abakpa ('Hausa') market in Yangedde district (Leslie 1936; Mathews 1933c; Idoma Native Authority *c.* 1930s).

Uterine groups have an ambivalent political status. On the one hand, traditional law prevents their members from assuming the clan headship; on the other, it authorises those groups to invest the clan head with a beaded wrist band, by way of insignia of office. According to various informants, this prerogative is sometimes employed to help arbitrate on chieftaincy disputes. In this way, uterine groups occasionally exercise an important, if subtle, influence on political life.

[7]Principles of clan organisation are discussed by Fortes (1945: 30–65).

[8]The concept of the 'stranger' in Africa has generally been applied to one who resides in another's territory (Skinner 1963: 307–20). The Idoma also designate as 'strangers' descendants of the marriage of an Idoma woman to a non-Idoma (e.g., the uterine *AiArobi*) and of Idoma parents from different clans. These descendants are 'strangers' in the mother's clan.

The Idoma: a cultural overview

Before embarking on an examination of the Idoma cosmology, it is necessary to consider yet another aspect of social structure: the position of women. The position of Idoma women can best be described as ambivalent. Generally speaking, their social status is fairly high. This is evidenced by, among other things, the titles, formal salutations, and elaborate funerals which they are accorded in most clans. Moreover, women are rarely characterised as weak or indolent. On the contrary, their substantial contribution to the economic life of the society as petty traders and farmers is widely acknowledged, if seldom acclaimed. At the same time, however, there is much evidence of sex antagonism and discrimination against women. Idoma men often boast that women are their inferiors and must be kept in their place. They pursue this objective both politically and ritually.

Women are systematically excluded from Idoma political life. They are prevented from participating in the *ojira* assembly at all levels of the society – from the clan down to the compound family. The prohibition also extends – extralegally – to the modern political sector. Women fill no office in the Idoma Native Authority. Their attendance at District Council meetings is infrequent; and they are rarely consulted on local affairs, official or otherwise. Interestingly, even the petty traders among Idoma women have so far failed to translate their social status and occupational talents into political power and influence. Unlike their counterparts elsewhere in West Africa, they remain unorganised and politically quiescent. This condition is probably reinforced by the principle of traditional law that all property accumulated by a married woman belongs to her husband and his heirs.[9]

The general inferiority of women is further emphasised in certain ritual practices. For example, they cannot participate in most of the activities of men's secret societies and dance groups and the ancestral cult. Moreover, as with the Nupe *ndako gboya* society (Nadel 1954: 188–97), many secret societies and dance groups in Idoma employ ritual masks and the threat of mystical sanction to intimidate women. Idoma women believe that seeing the masks will cause them to become barren. By exploiting this fear, the traditional associations are able to assert male superiority and dominance (Magid 1972: 294, 302).

[9]While Idoma women sometimes dispose of property without consulting their husband and his heirs, the fact that most adhere to the principle underscores their subordinate status in the society.

33

Cosmology
The Idoma cosmology is a system organised around a supreme being; a sustaining earth; and a guiding ancestral force. Together these elements define the spiritual life of the people and, as we shall see presently, shape the main principles of their constitutional polity.

The supreme being
Owoicho, the impersonal god above, is perceived as the prime mover. The Idoma believe that *Owoicho* chooses to govern the universe through an intermediary, *Enyangu*. Unable to communicate directly with their god, they make supplications to *Enyangu* whenever divine assistance is needed. Shrines for the latter are prominently displayed in most households.[10]

The Idoma further believe that the power of *Owoicho* is transmitted to them through diverse media, including charms and mounds. Perhaps the most important media are the earth and the ancestors, the former embodied in the *aje* cult, the latter in the *alekwu* cult.

The earth
On a day fixed annually by the clan head, usually when the hunting season is about to begin, prayers and sacrifices are offered at various shrines by elders who are priests of the *aje* cult. Hopeful that *Owoicho* will bless the *aje* with a bountiful harvest and hunt, the Idoma proceed to engage in joyous feasting. While the rule of annual celebration is generally adhered to, a measure of flexibility is permitted and even encouraged. Thus, Elliott (1937b) reports that an outbreak of smallpox caused the Boju clan to postpone its ceremonies in 1937. Drought, locust invasion, and other natural disasters may require special appeals to the *aje*.

The ancestors
The *alekwu* cult symbolises the bond between past and present. To strengthen that bond, each individual must choose propitious occasions on which to make offerings to the ancestors (Abraham c. 1935; Monckton 1927–8: 165–6; Meek 1925; Elliott 1937b; Wright 1936). The essential character of the cult is social, not religious. The Idoma esteem their ancestors. They do not worship them (Wright 1936).[11]

[10]The omnipresent energy of *Owoicho* is symbolised in each household by a white silk-cotton tree or a species of fig tree (Armstrong 1955: 100).

[11]Idoma informants rejected the view that the ancestors are essentially objects of worship (Abraham c. 1935; Elliott 1937a).

34

The Idoma believe that the living and the dead together constitute the membership of the society. As members, the ancestors occupy much the same position as the elders do. Neither group is worshipped. Rather, both are deferred to as sages. Each has a right to the food and drink which symbolise deference paid to those with superior wisdom gained from experience. Each, in turn, is obliged to provide assistance to supplicants.

Mannoni's theory (1964: 39–97) of the dependent personality helps to illuminate the relationship between the living and the dead in Idoma society. In a study of the Merina ancestral cult (in what is now the Malagasy Republic), he concludes:

It would be no exaggeration to say that the dead and their images form the highest moral authority in the mind of the 'dependent' Malagasy, and that for him they play the part filled for the European by the moral conscience, reason, God, King, or party . . . (*ibid.*: 55–6).

In that circumstance, actual or even threatened abandonment is apt to have dysfunctional consequences for the dependent personality (*ibid.*: 61–88). An analogue is suggested in Idoma.

Responding to a series of questions, twenty-eight district councillors observed that the elders would 'curse' them for not fulfilling a particular role-expectation – that is, they expected the elders to invoke the ancestors' wrath against a recalcitrant councillor. When asked to explain the significance of that sanction, eight councillors reported that it would immediately cause them to die. For the remaining twenty, the augury was still worse. As one councillor put it, 'I would be lost!' Other questions elicited the source of their anxiety: the Idoma believes that he is not equipped to master the environment without assistance from the ancestors. Abandoned by the *alekwu*, he is, in effect, bereft of a critical 'sense'. Furthermore, he fears that this loss may extend to the power of *Owoicho*. His god may now have abandoned him completely through the medium of the *alekwu*. Until death overtakes him, the accursed Idoma is lost among his contemporaries. And he fears that death may be an extension of his isolation into a kind of spiritual limbo.

Polity

Past, present, spirit, and matter unite in the Idoma cosmology. Their unity is expressed in several ways. First, in the power of *Owoicho* as it is transmitted through the *aje* and the *alekwu* cults; second, in the obligation of the Idoma to participate in various cult activities. In the

35

former case, the power of *Owoicho* affirms the bond between a supreme being, earth, and the ancestors; in the latter, each Idoma helps to promote the unity and continuity of the society by participation in its cult life.

Consistently with this outlook, unity constitutes the highest ideal in political life.[12] At the same time, however, the Idoma are acutely aware that conflicting interests conspire against its attainment. For example, rival groups and individuals compete for the clan headship; and the clan head, in turn, competes for political ascendancy *vis-à-vis* other members of the clan unit. To check the divisive effects of such competition the Idoma devised an elaborate constitutional system rooted in three principles: democracy, gerontocracy, and chieftaincy. It is to this system that we now turn.

The constitutional polity included the following sources of authority and influence: the assembly (*ojira*); the clan head (*oche*); the titled clan spokesmen (*aiigabo*); the market-master (*okpoju*); the constabulary (*aiuta* or *aioga*); the hamlet head (*oteyi*); and the secret societies (*aiowa*) and dance groups (*aiije*), which frequently overlapped with the constabulary (Magid 1972: 294–5, 297–8, 301–2).

The assembly

The word *ojira* denotes (1) the council area around which related sublineages or *ipooma* reside, and (2) a loose assembly of adult men – in age groups (*aiego*), secret societies, and dance groups as well as clan, lineage, sublineage, and compound-family units.

Convened *ad hoc* to deal with daily affairs, the traditional *ojira* also served as a check on its members' ambitions. A consensual democratic principle governed the decision-making process, rendering it difficult for an individual or faction to control the assembly. While the titled clan spokesmen and the 'owners' of the ancestral cult and the earth shrine formed a gerontocratic elite in the *ojira*, they were never able to convert that body into a select council of elders. From its inception, the *ojira* was essentially a democratic assembly of all the men of a particular unit (Smith 1931; Money 1935a; Armstrong 1955: 107; Elliott 1937a; Mathews 1936a).[13]

---

[12]The importance of this ideal in modern times is noted in Magid (1971: 346, 355).

[13]The unconfirmed thesis that the *ojira* was a select council of elders is presented in Macleod (n.d.) and Munshi Province (*c.* 1925).

The clan head and the clan spokesmen

Previous investigators have discerned a paradox in the Idoma tradition of chieftaincy. Despite an ideology of proud and vigorous chieftaincy, the institution appears to have been moribund when colonial rule began (Armstrong 1955: 95–6). For example, Shaw (1934) reports that the clan headship and the spokesman titles were filled in only two of the fourteen clans in present-day Ochekwu district. Neither the extensive unpublished literature on the subject nor the testimony of Idoma informants indicates that such officials were systematically hidden from enquiring British administrators. Accordingly, it seems reasonable to conclude that the traditional ideology of chieftaincy reflects what Lasswell (1960: 195) has termed 'political symbolisation' – that is, strong emotional commitment to a political institution which existed sporadically and achieved only symbolic greatness.

The emotional commitment of the Idoma to chieftaincy can be traced to their contact with the Jukun, the Igala, and the Fulani (Elliott 1937a; Benue Province 18 January 1935). For the most part, however, the Idoma were unable to reproduce the sophisticated state machinery and chieftaincy institutions of these peoples. Only among the Agala in southern Idoma and some clans further north is there evidence of state organisation and kingship. With its royal lineage and civil and military titles, the Agala clan represents the closest approximation to a state system in Idoma (Abraham c. 1935; also Fortes and Evans-Pritchard, eds. 1961: 15–23). In the Boju and Oturkpo clans as well as clans near the Benue River, the institution of clan headship combines the functions of chief priest and secular monarch (Mathews 1933a; 1933b; Elliott 1937a).

Throughout Idoma, the clan head had considerable power. As secular leader, he bestowed graded *aiigabo* titles on clan spokesmen, thereby designating both his aides and the line of chieftaincy succession; appointed the *aiuta* constabulary; received a share of fines imposed by the *aiuta*; acted as an appellate court in inter-family disputes; and took action to apprehend murderers. Acting with the *aiigabo*, he could promulgate ordinances (*ine*) which had the force of law. According to Meek (1925), the day-to-day exercise of secular authority depended at least as much on the character of the clan head as on the formal rules of office. Great secular power might accrue to the incumbent endowed with a strong personality and supported by a large and influential family. The power of the office was further

37

enhanced in central and northern Idoma, where the clan headship combined secular and spiritual authority. The spiritual power of the clan head derived from his mastery of magic and presidency of the cults.

Lest autocratic chieftaincy and disunity result from the abuse of such power, the Idoma took elaborate measures to limit the initiative of the clan head. His behaviour was strictly regulated by three constitutional devices: the authority of the *ojira*, the rituals of office, and the principles of rotation and seniority in chieftaincy succession.

The power of the clan head was circumscribed by public opinion in the *ojira*. He could not declare war without the express consent of that body. Nor could he bestow the *aligabo* titles on clan spokesmen without its approval. Frequently the clan head would assign the titles *pro forma* to men nominated by the *ojira* (Shaw 1934). In this way, the assembly influenced both the selection of the clan head's aides and the future course of chieftaincy succession.

Limitations were also placed on the power of the clan head by ritually emphasising the majesty of his office. This objective was often pursued by restricting the movements of that official. For example, a newly-appointed head of the Akpa clan (in Akpa district) was forbidden to leave his compound for two years. Similarly, the Agadagba clan (in Yangedde district) prohibited its clan head from entering the political world of the market-place (Meek 1925; Elliott 1937b).

The principle of lineage rotation checked the concentration of chiefly power in a single unit; and the principle of seniority virtually ensured that the clan head would be too old and infirm to participate actively in political affairs.[14] In central and northern Idoma, aged clan heads often preferred to delegate their political power to more efficient young men so that they might concentrate on their duties as chief priest and president of the cults.[15]

The market-master, the hamlet heads, and the constabulary

The most important recipients of delegated chiefly power were the market-master (*okpoju*), who was appointed by the *ojira* assembly,

[14]While this principle was often violated in succession to chieftaincy, the available evidence does indicate that the office of clan head was generally filled by a very senior – albeit not the most senior – member of the eligible lineage.

[15]Mathews (1933b) dissents from the widely-held view that only secular authority could be delegated.

and his assistants, the *aiuta* or *aioga* constabulary. The constabulary included hamlet heads (*oteyi*) and members of secret societies and dance groups. Individual *oteyi* administered the sublineage units in which they resided. The market-master and the heads of hamlets attending the market administered the site and adjudicated disputes arising on it in accordance with the customary criminal law (*uta*).

Having been encouraged to establish control over individual hamlets and market areas, these agents were in a position to challenge the secular authority of their seniors.[16] Thus, political discord between generational groups was the unintended consequence of a division of labour designed to strengthen the constitutional system. But such challenges were sporadic and short-lived. Similarly, the periodic emergence of an autocratic clan head signified only a temporary disruption of the constitutional equilibrium rooted in principles of chieftaincy, gerontocracy, and democracy in the *ojira*. As we shall see, the legitimacy of the traditional system was not permanently challenged until the era of colonial rule.

[16]This challenge was reflected in periodic attacks on what Eisenstadt (1964: 30) has termed 'the basic asymmetry of power and authority'.

Chapter Three Colonial Idoma: a study in normative and institutional change

Theorists of Indirect Rule assumed a relationship between colonial strategy and the degree of political development in African societies (Lugard 1920: 1ff.; 1923: 1ff.; Cameron 1934: 1ff.; Perham 1962: ch. 20).[1] An important consequence of that assumption was a tendency to define in largely normative terms colonial responsibility *vis-à-vis* societies with more highly developed administrative structures. For example, given the 'intelligence and powers of the Fulani caste', the primary objective of the British Administration in Moslem Northern Nigeria was to inject a catalytic agent into the emirate system: the presumed wisdom of a 'higher civilisation', including such alien notions as 'progress' and 'administrative efficiency' (Cameron 1934: 4, 5).

In theory, British rule in the Moslem North represented an exercise in plant maintenance and accretion: a well-constructed engine (the indigenous hierarchy, including Emir, district and village heads, and *alkali* or Islamic Courts) would be incorporated into a still wider politico-administrative network (including a bureaucratic engine with European administrative, judicial, and technical components). Together they would constitute, in Smith's words (1956: 63), a 'contraposition of coordinate units'.[2] This scheme predicated that European norms would govern behaviour in the indigenous sector. Moreover, it projected the expansion of the latter to include modern treasury, education, and technical components; these were also to be lubricated by alien norms.

Different structures were encountered, however, among primitive pagan tribes south of the Benue River (Laird and Oldfield 1837:

[1]Sir Frederick (later Lord) Lugard was the architect of indirect rule in Nigeria. High Commissioner of the Northern Nigeria Protectorate at the turn of the century, he was made Governor-General of Nigeria in 1914 (when the Protectorates of Northern and Southern Nigeria were joined with the Colony of Lagos to form a single political entity called the Colony and Protectorate of Nigeria).

Sir Donald Cameron, another exponent of indirect rule, was Governor of Tanganyika (1925–31) and Nigeria (1931–5).

[2]Also see Smith (1960: 1ff.) and Last (1970: 345–57).

442ff.; Crowther 1855: 53ff.; Burdo 1880: 239ff.; Mockler-Ferryman 1892: 72ff., 132–4). Difficulties were experienced with these peoples. For example, Mockler-Ferryman (*ibid*.: 76) observed in 1892 that 'the Mitshi [i.e., Munshi or Tiv] are a difficult people to deal with, since they acknowledge no one as head of the whole tribe, and live in independent families'.

The history of colonial administration among the contiguous Idoma underscores that early observation. Two dilemmas confronted the British in Idoma: How to reconcile a persistent, even if varyingly intense, commitment to indirect rule with a desire for institutional change? And how to reconcile a synthesis of the two with the long-range objective of normative change? Their response to those problems reflected a shift of emphasis in the definition of colonial responsibility. While normative change remained a long-range objective, institutional change assumed the highest short-range priority.[3] That priority was pursued until Nigeria's independence in 1960.

This chapter examines the evolution of administrative policy in Idoma as a response to the two dilemmas (Magid 1968: 299–313). It also illuminates, in due course, the relationship between colonial rule and role conflict confronting district councillors in that society.

Colonial policy in Idoma evolved through three phases. (1) 1908–30: occupation, boundary adjustment, pacification, and the quest for an indigenous leadership; (2) 1931–45: systematic implementation of, and subsequent retreat from, the policy of indirect rule; and (3) post-World War II: centralisation and 'democratisation' of the Idoma Native Authority or local government organisation.

1908–1930
Occupation, boundary adjustment, and pacification
Occupation of the area comprising Idoma Division commenced in 1908.[4] Early boundary adjustments were part of a larger effort to demarcate the boundary between the Southern and Northern Provinces of Nigeria. Modern Idoma Division came into existence in

---

[3]Perham (1962: ch. 10) notes that European personnel generally emphasised institutional change rather than Lugard's 'primarily educative' function or normative change.

[4]The area was penetrated as early as 1899 (Bassa Province *c*. 1910).

1928, as part of the new Benue Province in Northern Nigeria.[5]

Throughout the period 1908–30, European officers concentrated on eliminating such practices as slave-dealing, homicide, and headhunting – the stigmata of a primitive people[6] – and on achieving 'political pacification'. The last objective was pursued mainly by seeking to reduce the instability associated with disputes over succession to chieftaincy (Munshi Province 30 June 1919). That attempt was undermined to a great extent, however, by the decision to encourage indirect rule. With the injection of a new reward into the traditional 'game' of succession, power and prestige deriving from the Crown's paramount authority, competition for positions of *och'mbeke* ('chief of the white man')[7] intensified, and political instability increased.

The quest for an indigenous leadership

According to Lugard (1920: 22; 1970: 320), the character of indigenous organisation affected only the *degree* to which indirect rule might be applied. Thus, in Northern Nigeria, the contrast was not between indirect rule in the Moslem emirates and direct rule in pagan areas. Rather, it involved differences in the extent to which indigenous authorities were assigned tasks by the Administration.

In Idoma, it was apparent that a handful of European officers could not exercise political control if also required to collect tax and maintain law and order (Munshi Province 31 December 1919). Accordingly, the Administration mobilised an indigenous leadership to be responsible for such tasks.

[5] In 1924, the railway connecting Enugu (Southern Nigeria) and Kaduna (Northern Nigeria) passed through Oturkpo Town in Okwoga Division. Four years later, Okwoga Division and the old Idoma Division, comprising the southern and northern Idoma districts, respectively, were combined to form modern Idoma Division. Oturkpo Town has served as its headquarters since 1928.

[6] 'Pagan' peoples inhabiting Nigeria's 'Middle Belt' were generally regarded by European officials and missionaries as 'primitive' and inferior to the Moslems further north. And among the 'primitive pagans', the Idoma were often considered the lowest. Up to World War II the Idoma – or 'Okpoto', as they were called contemptuously by African and European alike – were viewed as a singularly barbaric people, ill-tempered, intransigent, and of low intelligence. Even their Tiv neighbours to the east – an acephalous society whose members had also practiced headhunting and resisted colonial rule in the early years – were more admired by the Europeans (Great Britain. House of Commons 1906: 179–240; Great Britain. Colonial Office 1934: 5–6; Crocker 1936: 63ff.; Heath 1941). Strong negative feelings towards the Idoma undoubtedly contributed to the failure before the war to incorporate their traditional constitutional system into the evolving local government organisation.

[7] *Och'mbeke* refers generally to any Administration-appointed 'chief' or village headman. Since World War II the term has been applied to the district heads.

The village level. 'Village areas' were created at the base of Idoma society. Theoretically, their headmen were appointed in accordance with native law and custom; in fact, appointments were often made by European officers alone. Occasionally, a traditional *oteyi* (hamlet head) was selected by elders and/or the Administration (*ibid*.; Munshi Province 1920).

The use of *oteyi* for administrative purposes did not involve incorporation of the *aiuta* constabulary. The *aiuta* system had largely decayed prior to 1908. European officers were now loath to revive a constabulary whose members were traditionally drawn from secret societies and dance groups known for their rebelliousness and headhunting activities.

The district level. Single- and multi-clan districts were created at the next higher level. Prior to 1914, these were governed with the assistance of Hausa and Yoruba headmen. By 1919, the decision was taken to rely on Idoma personnel and institutions.[8]

Those encouraged to accept district headships were not necessarily traditional office-holders. The Administration's decision to use such elements reflected the moribund condition of Idoma chieftaincy prior to World War I. Two developments did, however, endow many of the new district headships with a measure of traditional legitimacy. First, European revival of the *oche* (clan head) and *aiigabo* (clan spokesmen) titles produced traditional office-holders to serve as district heads. Second, appointees often enhanced the legitimacy of their positions by later obtaining the *oche* title. An alliance between European officers and the district head generally ensured the latter's acquisition of that title.

Having constructed an administrative apparatus, the Administration next attempted to organise an efficient judiciary. A Native Court was established in each district. Lacking real power, these courts were largely ineffectual in the period 1908–19.

The judicial system was reformed after World War I. A Native Court resembling the traditional *ojira* was established in each district. The salaried district head presided over a court composed of lineage and sublineage representatives.

Judicial reform along traditional lines appeared to underscore a commitment to indirect rule. In this vein, the Administration noted in

[8]This change was encouraged by Idoma resentment of 'stranger' chiefs and by the hostility of the Northern Provinces Administration toward the 'Warrant Chief' system in the Southern Provinces.

1922 that 'there can be not the slightest doubt that the re-creation of the Okpoto [i.e., Idoma] system of native rule is worth any exertion' (Munshi Province 31 December 1922).

The commitment implied a restoration of the constitutional equilibrium rooted in principles of chieftaincy, gerontocracy, and democracy in the *ojira*. That objective was avowed in 1923: 'It is now the policy of this Division to make the indigenous *ojira* the authority and do away with the system of rule through [largely autonomous European-] "made" chiefs . . .' (Munshi Province 30 June 1923).

Yet only six months later the Administration noted that 'the *ojira*, . . . from which it was once hoped that a native administration would spring, [has] proved . . . a barren seed' (Munshi Province 1923). Disillusionment with this attempt at indirect rule can be explained by re-examining that institution in traditional Idoma. The assembly was an arena in which public opinion crystallised. While that opinion could sanction individual or collective vengeance against wrongdoers, the *ojira* itself was neither an administrative nor a judicial agency.

In traditional Idoma, those functions had devolved for the most part on the *aiuta* constabulary. Reluctant to revive the *aiuta*, yet determined to govern through traditional institutions, the Administration turned instead to the *ojira*; it was to serve as a fulcrum for district administration and adjudication. This crucial exercise in institutional adaptation represented an attempt 'to create [an organ that had] no real counterpart in the indigenous social structure' (Heath 1941). Failure was predictable. The notion of the *ojira* as a fulcrum was, at least for the time being, abandoned.

The divisional level. Aware of the difficulty involved in governing an acephalous polity, the Administration sought a remedy in the decade after World War I. Ostensibly resorting to indirect rule, it formed the Idoma Central Council, or *ojira* of district heads. The council was gazetted as the Superior Native Authority primarily responsible for advising European officers on matters affecting the whole division (*ibid.*). It was also expected to serve as the Appellate Court in Idoma Division (Benue Province 1930).

In fact that body was not a Superior Native Authority. It met only infrequently and lacked real executive authority (Heath 1941; Crocker 1936: 66–7). European officers continued to exercise direct rule at the divisional level. Neither was the Central Council an *ojira* properly understood. Its generally compact form, prescribed membership, and scheduled meetings were only infrequent attributes of the traditional assembly. More important, however, the council operated at a political level that did not exist in pre-colonial Idoma. It was, in the final analysis, an organ of the Administration rather than a genuine representative of the Idoma people. As such, it reinforced a centralising tendency that was not compatible with Idoma constitutional ideas and organisation.

Implications of colonial rule in the period 1908–30

During the formative period of colonial rule in Idoma, the Administration had been greatly influenced by the Fulani model of government. Village areas and districts established in Idoma paralleled those found in the emirates. Fascination with that model is also indicated in the Administration's reaction to failure at the district level. Unable to reconcile administrative needs with the democratic and gerontocratic principles, it turned to the principle of chieftaincy. Colonial officers sought to construct an efficient Native Authority system by strengthening chieftaincy at the district and divisional levels. They succeeded at the district level only. Yet as early as 1927 the Central Council was perceived as the precursor of a divisional chieftaincy in Idoma (Benue Province 1927). The Administration envisaged a paramountcy modelled after the Fulani emirship.

Before turning to the second administrative phase, it would be well to summarise the effects on Idoma constitutionalism of developments examined above. While clan heads in traditional Idoma periodically behaved as autocrats, there is no evidence that *de facto* autocracy permanently challenged the legitimacy of the constitutional system: chiefly usurpation appears to have been extra-constitutional if not unconstitutional behaviour.

In contrast, the Administration's cultivation of strong chieftaincy tended to subvert that legitimacy. The regulatory mechanism in the Idoma constitution was eroded by the failure to integrate elders and the *ojira* into district administration. This did not, of course, remove the district head from the arena of traditional control; in theory, he was subject to its sanctions. Rather, the competitive legitimacy of the colonial authority system largely insulated him from this regulatory mechanism. Encouraged by European officers, the district head had moved from a traditional position of *primus inter pares* to one of undisputed primacy.

1931–1945

The implementation of indirect rule

During the early 1930s British rule in Africa was subjected to critical re-examination – both officially and unofficially (e.g., Cameron 1934: *passim*; Crocker 1936: 5ff.). Among the most influential critics was Margery Perham, student of colonial administration, apologist for the policy of indirect rule, and later Lugard's biographer (Perham 1956). Perham (1962: *passim*; 1931: 310–11; 1934a: 321–34; 1934b: 622) lamented the frequent assumption that indirect rule required autocratic chieftaincy. She argued contrarily that it ought to favour the restoration of traditional conciliar democracy.

In Idoma the Administration moved swiftly to strengthen the constitutional system. It proposed to adhere more closely to indirect rule by

... organis[ing] (but not ... over-organis[ing] and ... reduc[ing] to the lifeless formality of the average parliament or conference) the mass meetings of the clan (where even in the past only the leaders and men of influence had any real say) into District *Ojiras* of village heads and leading men, who in their turn choose the *Oche* or chief who becomes the district head (Idoma Native Authority 31 August 1931).

A series of anthropological investigations undertaken by European officers (e.g., Leslie 1936; Money 1935b) affirmed that the *ojira* had in fact controlled all actions of the *oche* in traditional Idoma. Restoration of the constitutional equilibrium was now viewed as necessary for successful administration in the division (Idoma Native Authority 11 November 1933).

The Native Authority was reorganised. A conciliar system replaced that based on village area and district units. 'Chief-in-Council' organs were gazetted as Superior Native Authorities in the former single-clan districts. The *oche* in each was designated lifetime president of an *ojira* comprising *oteyi*, kindred heads, and elders. In the former federated districts, each clan *ojira*, including the *oche*, became a Subordinate Native Authority. Subordinate Native Authorities were empowered to collect tax and maintain law and order. Clan *ojiras* or their representatives formed a Federal Council or Superior Native Authority. The council was responsible for enforcing the law, supervising markets, and disbursing funds. It, in turn, chose a lifetime president in accordance with the principle of clan rotation (Leslie 1936; Money 1935b).

Superior Native Authorities were granted some financial responsibility. They received tax revenues, and paid scribes, messengers, police, and, in federated areas, Subordinate Native Authorities.[9] They also sat as unpaid Native Courts which could imprison persons convicted of praedial larceny for a maximum term of nine months. An attempt was even made to have secret societies and dance groups act as agents of the courts (Magid 1972: 298–9).

Finally, in 1935, the Idoma Central Council was gazetted as an advisory body. European officers continued to head the Native Authority until 1947, when an Idoma Chieftaincy was inaugurated. The Council retained its judicial function until 1937, when Regional Appelate Courts were established for Northern, Southern, Western, and Eastern Idoma (Leslie 1936; Money 1935a).

The retreat from indirect rule

Native Authority reorganisation appeared to indicate a commitment to indirect rule based on Idoma constitutionalism. Yet there was evidence to the contrary. For example, we note the Administration's equivocal response to Perham's plea for reform, and the implications of that response for later developments in Idoma.

The Secretary of the Northern Provinces of Nigeria stated that, while his superior, the Chief Commissioner,

agrees with the views expressed in theory [by Perham], . . . the difficulty is that the people themselves do not want councils but prefer chiefs since they have been taught the Moslem system of district heads by administrative officers. In one case His Honour was told by the people that their original organisation was democratic, by council, but that they now know better and had progressed into having a chief (Benue Province 11 May 1934).

A retreat from indirect rule had been signalled. European officers reported that formal abolition of the Fulani district system had not fundamentally altered the *status quo*; conciliar administration had merely caused salaries to be redistributed (Leslie 1936; Money 1935b). Other officers assailed Perham's thesis that traditional political organisation was essentially conciliar. Pointing to autocratic chieftaincy in pre-colonial Idoma and to public opinion which allegedly favoured district headships, they urged that district administration be formally reinstituted (Benue Province 22 August 1938).[10]

[9]European officers still controlled the appointment and dismissal of scribes, police, etc.

[10]The decision taken by the Administration to strengthen chieftaincy at the expense of the *ojira* assembly was an expression, too, of impatience with a body which appeared to

Even as indirect rule was being subverted in the name of 'democracy', the Administration continued to express its predilection for traditional constitutional practices. For example, as late as 1939, the Senior District Officer in Idoma posited that the only alternative to a district head system was 'the Ioma . . . [being] left to himself, with tactful guidance and encouragement, to work out his own democratic salvation' (Benue Province 1939). But he was soon to concede that the Idoma had not yet attained 'his own democratic salvation': ' . . . here we are dealing with a more or less artificial creation of our own and not with the reform of an old established system as in the [Moslem] North' (Heath 1941).

Post-World War II

Centralisation and 'democracy' in the Native Authority

The Administration's final exercises in institutional change involved centralising and 'democratising' the local government establishment. Plural Native Authorities created in the 1930s were replaced by a central administration and judiciary designed to promote unity and efficiency in the division (Benue Province 1948). The focal point of the new system was an Idoma Chieftaincy created in 1947. The Idoma Central Council designated Ogiri Oko, the combined clan head/district head of Adoka, *Och'Idoma* (Chief of Idoma) for life; whereupon the Council was replaced by a five-man Advisory Council established to assist the Chief in administering the division. In 1948 the Chief and his council were gazetted as the Idoma Central Court, with power to hear appeals passing from Native Courts in the districts through four Intermediate Area Courts.

The process of 'democratising' the Native Authority commenced in 1947 with the abolition of all Superior and Subordinate Native Authorities. Their administrative responsibilities were assumed by Native Authority departments in Oturkpo Town. With the exception of their judicial function, retained until 1952, district *ojiras* had only to serve as the base in a new multi-tiered electoral system. Each *ojira* elected a representative to one of four Intermediate Area Councils in

---

eschew formal procedures (Crocker 1936: *passim*). Similar impatience with traditional councils could be found throughout sub-Saharan Africa (Richards and Kuper, eds. 1971: 9).

the division. Members of each council, in turn, elected one representative to the *Och'Idoma*'s Advisory Council. In addition to a co-opted scribe, the first Advisory Council included three elderly clan heads and a district head – all four illiterate (Benue Province 1950).

The implications of that election are made clearer by reference to forces operating in a wider context. In the aftermath of World War II, educated elements throughout British Africa were agitating for a larger share in the political and economic life of their territories. Nationalists were especially vocal in demanding greater participation in government and administration as a prelude to independence (e.g., Coleman 1958: 271–95; Apter 1955: 141ff.).

In Nigeria many basically in sympathy with these aspirations were at the same time committed to a gradual approach. According to Perham (1962: 362), for example, 'democratisation' of the Native Authority system was more desirable than either the immediate recruitment of Africans into upper echelons of the civil service or the expansion of powers in the Legislative Council. The gradual approach was reflected in post-war constitutional developments. In March 1945 Governor Sir Arthur Richards presented the Legislative Council with a plan for constitutional revision whose nucleus was embodied in the so-called 'Richards Constitution' that governed Nigeria until 1951 (Great Britain. House of Commons. 1945). The most significant portions dealt with the organisation of a Nigerian state and the place within it of a Native Authority system. A series of compromises between contending federalists and separatists produced a state divided into three Regions (East, West, and North). Each had an administrative service and a House of Assembly; the latter was empowered to prepare the regional budget and discuss legislation. Native Authorities in each Region nominated the members of the Assembly. That body, in turn, nominated five representatives to sit on the Legislative Council at the centre. By establishing a hierarchy of indirectly elected councils connecting apex and base, the British perpetuated a Native Authority system as the basis for local administration. Not surprisingly, many Africans opposed the conservative bent of government and constitution.[11]

[11]Tribal nationalism helped to quicken the pace of political development in Nigeria. Constitutional changes wrought between 1951 and 1957 left the country with these arrangements on the eve of independence (Ezera 1964: 39ff.): three Regions each had a bicameral legislature (an appointive House of Chiefs and a popularly-elected House of Assembly); an executive; a judiciary; and an administrative service. The executive was headed by a Premier appointed by the Regional Governor from among the majority

Opposition to official conservatism pervaded the Nigerian political system. Even as Nnamdi Azikiwe, Obafemi Awolowo, and others worked at the centre for change, lesser lights engaged in parallel activities nearer the periphery. For example, literate youths in the reformist Idoma Hope Rising Union (IHRU) agitated for greater participation in the Native Authority (Magid 1971: 354–9).[12] The election of four illiterates, including three traditional office-holders, to the Advisory Council in 1948 provoked even more vehement demands for change.

The dissidents called for immediate doubling of Intermediate Area Council representation on the *Och'Idoma*'s Advisory Council (Benue Province 1950). The Administration proposed that they join the Intermediate Area Councils as 'unofficials', and participate at the centre as an 'advisory committee' (*ibid.*). Predictably, the youths rejected a proposal which seemed to reaffirm the *status quo* in Native Authority affairs.

The dissidents sought to force the issue. Preparing for indirect elections to the Northern House of Assembly in 1951, they managed to gain control of electoral colleges at the district and divisional levels. Their demands for local government reform could now be more effectively expressed. Agitation continued unabated.

party in the Assembly. The Premier, in turn, recommended to the Governor the appointment of Government Ministers from among the members of the Assembly. In every case the Regional Government was dominated by a single party organised around a major tribal grouping: the National Council of Nigeria and the Cameroons (Ibo) in the East; the Action Group (Yoruba) in the West; and Northern Peoples' Congress (Hausa-Fulani) in the North.

By 1957 the central government also included legislative, executive, judicial, and administrative institutions. The members of the House of Representatives at Lagos were popularly-elected in the three regions. The Governor-General was empowered to appoint as Prime Minister the person who commanded a majority in the House. That official then recommended to the Governor-General the appointment of (1) Government Ministers (comprising the Council of Ministers) from among the members of the House, and (2) the members of the Senate soon to be established. A Public Service Commission advised the Governor-General on matters affecting public officials in the Nigerian Federation.

As a result of the federal parliamentary election of 1959, a coalition government was formed at the centre by the conservative NPC and its junior partner, the nationalist NCNC. Sir Abubakar Tafawa Balewa, an NPC man from the far North, was designated the Prime Minister. The stage was set for independence a year later.

[12]The tribal union initially favoured Native Authority centralisation under a strong divisional chieftaincy in order to break the political stranglehold of the district heads. By 1949, however, many members opposed the *Och'Idoma*'s formal inauguration, alleging his corruption and his alliance with those elements.

Finally, in 1953, the Administration relented. The Advisory Council was expanded to include a scribe and two members elected to three-year terms by each Intermediate Area Council. With six literates averaging 35–40 years in age, the Advisory Council was transformed, in the words of one observer, into a 'useful blend of traditional office-holders and educated progressives' (Benue Province 1952). Each district *ojira* was authorised to nominate one person to sit with the district head on the Intermediate Area Council. And the Native Courts based on the *ojira* were replaced by District Courts, whose members were elected from officially recognised, kindred-based constituencies.

In retrospect, it appears that the Administration was influenced only in part by local pressures for reform. Important developments were taking place at the regional level. In 1950 a commission was established in the Northern Region to inquire into the state of local administration.[13] Later that year it reported the existence of a wide variety of largely ineffective councils, committees, and conferences. The commission confirmed a trend towards conciliar administration at the local level (Maddocks and Pott 1951: 1–35).

The Northern House of Assembly, perhaps sensitive to 'democratisation' of local administration in the Eastern and Western Regions, adopted a programme of reform. Sole Native Authorities (i.e., emirates and chieftaincies without formal responsibility to councils) were gradually replaced by gazetted 'Chief-in-Council' or 'Chief-and-Council' organs.

A Native Authority Law was enacted in 1954 (Northern MLG 1961; Wraith 1964: 125–44). Essentially a codification of existing legislation, it recognised the abolition of Sole Native Authorities and outlined the formal relationship between local councils and the Native Authority system. All informal councils operative as of July 1954 were rendered statutory bodies. While the law did not establish any new organs, it did provide that Native Authorities could establish local councils for administrative sub-areas (section 55). The North's *formal* commitment to 'democratisation' of the Native Authority system was embodied in section 59: local councils were to include elected majorities.

In sum, Native Authority reforms in Idoma resulted from a convergence of forces: (1) agitation by a clamant minority in the division;

[13] I have drawn from Cowan (1958: 79–83) for the discussion of Northern developments.

and (2) the Administration's post-war commitment to gradual, controlled change. A gradual approach, forming the thread with which both the 'Richards Constitution' and Native Authority Law were woven, guided future developments in Idoma.

The Idoma Native Authority proceeded to establish a District Council system. These bodies – with elected majorities and minorities appointed by the Native Authority – were empowered to act as agents of the local government organisation and representatives of the district population (Northern MLG 3 March 1958; 19 April 1962). The first triennial elections were held in 1955.

Having established a hierarchy of councils connecting apex and base in Idoma, the Administration next turned to the problem of normative change. It sought to reconcile 'democratisation' with the objective of an *efficient* Native Authority. In 1958, after lengthy experimentation, the four Intermediate Area Councils and the *Och'Idoma*'s Advisory Council were abolished. The former were replaced by a Representative Council linking district and divisional levels. Sixteen of the twenty-two District Councils each elected one person to a three-year term on the Representative Council; councils of the six most populous districts each elected two representative councillors.

A General Purposes Committee replaced the Advisory Council as the policy-making body in the Native Authority. The Committee included the *Och'Idoma* (President), two administrative councillors elected by representative councillors from each of the former intermediate areas, and representative councillors chosen in rotation (Idoma Native Authority 20 August 1958).[14] Two years later the unwieldy Committee was overhauled: The eight administrative councillors were replaced by four portfolio councillors elected in the same manner and assigned similar functions.[15]

The Administration's final exercise in normative and institutional change involved the judiciary. Administrative and judicial functions were separated in 1957, presumably to enhance Native Authority efficiency at the district and divisional levels. The *Och'Idoma* and the

---

[14]Administrative councillors were elected for a three-year term. Each headed a department in the Native Authority – Finance, Local Government, Police-Judiciary, or Works.

[15]The portfolio councillor was nominally a consultant, the administrative councillor an executive (Northern MLG 12 September 1962). In fact, both were executives.

district heads were replaced as court presidents (Idoma Native Authority 6 June 1957). The four Intermediate Area Courts were abolished one year later (Idoma Native Authority 22 January 1958). In 1961 the District and Central Courts were replaced by six 'professional' Circuit Courts of first instance (see p. 127). Civil and criminal sections convened separately under a single court president. Appeals from both sections passed directly to the Provincial Court at Makurdi.

Colonial rule in Idoma: a summary

An examination of administrative policy in colonial Idoma has revealed a pendulating course of development: on the one hand, cultivation of strong chieftaincy and centralisation based on the Fulani model; on the other, 'democratisation', rooted first in Idoma constitutionalism, and finally in Western notions of majoritarian local government. Those alternating movements have illuminated the two dilemmas confronting the British in Idoma: How to reconcile a persistent, even if varyingly intense, commitment to indirect rule with a desire for institutional change? And how to reconcile a synthesis of the two with the elusive long-range objective of normative change?

The irreconcilability of long-range objectives with the mandate of indirect rule was evident as early as 1922. In that year, indirect rule based on Idoma constitutionalism waxed and quickly waned. Yet it survived as an influential myth for nearly two decades until a candid Senior District Officer affirmed the contrast between artificiality in Idoma and reform in the emirates.

Having abandoned all pretence of indirect rule, the Administration sought to create that which was envisaged twenty years earlier. In 1947 the Native Authority was centralised under a divisional chieftaincy. However, post-war conciliar 'democratisation' augured a Pyrrhic victory for the Administration. Could one expect councils hastily formed to contribute any more to the viability of the Native Authority than had the *ojira* earlier? Prophets of doom discerned in 'democratisation' a reverse trend toward decentralisation and a harbinger of the disorderliness which often seemed to characterise Native Authority affairs prior to World War II.

What of the prophecy? The evidence points to the contrary. It can be argued on several grounds that 'democratisation' promoted centralisation under an even stronger Idoma Chieftaincy. First, the *Och'Idoma* consolidated his position *vis-à-vis* the district heads by appearing to support both the IHRU clamouring for 'democracy'

53

c

(i.e., participation) and the Administration insistent on efficiency. District heads were excluded from the Representative Council and the General Purposes Committee. This 'reform' limited the district heads' ability to exert direct influence at Native Authority headquarters. Second, the separation of administrative and judicial functions engendered competition for power, prestige, and income between district heads and court presidents appointed by the Native Authority leadership. Predictably, the district heads protested against both 'reforms', but to no avail. At the same time, the *Och'Idoma* maintained control of the upper judiciary by appointing a brother to the Presidency of the Central Court. Third, abolition of the Intermediate Area Courts, on which district heads sat, eliminated four strategic points around which opposition might organise. Fourth, the ability of the District Councils to rival the centre was circumscribed by their rural isolation, limited powers, and continued dependence on goodwill in Oturkpo Town. Fifth, as President of the General Purposes Committee, the *Och'Idoma* controlled policy-making in the Native Authority. This enabled him to wield considerable influence in the day-to-day operations of the Native Authority departments.

In sum, changes wrought in Idoma between 1947 and 1960 were most beneficial to the centre. By combining institutional change, prestige of chiefly office, and consummate skill as a politician, Ogiri Oko had outmanoeuvred his foes in both the IHRU and the Native Authority. Concomitantly, midway through his administration he could claim much support among the essentially conservative Idoma for defending the institution of chieftaincy in the face of IHRU attacks upon traditionalist clan heads and district heads, and for appearing to favour both the elimination of autocratic district headships and the restoration of the traditional constitutional equilibrium. (Despite competition from the court presidents, most district heads remained virtual autocrats in their administrative units.) By 1960, when Oko died and Nigeria became independent, it could fairly be said that the Administration's culminating exercises in institutional change had been successful. Politically and administratively, Idoma was centralised as never before. That it had yet to experience the efficiency which might have resulted from long-range normative change does not detract from that achievement.[16]

[16]Especially sensitive to administrative inefficiency in Idoma, the Administration conceded the lag between institutional and normative change (Idoma Native Authority 5 September 1958).

Between 1960 and 1963 the political and administrative climate changed significantly in Idoma Division. In 1960 Ajene Ukpabi was designated by a convocation of the twenty-two district heads in the division to succeed his father-in-law as *Och'Idoma*.[17] Despite considerable intelligence and governmental experience (Ukpabi had been an administrative councillor and a portfolio councillor in the Native Authority), he laboured under severe handicaps. First, many Idoma deeply resented the fact that an ethnic Egede – a 'stranger' – had been installed as Chief. The Idoma traditionally viewed their Egede neighbours as pariahs: in the words of one educated informant, 'chiefless primitives distinguished only for their service as slaves'.[18] Stigmatised by ethnic affiliation and lack of facility in the Idoma language, Ukpabi became the butt of contemptuous jokes. His frail, sickly appearance was also the object of considerable ridicule.

Second, some feared that installation of Ogiri Oko's son-in-law might encourage the substitution of the dynastic principle for the principle of rotation in succession to chieftaincy. They assailed Ajene Ukpabi as a foe of Idoma constitutionalism.

Third, the *Och'Idoma* lacked the political adroitness of his predecessor; Ogiri Oko alone could keep opponents off-balance and fighting among themselves. In the period 1960–3, Ajene Ukpabi's bitter rival in the struggle for succession – a Minister of State in the Northern Region Government and the son of a prominent district head (deceased) in western Idoma – led the opposition to his rule. Ironically, many of the *Och'Idoma*'s actions encouraged unity among his opponents, both within the Native Authority and in the division at large. For example, his decision in 1963 to rotate the court presidents among the six judicial units in Idoma Division – presumably to enhance efficiency and to reduce official corruption (Idoma Native Authority 22 October 1960) – was generally interpreted as an assault on powerful vested interests. The judicial reform of 1961 had already deprived the *Och'Idoma* of an important power base: the Idoma Central Court. By risking the alienation of its successors – the six

[17]According to various informants, including some who participated in the selection process in 1947 and 1960 (and who were political allies of the two Chiefs of Idoma), both men had been designated by the district heads after lengthy negotiations with European officers. Viewing Ukpabi as somewhat more flexible than his autocratic predecessor, the district heads chose him over a powerful and ambitious rival.

[18]The Egede reside in Ito, Worku, and Egede districts. (See Map 3, and Frampton 1935; Armstrong 1955: 140–70; Idoma Native Authority 23 May 1933.)

Circuit Courts and their presidents – Ukpabi was unwittingly serving the political interests of his principal rival. Significantly, this occurred at a time when the Northern Government was expressing its dissatisfaction with the performance of the Native Authority. In 1963 the regional Minister for Local Government responded to the Native Authority's chronic tardiness in tax collection by reducing the status of its treasury from Grade 'B' to Grade 'C'. This action accelerated the decline in Ukpabi's personal prestige. It also caused him to lose control over the financial affairs of the Native Authority; the District Officer in Idoma, responsible to the Minister for Local Government, was now empowered to administer the Native Treasury. Forced by his new assignment to forgo systematic touring of the districts, the District Officer was unable to assist the Chief in checking rural opposition to his rule.[19] By 1963, opponents of the *Och'Idoma* among regional officials, district heads, court presidents, court members, and councillors at all levels of the Native Authority had seized the initiative. It was in this fluid milieu that I began my study.

Institutional and normative changes introduced during the colonial era and perpetuated after independence produced two types of strain in Idoma society: political instability and disunity engendered by disputes over chieftaincy; and role conflict. The first type, endemic in Idoma, was exacerbated by the fateful decision to make chieftaincy the keystone of the Native Authority. Cultivation of that institution hastened the decline of Idoma constitutionalism. This development was reflected in the weakening of mechanisms which traditionally regulated chieftaincy affairs: ritual, the principles of rotation and seniority, and public opinion in the *ojira* assembly. As the regulatory mechanisms became less effective, competition for the power, prestige, and emoluments[20] associated with positions of *och'mbeke* (chief of the white man) became more intense. This, in turn, caused political instability and disunity to increase. Centralisation of the Native Authority under a powerful Idoma Chieftaincy did not serve to diminish the convulsive effects of disputes over chieftaincy.

[19]Even without this onerous assignment, it is doubtful whether the District Officer would have been able greatly to assist the *Och'Idoma*. By early 1963 it was common knowledge that that post would shortly be 'Africanised'. Its last European incumbent was expected to have little influence in Idoma politics.

[20]The emoluments included salaries, bribes, and tribute.

The second type of strain – role conflict – derived from the pendulating course by which administrative policy developed in colonial Idoma. Various attempts at 'democratisation' – based initially on Idoma constitutionalism, and finally on Western notions of majoritarian local government – attended the cultivation of strong chieftaincy in the period 1919–60. Centralisation of the Native Authority – conceived in 1927 and accelerated after the creation of a divisional chieftaincy some twenty years later – did not halt the swing to 'democratisation'. Most Idoma hoped that the multi-tiered system of councils established after World War II would exercise a restraining influence on the bureaucratising impulses of district heads and the *Och'Idoma*. Because the establishment of councils reinforced the traditional abhorrence of autocratic rule, many felt betrayed when 'democratisation' was subsequently manipulated to promote Native Authority centralisation under a powerful Idoma Chieftaincy.

Feelings of betrayal were first provoked by the activities of portfolio councillors and representative councillors. As members of the policy-making General Purposes Committee, these officials were understandably loath to oppose strong chieftaincy and centralised political authority. They quickly joined forces with the first *Och'Idoma* and his allies among the district heads. Popular disillusionment with the two groups of councillors waxed in 1959.

Adding to the disillusionment was the widespread realisation that gradual, controlled change in the post-war era had encouraged an inexorable increase in the power of the Native Authority at the expense of all opposition elements. By now that power had prepared the way for the demise of the IHRU. Having failed to achieve its primary objective – a major policy role in a democratised local government establishment – the IHRU succumbed in 1959 to the combined pressures of erosion from within and coercion from without. Later that year, the Native Authority demonstrated its great power by leading three candidates of the conservative Northern Peoples' Congress (NPC) to easy victories in the federal parliamentary elections which preceded independence (Post 1963: 454). As a result, Idoma Division was firmly tied to the NPC, the political party which controlled both the regional government in Kaduna and the federal government in Lagos.

Those disillusioned by the failure to restrain chiefly power and centralisation were in a state of disarray, some responding to the events of 1959 by retiring from the fray; others by joining their former opponents in the Native Authority; and still others by seeking fresh allies for a renewed assault on vested interests in the Native Authority. Believing that the higher officials who opposed the second *Och'Idoma* were nevertheless advocates of strong chieftaincy and centralised political authority, this third group (which reflected the sentiments of a substantial majority of the rural population) turned in desperation to the District Councils operating near the base of Idoma society. Despite their rural isolation and limited powers, the councils were widely acclaimed as representatives of the traditional *ojira* assembly and, therefore, as a vanguard of the resistance to chiefly power and Native Authority centralisation. To some this function was further legitimised by the official policy which brought them into existence in 1955: the councils were to 'faithfully represent . . . the people of the various districts' (Idoma Division May 1955: 1–2). Curiously, many Idoma – including district councillors – either failed to appreciate or deliberately chose to ignore the fact that these bodies were, in the final analysis, dependent on goodwill in Oturkpo Town. As statutory agents of the Native Authority,[21] the councils were also expected (1) to recommend to the General Purposes Committee the appointment of district heads and local tax collectors; (2) to levy taxes on individuals and village units; (3) to authorise the expenditure of council funds; (4) to supervise work for the regional government and Native Authority in the district when required to do so; (5) to supervise the use of communal labour approved by the General Purposes Committee; (6) to maintain law and order within the district; and (7) to carry out duties delegated by the Committee (Benue Province May 1955: 2).

The District Councils' legal mandate underscored the tension in Idoma between centralisation and 'democratisation'. One manifestation of that tension was role conflict stemming from competition between bureaucratic and debureaucratic values and interests. As 'men in the middle', councillors at all levels of the Native Authority were subjected to conflicting role-expectations which were widely seen as reflecting, on the one hand, support for, and on the other,

---

[21]The Chief of Idoma, portfolio councillors, and district heads are salaried Native Authority officials; representative councillors and district councillors are paid sitting fees. District heads and the Chief are appointed for life and are pensionable; portfolio councillors, representative councillors, and district councillors may serve an unlimited number of three-year terms. Tax collectors serve indefinitely and are remunerated with a portion of the tax receipts.

opposition to, strong chieftaincy and centralisation.[22] Among these local officials, the district councillors were especially vulnerable to role conflict. Caught up in swiftly moving events and sometimes perplexed by their formal mandate, they were held hostage by all camps in the struggle over the character of the Native Authority. In due course we shall specify some of the cross-pressures which the councillors experienced as well as their responses. But it is first necessary to illuminate both their backgrounds and the process by which they came to hold office.

[22]The district heads served as permanent chairmen of the District Councils and could also be viewed as 'men in the middle'. Participant observation, conversations with district heads, and the testimony of many informants all revealed that those officials generally experienced far less role conflict than the district councillors. Predictably, the district heads' primary loyalty was to their Native Authority employer. See pp 228–40, 260–5.

Part III The men in the middle

Chapter Four The Idoma district councillors: social backgrounds and personal profiles

Two objectives are pursued in this chapter, viz. to orient the reader generally to the social environment in which fieldwork was undertaken, and to illustrate the social backgrounds of the seventy-one district councillors on whom the study centres. Data obtained by interviewing those officials (see pp 258–9, 268–9) are presented here in aggregate form and in profiles of selected councillors.

Tenure in office

In accordance with the Native Authority Law of 1954, the twenty-two District Councils in Idoma Division were comprised of popularly-elected majorities and minorities appointed by the central administration of the Native Authority upon the recommendation of the district head; 'the Native Authority councillors' served three-year terms concurrently with their elected colleagues. A system of triennial elections was inaugurated in 1955; elections followed in 1958 and, after some procrastination, in early 1962. The study was undertaken in Boju, Ochekwu, Oglewu, Oturkpo and Yangedde districts in the aftermath of the 1962 elections.

Among the seventy-one district councillors who took office in these districts in 1962, fifty-five (77 per cent) were elected to represent particular constituencies and sixteen (23 per cent) were appointed by the Native Authority. There was a high turnover that year: forty-five elected councillors and eleven 'Native Authority councillors' (together representing 79 per cent of the total) were serving for the first time. More light is thrown on this finding with some additional data: thirty-nine of the fifty-five elected councillors (71 per cent) stood in contested elections; of the thirty-nine, only five confronted an incumbent councillor. Interestingly, the five defeated incumbents were subsequently appointed to serve as 'Native Authority councillors'. Among the factors which accounted for the reluctance of most councillors to seek re-election in 1962 were the following: the press of council business; inadequate remuneration (a five-shilling sitting-fee per month); feelings of powerlessness *vis-à-vis* superiors in the Native Authority; and deference to the principle of rotation in succession of councillors.

Age

Despite the fact that the adult Idoma cannot specify his age, it was possible to establish a fairly reliable approximation for the district councillors with this procedure: each councillor was asked to recall an important historical event and any youthful experience he had had about the same time. (Nine events were identified, seven by more than one councillor; seven youthful experiences were also cited, six by more than one respondent.) Since the agricultural cycle in Idoma is roughly equivalent to a year, each councillor was then asked to estimate the number of cycles which ordinarily pass between the birth of a child and the experience cited. Estimates for the six experiences cited by more than one councillor were compared. In all cases the differences were slight, ranging from one to three cycles (or years). Councillors' estimates for each of the seven youthful experiences were also compared with estimates solicited from other Idoma informants. Here, too, the differences ranged from one to three cycles (or years). The dates of historical events cited by the councillors were culled from official files in the Divisional Office at Oturkpo Town.

These events were identified by the district councillors: an influenza epidemic (1917); a murderous battle between the Boju and Oturkpo clans (1921); the commencement of railway construction in Oturkpo district (1922); the establishment of an administrative centre at Oturkpo Town (1924); the opening of Methodist Mission primary schools in central Idoma (1925); the public hanging of a convicted headhunter (1928) ; the creation of modern Idoma Division (1928); a destructive locust invasion (1935); and the return of Idoma soldiers from wartime service in India and Burma (1946). The youthful experiences cited by the councillors included bathing alone in a stream for the first time (4–5 years of age, based on estimates of agricultural cycles); enrolment in a primary school (5–6 years of age); farming alongside a father for the first time (6–8 years of age); circumcision (13–14 years of age); sexual intercourse for the first time (16–18 years of age); farming alone for the first time (16–18 years of age); and taking of the first wife (18–20 years of age). Thus, a councillor who recalled the influenza epidemic as an event which occurred when he first farmed alongside his father was estimated to have been 52 years of age when interviewed in 1962. Another who recalled the return of Idoma soldiers as an event which occurred when he first farmed alone was estimated to have been 33 years of age.

The ages of the seventy-one district councillors ranged from 32 to 64.[1] Of the total, only eight councillors were under 40 years of age. Nearly double that number, fifteen, were over 60. In between, twenty-eight councillors were in the 40–49 age bracket, twelve in the 50–59 age bracket. The mean age for all respondents was 50, the median age 49.

While age need not correspond with seniority based on genealogical status – for example, where a man's son is older than the former's brother – it usually does. Comparing two clan members, we are apt to find that the older one is also closer to the putative common male ancestor. Young men with low seniority are rarely elevated to leadership positions – traditional or modern – at the district level in Idoma. The data underscore a preference for older, more senior leaders.

Residence

The district councillors had deep roots in the area in which they resided. Thus, forty-six (65 per cent) of the seventy-one councillors lived in the rural settlement where they were born. Twelve (17 per cent) lived in the district where they were born, but in a settlement other than their birthplace. Only thirteen councillors (18 per cent) were born in another district. Of the fifty-five elected councillors, thirty-nine (71 per cent) represented constituencies which were coterminous with or included their birthplace.

Those district councillors who were either members of a uterine group or descendants of the marriage of Idoma parents from different clans were 'strangers' in the genealogical sense alone. As one 'stranger' put it: 'Why am I insulted for having a Hausa father [i.e., for being a member of a uterine group descended from the marriage of a Hausa man to an Idoma woman]? The circumstances of my birth are not important. I am an Idoma man. I am in my mother's place.' Of the fifteen 'stranger' councillors, all but four lived in the settlement where they were born. Two resided in the district where they were born, but in a settlement other than their birthplace. Only two

---

[1]Where the estimates involve a three-year span (for example taking the first wife), the middle year is employed in the analysis. Where the span is two years (for example circumcision), the lowest estimate is employed.

'stranger' councillors were born in another district. Finally, ten of the 'strangers' were elected councillors who represented constituencies which were coterminous with or included their birthplace.

Religion

Christianity came relatively late to Idoma, in the aftermath of World War I. The Methodists were the first to enter the field, commencing regular operations in the mid-1920s. Shortly thereafter Roman Catholic activity began. After a slow start, Catholic efforts were accelerated and soon the two groups were bitter rivals for the allegiance of the Idoma.[2]

Until the end of World War II the European missions held a monopoly over education in the division. In the ensuing years, a primary school system was established under the auspices of the Idoma Native Authority and gradually expanded. Notwithstanding, the Methodists and Catholics together continued to control much of the educational life of the Idoma. Paradoxically, this situation proved to be a mixed blessing to the missions. On the one hand, it endeared them to the many Idoma who associated Western education with occupational advancement and high social status; on the other, it forced them to divert scarce energies and resources from what was ostensibly their primary objective: spiritual training and the salvation of souls. The essentially conservative Idoma had managed to distinguish between missionary schooling and Christianity, generally embracing the former while resisting the inroads of the latter. Addressing this paradox, a Methodist official confided to me: 'It would be a good thing if government took control of the schools. Perhaps then we could get on with the job of making proper Christians of these people.'[3] Sharing his distress over the sluggish pace of spiritual activity, a Catholic missionary observed: 'At this rate, we shall not have true Catholics for several generations. Even now it is difficult to find Idoma youths for the priesthood.'

The disparity between educational and spiritual achievement in the missionary enterprise is reflected in the data on the religious backgrounds of the district councillors: forty-one (58 per cent) of the seventy-one councillors rejected Christianity out of hand. Twenty-

[2]Another group, the Christian Mission in Many Lands, had made little headway in Idoma.

[3]This official averred that he had never thought that a Moslem-dominated administration in the Northern Region might then curtail Christian religious activity.

nine (41 per cent) described themselves as 'Christian' and one was a Moslem. But most of the fifteen 'Methodists' and fourteen 'Catholics' were only marginally involved in the life of the church. Twenty-one (72 per cent) of the 'Christians' attended the weekly service on an irregular basis – no more than once per month. Significantly, only one 'Christian' eschewed organised cult activities. And he, too, acknowledged the importance of the cults for every Idoma: 'As a practising Christian [he is an elder in the local Methodist church and frequently presides over its weekly service and other religious functions], I cannot take part in the rituals of the *aje* and the *alekwu*. As an Idoma man, however, I cannot renounce the earth and my ancestors. When I became a Christian, I did not cease to be an Idoma man.'[4]

Fifty-five (82 per cent) of the seventy-one district councillors praised Western education in general and mission education in particular. This group included twenty-six of the forty-one councillors who disapproved of Christianity as such. Of the twenty-nine 'Christians', twenty-three professed the new faith as a way of ensuring that Idoma children were properly educated; only four 'Christians' avowed a strong interest in Methodism or Catholicism. Interestingly, two 'Christians' viewed their adopted faith as a hedge against future calamity. One of them asked: 'Would a dying man refuse the services of a second doctor?'

Despite evidence that some youths were losing interest in traditional cult activities, fifty-five (77 per cent) of the seventy-one district councillors were confident that neither Western education nor Christianity would destroy 'the ways of Idoma'. Included in this group were the twenty-nine 'Christians' and twenty-six of the forty-one councillors who rejected Christianity while supporting Western education under mission auspices.

Education and language competence

The relatively advanced ages of the district councillors combined with the late arrival of European missionaries in Idoma account for the councillors' low educational attainment. Forty-five (63 per cent) of the councillors were unschooled. The breakdown for the twenty-six (37 per cent) who attended school is as follows: eleven completed Infant I in primary school; four, Infant II; two, Standard I; four, Standard II; one, Standard III; one, Standard IV; one, Standard V;

[4]See Mannoni's discussion (1964: 51–3) of Christianity as a social mask.

and one, Standard VI. One councillor completed the basic course in a Koranic school.

The district councillors' enthusiasm for Western education is reflected in the high hopes they had for their children who were of pre-school and primary school age. Among the thirty councillors in this category, twenty-seven anticipated that at least one child would eventually attend a teacher training college or secondary school. Twenty-four of the twenty-seven also expected that the child (or children) would attend what the Idoma refer to as the 'higher high school', i.e., the university. Among the forty-one councillors who either had no children or whose unschooled children had passed school age, all but fifteen held affirmative views of Western education. The fifteen 'negativists' believed that such education, in league with Christianity, was subversive of 'the ways of Idoma'.

Reflecting limited educational experience, among other factors (see pp. 69–70), is the low level of language competence among the district councillors. While several were literate and fluent in as many as five languages, forty-seven (66 per cent) of the seventy-one councillors were illiterate and thirty-four (48 per cent) spoke Idoma alone. Seven councillors could speak and were literate in English. Sixteen had similar proficiency in Hausa, five in Ibo, and three in Yoruba (major Nigerian languages); twenty-one each in Tiv and Igala (languages spoken by neighbours on the eastern and western borders of Idoma Division); and three each in Akweya and Egede (languages spoken by other ethnic groups in the division).

Except for Idoma and English, literacy was acquired without formal training. The Yoruba-speakers had been seasonal labourers in the cocoa fields of Western Nigeria; the Hausa-speakers were previously clerks, labourers, or traders in the Moslem north. English was learned in primary school, in the employ of Europeans, or during wartime military service. Finally, twenty-one councillors learned to read and write Idoma by enrolling in the Native Authority's Adult Education Literacy Course; the other three who were literate in Idoma acquired their skills informally with the aid of a friend or relative.

Work experience and economic status

Following in their fathers' footsteps, the seventy-one district councillors were all self-employed farmers.[5] Five supplemented their income

[5]Several supplemented their farm income by hunting and petty trading.

by occasional petty trading and one councillor was a salaried vaccinator with the Native Authority. Thirteen councillors also served as
local tax collectors and three as representative councillors. (Tax collectors and representative councillors were compensated with modest
fees. See p. 58, note 21.)[6]

Fifty-four (76 per cent) of the district councillors had never held a
salaried position. The other seventeen (24 per cent) included the
councillor who was a Native Authority vaccinator, eight ex-soldiers, a
onetime member of the Nigeria Police, and seven former petty clerks
and road and railway labourers. In past years, twenty-three councillors combined farming with petty trading, seven had been tax collectors, and eight had been unsalaried members of various District
Courts.

Operating on the periphery of the cash economy, most Idoma farmers could not specify their income as such. Accordingly, they generally relied on these traditional criteria in assessing the economic
status of members of the society: the number of yam heaps cultivated
yearly[7] and the number of wives for whom brideprice was paid or
pledged. Five levels of economic status based on yam cultivation were
distinguished by the Idoma: very poor, denoting cultivation of fewer
than 2,000 yam heaps yearly; poor, 2,000–3,999; modest, 4,000–6,999;
prosperous, 7,000–9,999; and very prosperous, more than 10,000.
Fifty-four (76 per cent) of the seventy-one councillors were poor or
modest farmers. By Idoma standards, abject poverty and prosperity
had thus far eluded most councillors.

Despite legislation restricting brideprice payments to £30 in
Northern Nigeria, Idoma men often expended considerably more for

[6]Some tax collectors, district councillors, and representative councillors also exploited
their offices illegally for personal gain.

[7]Idoma farmers normally cultivate a yam in each conical heap, Egede farmers two
yams in each heap.

Tax data were not useful in assessing economic status. Most farmers paid the annual
poll tax (£1·75 in 1960, £2 in 1961). Where income tax was also paid, it was usually
assessed on all the adult males in a community to help defray local costs (e.g., to
construct a rural dispensary). Some Idoma were made to pay income tax (up to 50p) in
reprisal for their political opposition to the district head and/or the Native Authority.

While some district councillors did hire transient farm labour, this, too, was not
useful in assessing economic status. Few farmers in Idoma could specify the number of
labourers employed or their remuneration (in cash and/or in kind).

Idoma farmers assess their economic status based on yam cultivation without referring to their wives' agricultural production. Wives often helped farm the district councillors' fields; some cultivated their own fields, usually between 800 and 1,400 yam
heaps yearly. Two wives were also petty traders.

a 'good wife'. The brideprice on a young literate girl or the daughter of a prominent district head ranged up to £150 – payable in cash and/or in kind. It is not surprising, therefore, that the ability to pay brideprice is an important indicator of economic status. The Idoma expect 'strong farmers' to take more wives than 'weak farmers'. Not unexpectedly, then, very poor and poor farmers among the district councillors had proportionately fewer wives than modest, prosperous, and very prosperous farmers. All six who were very poor, and nineteen of the twenty-eight who were poor, had only one wife. Of the twenty-six councillors whose status was modest, twenty-one had between two and four wives. All eight councillors who were prosperous, and all three who were very prosperous, had between two and five wives. This lament sums up the feelings of most councillors who had but one wife: 'I am a weak farmer. It is sad. I am too poor to take wives.'

The economic status of the district councillors is further illuminated with data on the ownership of sturdy tin-roofed houses, radios, and bicycles. Here, too, the proportion of councillors who owned these costly items increases with the level of economic status based on yam cultivation. It cost from £70 to £125 to construct a tin-roofed house in rural Idoma. Such houses were owned by eight of the eleven councillors who were prosperous or very prosperous; by only five of the sixty councillors in the lowest three status categories. Relatively few radios (nine in all) were owned by the councillors. While most could not afford a radio, some did not own one because of their inability to understand the broadcasts. Bicycles were owned by thirteen of the thirty-four councillors who were very poor or poor; by twenty of the twenty-six whose status was modest; and by all eleven councillors in the two highest status categories.

Travel experience

Several factors conspired to tie the district councillors to their home areas. Caught up in the alternating routine of a subsistence economy[8] – burning the bush and hunting in the dry season, farming in the rainy season – most councillors were understandably loath to take extended leave of their fields. Meagre funds and limited competence in languages other than Idoma also restricted movement far afield. Finally, lack of curiosity and fear of other peoples and places inhi-

---

[8]With large extended families to feed, few district councillors had substantial farm surpluses to barter or sell.

bited travel. All of these factors are reflected in the comments of various councillors:

Who will hunt guinea fowl and build yam heaps if I leave? My place is here.

How will a poor farmer go to Kaduna or Enugu?

I speak only Idoma. Who will lead me when I am among strangers?

Lagos? A Yoruba place. I have no need to know the Yoruba man.

The Hausa man is my ancient enemy. The Ibo man would steal my eye.[9]
What will become of me if I leave this place?

The infrequency with which the district councillors ventured from familiar surroundings is indicated by the following: as many as forty-four (62 per cent) and forty-eight (68 per cent) of the councillors had never visited nearby Igalaland and Tivland, respectively (see Map 3). Only six councillors (8 per cent) visited any area(s) outside Idoma Division more than six times a year. And between forty and sixty-two councillors (56–87 per cent) had never visited twelve of the twenty-two districts in Idoma Division – all in the southern sector. Travel outside the home district was usually to neighbouring districts in central and northern Idoma – from Agatu on the Benue River south to Yangedde, Oglewu, and Oturkpo. The world of most of the councillors was thus effectively bordered by the great river to the north, Igalaland to the west, Tivland to the east, and the upper portion of the southern Idoma districts to the south. The north–south length of this world was nearly sixty miles. East to west, it ranged from seventeen miles at the narrowest point to just under thirty-five miles at the Benue.[10]

Media exposure, political information, and political perspectives

The findings on travel would seem to warrant the conclusion that the district councillors were, with few exceptions, a parochial group. Thus, despite modern transport nearby – Idoma Division is traversed by a major north–south railroad and a tarmac highway plied by passenger lorries – most of the councillors had never journeyed any considerable distance from their homes. And among those who had, such travel had generally been infrequent and sporadic. Notwith-

[9]Viewing the Ibo as clever, deceitful, and exploitative, most Idoma evinced great hostility toward Ibo entrepreneurs in the division.

[10]Enlisting in the armed forces during World War II, eight district councillors were posted to the Gold Coast, Sierra Leone, Egypt, India, and Burma.

standing this, caution is advised in inferring parochialism from travel experience alone. Because breadth of outlook need not be congruent with the bounds of physical mobility, other kinds of data are required to affirm the aforementioned conclusion. The essentially parochial character of a great majority of the councillors is better illuminated with data on media exposure, political information, and political perspectives.

If, as Lerner (1965: 399ff.) suggests, exposure to mass media is the great liberator, then it can be said that most Idoma were still in virtual bondage. There was no cinema to promote what Lerner (*ibid*.: 401) calls 'psychocultural modernisation' – either in Oturkpo Town (the 'urban hub' of the division) or in the rural districts.[11] Newspapers were practically unknown in the latter. And in the town, the *literati* hoped each day that Ibo shopkeepers would receive their precious supply of the national and regional press.

Radio was another matter – in Oturkpo Town, at any rate. Wending one's way along narrow, criss-crossing alleys, one's ears were assaulted by the electronic sounds of the popular 'hi-life'. Radio gripped Oturkpo Town – by day and by night. After dark, traditional drums strained to rival the new sounds. They contended until midnight, when radio finally gave way. Under the reign of the drums, the town soon slumbered. At dawn 'hi-life' shattered the quiet and the cycle began anew.

A very different pattern was encountered in the rural districts, where fully 95 per cent of the population lived. Here the men rose in silence before dawn and departed quickly for the fields. Wives and daughters awakened soon after and began the daily round of household chores. The dominant sounds of rural Idoma by day were of work, gossip, and children at school and play. 'Hi-life' rarely assailed the equanimity of compound or field. When the dinner meal had been taken, villagers usually gathered in small knots – inside huts, on the council ground, or off in the bush. The talk and gossip were of local matters – birth, marriage, death, farming, wife-chasing, district politics, and the school. A local teacher or schoolboy would occasionally hold forth on the affairs of Lagos or Kaduna. He would know that these were of little import to the listener. Rural Idoma was not Oturkpo Town. Here the traditional drums did not strain to rival the new sounds.

[11]The Roman Catholic Mission occasionally provided cinema for small audiences in Oturkpo Town.

The marginal impact of modern communications media on rural Idoma is reflected in data obtained on exposure to the press and radio. General uninterest, physical isolation, and a high rate of illiteracy combined to minimise the district councillors' exposure to the press. Fifty-two councillors (73 per cent) had had no contact with a newspaper. Of the nine who did read a newspaper more or less regularly (i.e., daily or weekly), all but one resided in or near Oturkpo Town. Their strong preference for political news called attention to a continuing interest in national and even international affairs.[12]

Contrastingly, only two district councillors had never listened to a radio. Since large settlements and the district headquarters were usually equipped with at least one set, there was understandably greater contact with this medium. Radio was also more accessible to those with some competence in another language – especially English, Hausa, Ibo, or Yoruba. But the data also reveal a striking imbalance in programme preferences. As many as forty-eight councillors (68 per cent) strongly preferred the traditional music and folklore presented on the weekly 'Idoma Magazine' programme; four respondents chose foreign music or 'hi-life' over all other programmes. Only eleven councillors, including the nine who regularly sought political information in a newspaper, preferred to listen to news broadcasts; they listened to at least one such programme daily. For most councillors, then, radio was not the liberating bridge to an external world,[13] but a useful device for reaffirming and deepening the commitment to traditional, parochial ways.

The depth of that commitment is further illuminated with data on the district councillors' awareness of political events and personalities – both within the division and elsewhere in Nigeria. During the course of the study, political conflict throughout the country was undermining stability at the local, regional, and national levels. Within Idoma Division, for example, there was mounting opposition to the second *Och'Idoma*. And outside Idoma, certain political developments were destined to shake Nigeria to its foundation. I shall resume the discussion of councillor parochialism after identifying these developments and the historical context within which they were rapidly evolving.

[12]Two district councillors could discuss French nuclear testing in the Algerian Sahara and the evolving American role in South Vietnam.

[13]The district councillors evinced little interest in sports news, serials, religious formats, special features, and advertising in the two media.

The first independence government was formed in the aftermath of the 1959 parliamentary elections by the conservative NPC and the progressive National Convention of Nigerian Citizens (NCNC).[14] (The NPC, the senior partner in the coalition, already controlled the Northern Region Government; the NCNC, the Eastern Region government. The Western Region Government was in the hands of the leading opposition party at the centre, the Action Group.) Both NCNC and AG viewed the coalition arrangement as temporary; each was convinced that NPC power would soon be broken either by dismembering its base in the Northern Region[15] or by victory at the polls. To their dismay, the NPC instead tightened its hold on the North in the 1961 regional elections. One year later, the first post-independence census established the North's ascendancy in population *vis-à-vis* the other two regions and strengthened the NPC's hold on the federal government. Mutual charges of fraud by the NPC and the NCNC intensified strains on the governing coalition. The census was nullified; a new one organised in 1963–4 affirmed NPC political dominance at the centre.

At about the same time the Action Group was being subjected to a series of smashing blows. In May 1962, the Federal Prime Minister responded to a bitter conflict between AG factions in the Western House of Assembly – one headed by the Premier, Chief Samuel Akintola, the other by his predecessor, Chief Obafemi Awolowo – by declaring a state of emergency in the Region. The regional government was suspended and official responsibilities assigned to a Federal Administrator. Shortly thereafter, the Coker Commission of Inquiry impugned the integrity of the AG in its relationship with the Region's statutory corporations (Nigeria 1962). Later that year, the top leaders of the party were charged with treasonable felony and imprisoned; during the trial Ghanaian President Kwame Nkrumah was accused of having aided the conspirators. In January 1963 the emergency was terminated and Akintola was restored as Premier (without elections), his new United People's Party (UPP) joining in a coalition with the NCNC. Six months later the Mid-West Region was carved out of the

[14]Before independence in 1960, the NCNC was known as the National Council of Nigeria and the Cameroons.

[15]The NCNC and the AG both favoured creating a separate 'Middle Belt' Region in the lower North. In 1958, the upper (Moslem) North had successfully withstood pressure to establish such an entity (Great Britain. Colonial Office 1958: 71–3, 87; Ezera 1964: 251–2; Sklar 1963: 138–40, 349, 354; Magid 1971: 360–4).

eastern sector of the Western Region. As the AG was being smashed and the Western Region emasculated, the power of the federal government was visibly increasing. Practically speaking, this meant that the NPC was establishing a stranglehold over the country's political life. During 1964 a political realignment occurred when the NPC and the UPP united against the NCNC and the old AG. In that year, the NPC–UPP alliance won a resounding victory in the federal parliamentary elections. All of these events together helped spark the military *coup* of January 1966, during which Ibo officers apparently arranged the assassination of the Prime Minister, the Northern Premier, and the Western Premier, among other officials (Mackintosh 1966: 17ff.; Sklar 1966: 119ff.). Nigerian political life continued to deteriorate under military rule and finally, in 1967, the Eastern Region seceded and constituted itself the Republic of Biafra. This precipitated the bloody Nigerian–Biafran conflict. Needless to say, these events were all widely publicised in Nigeria.

Pursuing the inquiry into councillor parochialism still further, the seventy-one district councillors were queried as to their awareness of the political forces operating at various levels in Nigeria. Each councillor was presented with two sets of questions, the first probing his knowledge of key events in the period 1962–3, the second his familiarity with prominent figures involved in them. After being apprised of an event, the councillor was asked if he was already aware of its occurrence, and if he was able to tell me anything about it. For example, after being told that a state of emergency was recently declared in the Western Region, the councillor was asked if he had already known of this development, and if he could speak about it. Following that, he was presented with the offices of two participants in the event and then asked to identify the incumbents by name.[16] Thus, after being told that the Premier of the Western Region and the Federal Prime Minister were both involved in the emergency, the councillor was asked to name those officials. The entire procedure was repeated for four more political events.

[16]Some offices were matched with more than one event. The matchings were as follows: opposition to Chief of Idoma (the *Och'Idoma*, Ajene Ukpabi, and the four portfolio councillors in the Native Authority); Coker Commission investigation of Western Region statutory corporations (the AG leader, Chief Obafemi Awolowo, and the Western Premier, Chief Samuel Akintola); controversy over federal census of 1962–3 (the Eastern Premier, Dr Michael Okpara, and the Northern Premier, Alhaji Sir Ahmadu Bello); emergency in Western Region (the Governor-General, Dr Nnamdi Azikiwe, and the Prime Minister, Alhaji Sir Abubakar Tafawa Balewa); trial of AG notables (AG leader, and Western Premier).

As expected, the district councillors were better informed of political affairs within Idoma Division than elsewhere in Nigeria. Nevertheless, we are struck by the extent of the differences. Thus, sixty-three councillors (87 per cent) were aware of the mounting opposition to the *Och'Idoma* – indeed many were themselves foes of the Chief – and fifty-six could discuss some aspect(s) of the conflict. In contrast, the number who were at once aware of political events outside Idoma and able to discuss them ranged between 13 per cent (the Coker Commission investigation) and 22 per cent (the trial of AG leaders). Between 34 per cent and 68 per cent were unaware of highly publicised developments at the regional and national levels. (The former figure refers to the trial of AG leaders, the latter to the Coker Commission investigation.)

Parallel data were obtained on the district councillors' ability to identify prominent officials involved in those events. While all of the respondents could name the central figure in the chieftaincy conflict – Ajene Ukpabi – between 45 per cent and 86 per cent were unable to name various political figures outside Idoma. (The former figure refers to Alhaji Sir Ahmadu Bello, the Northern Premier, the latter to Dr Michael Okpara, the Eastern Premier.) Interestingly, nearly half of the councillors (45 per cent) were unable to identify Bello, leader of the NPC and reputedly the most powerful politician in Nigeria, as the Premier of their own Region; and nearly two-thirds (65 per cent) were unable to identify Dr Nnamdi Azikiwe, the great West African nationalist, as the Governor-General of Nigeria. Interesting, too, are the data on other leading participants in Idoma's chieftaincy conflict: only thirteen councillors (18 per cent) could name all four portfolio councillors in the Native Authority; 17 per cent were unable to name the portfolio councillor elected from their own area in the division. And as many as forty-three councillors (61 per cent) were unable to identify a portfolio councillor from outside their own area.

These data draw attention to councillor parochialism in several ways. First, they reveal the narrow political purview of the district councillors as citizens of Nigeria. All but a few councillors were either unaware of or not especially interested in the great events and personalities shaping that country's political destiny. Second, the data reflect the extent to which they were isolated within Idoma Division itself. The findings on the portfolio councillors are particularly enlightening on this point. Most of the councillors were unable to

75

name one or more of the portfolio councillors who were from areas other than their own – and follow-up probes revealed that few had ever met any of the unnamed officials. This finding reinforces another in the study: while many of the councillors were bitterly opposed to strong chieftaincy and Native Authority centralisation, hardly any could identify adversaries – excluding the *Och'Idoma* – sympathisers, or potential allies elsewhere in the division. Their opposition was essentially unorganised, verbal, and diffuse. It usually took the form of lengthy speeches at council meetings attacking the *Och'Idoma*, the district head, or a kind of 'generalised foe', the Native Authority.

Several factors which help explain councillor parochialism have already been noted: low educational attainment and illiteracy, limited occupational and travel experience, and low exposure to the political content of mass media. Another factor, as yet unidentified, also helps explain that phenomenon – both within the division and *vis-à-vis* the rest of Nigeria. It is a profound antipathy towards organised political activity in general and political parties in particular. As we shall see in Chapter Five, such traditional considerations as kinship, personality, and gift-giving still constituted the basis for political life in rural Idoma. Fearful that political life organised alternatively around party, programme, and ideology would 'spoil the land' by engendering permanent disunity, most rural dwellers anathematised these modern considerations (Magid 1971:346, 355, 358). The practical effects of this outlook were twofold: on the one hand, it turned most Idoma away from the party political world outside the division and dampened interest in related events and personalities; on the other, it localised political activity in the districts and discouraged the organisation of political dissent within the division.[17]

Associational activities and traditional offices

Theoretically, associational life in rural Idoma was rich in diversity. In addition to secret societies, dance groups, and age groups, there were co-operative societies, political parties, and religious bodies with which an individual could affiliate. On closer examination, how-

[17]Both effects were undoubtedly reinforced by a powerful impulse to direct one's loyalties to the clan and to one's membership groups within it: the compound family, the sublineage, and the lineage. Most Idoma distinguished these from other such groups in the division and, indeed, from all other peoples. Fortes (1948: 20) has noted a similar tendency in the Gold Coast, among the Ashanti.

ever, we observe a considerably narrower range of choice. Co-operative societies provided credit and marketing assistance to farmers. But since most of these organisations served no larger social or recreational purpose, they tended to draw few members. Among the seventy-one district councillors, for example, only two were members of a local co-operative society.

Despite their unpopularity, political parties tended to attract a larger following. Among the three major parties – the NPC, the AG, and the NCNC – the NPC had the strongest support by far. Few Idoma were attracted to the Yoruba-dominated AG and the Ibo-dominated NCNC. Fewer yet were injudicious enough to alienate the NPC – all but eight of the district councillors were dues-paying members or supporters of the Region's governing party. (Five councillors were AG members, two others members of the NCNC.) Significantly, none of the major parties in Idoma took the question of discipline very seriously. None sought to serve the totality of its adherents' needs. Rather, each better fitted the description of the 'elite' or 'cadre' type party: they were dominated by notables – or would-be notables – whose party activities were limited to the single goal of winning elections (Duverger 1955: 61ff.; Hodgkin 1961: 68–75). Party branches were normally dormant. They were revived every five years to contest a regional or federal election and then quickly lapsed back into that state.[18] No other purpose was served by these political organisations in rural Idoma.

The European missions in Idoma Division were preoccupied with educational work. Their weekly services, Sunday School activities, and other periodic convocations were hardly sufficient to meet the day-to-day social and recreational needs of most Idoma. To meet those needs, rural dwellers were constrained to seek out associations which had always been close at hand – secret societies, dance groups, and age groups.

Despite periodic suppression by the authorities, secret societies and dance groups flourished in colonial Idoma – albeit clandestinely, and usually without renewing proscribed headhunting activities. Following independence, these associations continued to serve three

[18]Northern Peoples' Congress branches had no need to revive more frequently. As elsewhere in the North, NPC reliance on Native Authority personnel in political recruitment and election campaigning produced a virtual fusion of party and local government (Sklar 1963: 321–76; Dudley 1968: 116–64). Faced with this overwhelming power, and lacking financial resources, the opposition parties could hardly be expected to flourish between elections.

important purposes. First, they organised the social and recreational life of their members – and, occasionally, even non-members. Second, they provided a vehicle for asserting male superiority and dominance (Magid 1972: 301–2). No longer able or disposed to employ headhunting for that purpose, they relied on other traditional devices. For example, ritual masks and the threat of mystical sanction were still employed to intimidate the women. Third, they extended their social control by assisting – extralegally – in tax collection, mediation of land disputes, and maintenance of law and order in rural settlements not policed by the Native Authority. Age groups performed similar social, recreational, and administrative functions. Moreover, they periodically organised themselves as farming teams to assist members who were less fortunate or handicapped.

Among the seventy-one district councillors, fifty-six (79 per cent) were active in at least one secret society and fifty-eight (82 per cent) in at least one dance group. All but three councillors were active members of an age group. Significantly, a substantial number of the active members were also office-holders in at least one of the three types of traditional associations. Thirteen councillors were chairmen of secret societies, six spokesmen (this official speaks for the chairman), four masks, five dividers of food, three constables, and one a messenger. The active members of dance groups included nineteen who were chairmen, five spokesmen, five masks, six singers, and four messengers. Included among the active members of age groups were thirteen chairmen, eleven spokesmen, four treasurers, six dividers of food, and three constables. Overall, thirty-eight councillors were office-holders in at least one traditional association. When we add to this number the ten councillors who were not office-holders in an association but who were *aiigabo* or titled spokesmen of clans in the line of succession to chieftaincy,[19] we observe that fully two-thirds of the councillors held traditional offices. The modern district councillor was thus apt to be drawn from the ranks of traditional leaders.

While analysis of aggregate data is useful for illuminating general patterns in the social backgrounds of the district councillors, such an approach is still problematical. By itself, it may convey the misleading impression that the patterns adequately describe all of the council-

[19]Four more district councillors were *aiigabo* and office-holders in at least one traditional association. Fourteen councillors in all held these titles in the graded hierarchy of clan spokesmen: *alapa* (2); *itodo* (3); *amana* (2); *ochai* (3); *aidokaanya* (2); *omadachi* (2).

lors. Clearly this is not the case. To apprehend the many individual differences which are encountered among those officials, we must employ yet another approach – that of viewing at least some of them as individuals. Three profiles are presented pseudonymously to convey the rich variety which in fact existed among the seventy-one councillors.

Profile 1.   Audu Entonu: 'A Big Man'.

Audu Entonu is a 39-year-old farmer and occasional petty trader. Of modest means, he expects to prosper some day as a farmer and entrepreneur. Audu's considerable sophistication transcends both occupational achievement and a Standard V education at a Methodist primary school. Literate and fully conversant in five languages (Idoma, Tiv, Hausa, Ibo, and English), he has been a consultant to various social scientists in Nigeria. Audu reads three newspapers – 'my bibles', he notes irreverently – and listens to at least one news broadcast daily; he prefers the 'more objective' BBC. Audu is especially fond of works on nationalism and imperialism. He is quick to extol such nationalist luminaries as Nkrumah, Azikiwe, Awolowo, and Nehru; Audu speaks knowledgeably of their ideological perspectives, political strategies, and historic significance. Well-travelled (by Idoma standards), Audu is easily moved to expatiate on his numerous forays into the great cities of Nigeria. He also recalls a 'sweet visit' to Douala in the former French Cameroons.

In both outlook and personal style, Audu Entonu bears a resemblance to the sociological characterisation of the 'marginal man' (Park 1928: 887–92; Stonequist 1935: 3–12). A resident of Oturkpo Town since the late 1930s, Audu has not abandoned a distaste for European attire and monogamy. He is husband to three wives and dreams of the day when his many children will be physicians, barristers, and agronomists. Audu expresses considerable ambivalence towards Christianity and the European missionary enterprise. Nominally a Methodist, but an infrequent churchgoer, Audu praises aspects of Christian thought and mission educational policy. These are offset, however, by the condescension and hypocrisy which he associates with most missionaries. Audu thinks that Christianity will be eclipsed when the state establishes a monopoly over education. He contemplates this development with mixed emotions. A self-styled 'Idoma nationalist', Audu extols the symbolism of the ancestral cult, but, curiously, does not lament its weakening under the impact of

Western education and technology. Pressed to clarify this seeming paradox, he exclaims: 'I am pleased that my descendants will be Nigerian nationalists!' Audu belongs to an age group. When asked to explain his limited involvement in traditional group activities, he confides that they are not for 'a big man'.

Discernible in Audu Entonu's record as a politician is evidence of yet another sociological type, the compulsive 'opposition mentality' (Shils 1960: 329–68). Between 1943 and 1959 Audu was successively a member of the Nigeria Police, a minor official in the Native Authority, and President of the Oturkpo Town Court. Throughout this period, he was also active in opposition politics. Motivated by a strong social consciousness and personal ambition, Audu was in the vanguard of youths in the IHRU who campaigned against chiefly power, Native Authority centralisation, and official corruption. He was elected Secretary-General of the IHRU in 1958. Impatient with the organisation's meagre political gains, Audu sought another base from which to launch his attacks on the Native Authority and its ally, the NPC. In 1954 Audu joined the AG, a political party committed to progressive nationalism and the creation of a separate 'Middle Belt' Region (Sklar 1963: 231–320, 422–41). Three years later he was named leader of the Idoma branch of the party and a member of its Federal Executive Committee. The AG also rewarded him with membership on the Board of Directors of the Western Nigeria Printing Corporation. (Audu eventually lost this sinecure as a result of the Coker Commission investigation.) To many in Idoma, Audu was indeed 'a big man'. He was destined, however, to be a perennial loser in elections for high office. In 1954 and 1959 Audu failed to win a seat in the Federal Parliament; he suffered the same fate in the 1955 and 1961 elections for the Northern House of Assembly.[20] Audu has had to settle for a lesser office. In 1962, he was elected to represent a rural constituency on the District Council. His attacks on the NPC and the Native Authority leadership continued unabated.

Profile 2. Apochi Ichichi: 'A Fool Dreams of Freedom'.

Apochi Ichichi is serving his second term on the District Council. Admired for his acuity and boldness, he was first elected to the coun-

---

[20]Audu Entonu was one of only two district councillors who sought political office at the regional or federal level. The other councillor, also an AG member, failed to gain election to the Northern House of Assembly.

cil in 1958 and then re-elected four years later. Apochi is 48 years old and unschooled. A poor farmer with two wives, he is barely able to pay the fees of two sons who attend a Catholic primary school. Apochi complains that he will have no money to pay for the sons' apprenticeship with an Ibo mechanic in Oturkpo Town. Fearful that Ona and Ejembi, too, will be poor farmers, he notes sardonically: 'The Idoma man is a slave to his way of life. A fool dreams of freedom.'

Apochi Ichichi remembers having felt differently as a young man – in the late 1930s, when he was a servant to the Senior District Officer. Residing for the first time in Oturkpo Town and frequently accompanying that official on tours of the division, Apochi was introduced to a new way of life. He learned to speak English, 'small-small'. With the outbreak of World War II Apochi enlisted in a Nigerian regiment and was shortly despatched to India – via the Gold Coast, Sierra Leone, and Egypt. Based in New Delhi 1943–5, he became fast friends with a group of American GIs. Apochi recalls the experience as a personal triumph: 'Freedom for an Idoma man was drinking beer with white friends and going together to the harlots. I loved the Americans as brothers!'

Upon returning to Idoma in 1946, Apochi Ichichi settled again in Oturkpo Town. Working now as a Native Authority messenger, he tried to save money for a mechanic's apprenticeship. Frustrated in his efforts, Apochi returned home in 1949, where he took up farming, married, and began to raise a family. For a time Apochi was active in opposition politics as a member of the IHRU and NCNC (Sklar 1963: 143–230, 389–420). Concluding that such groups were doomed in Idoma, he resigned and joined the NPC in 1957. Within the district, however, Apochi continued to oppose the elderly tyrant who was serving in his twenty-eighth year as district head. Election to the District Council in 1958 provided a useful forum for this purpose.

In his middle years Apochi Ichichi has become increasingly active in the traditional life of the clan. Recently elected chairman of both the Echi dance group and Onyonkpo, a secret society, he also expects to be appointed an *igabo* or titled clan spokesman. Asked how he reconciles full participation in cult activities with frequent attendance at Catholic services, Apochi confides: 'It is not difficult. A clever man does not question the power of any god. And no god questions the loyalty of a clever man'.

Apochi Ichichi tries to keep up with events outside Idoma. Twice each month he cycles three miles to the district headquarters, where he greets friends, attends to council business, and listens to news broadcasts in Hausa and English. Occasionally Apochi visits friends in Kaduna and Enugu, where he hears of his country's grave political problems. On one of these trips, Apochi overheard two American Peace Corps workers discussing a war in a place called 'Indo-China'. Nostalgically, he asked one of them: 'Is it near India? Will your leader send a Nigerian regiment to Indo-China?'

Profile 3. Udo Okwu: 'True to the Ways of Idoma'.
Udo Okwu stands out among the seventy-one district councillors as the most tradition-minded and parochial. Born fifty-five years ago in a remote settlement in northern Idoma, Udo is proud of having personally withstood the challenge of *mbeke*, the white man. He is often given to boasting: 'I pay tax. That is all!' A poor farmer, Udo lives in a large compound with his two wives and their children – four infant daughters and a teenage son. Deprecating all foreigners and all things foreign, he refused to enroll Adikwu in the Methodist primary school. 'It was not the fee,' he insists. 'The Idoma man is a strong farmer. It is an insult to the ancestors!' Invoking several parables, Udo complicatedly emphasises the importance of remaining 'true to the ways of Idoma'.[21]

Content with his immediate surroundings, Udo Okwu rarely ventures far from home. He has never travelled outside Idoma and speaks no other language. Udo has visited Oturkpo Town on only one occasion, in 1963, to attend a reception for the Northern Premier; he was impressed with neither the town nor the visiting dignitary.[22] Until 1962, there was little reason for Udo even to visit the headquarters of his own district. In that year he was appointed to the District Council. Udo walks eight miles to the district headquarters to attend the monthly meeting of the council. He spends the night with a relative and returns home the next day. Reluctantly he pursues this schedule in the rainy as well as the dry season.

[21]Older, tradition-minded Idoma often invoke complex parables in a convoluted speaking style.

[22]Udo Okwu viewed sprawling Oturkpo Town, with its densely populated, unkempt streets and alleys, as a blight on the Idoma landscape; he also criticised the Ibos' dominant economic position in the town. Udo was particularly distressed that Idoma officials would pay homage to the visiting dignitary, Alhaji Sir Ahmadu Bello, a son of their traditional enemy, the Fulani.

Udo Okwu evinces little interest in political affairs outside his district. Asked to identify the Governor-General of Nigeria, the Prime Minister, and the three regional Premiers,[23] among other officials, he responds disdainfully: 'I know only the representative councillor in my place. We are of the same father.' Unable to identify the four portfolio councillors in the Native Authority, Udo observes laconically: 'They are strangers in my place.' When questioned about the controversial federal census, the emergency in the Western Region, and the mounting opposition to the *Och'Idoma* (among other political issues), he avers ignorance of all but the last. Probed on the opposition to Ajene Ukpabi, he merely observes that the Idoma man cannot be ruled by an Egede slave. Udo concludes a lengthy analysis of the conflict raging between the elected district councillors and the overbearing district head with this lament: 'They are all like the white man. They divide our people, they spoil the land. I fear the wrath of the ancestors. Who will appease the *alekwu* when the land is spoiled?'

Udo Okwu is absorbed in the traditional life of the clan. Recently designated an *igabo* or clan spokesman, Udo is an influential adviser to the elderly clan head. He is also chairman of Akpantla, a secret society. Discussing Akpantla, Udo is filled with nostalgia. He recalls when he earned the title of *ogbu* (headhunter) and sadly acknowledges that the suppression of headhunting has caused the society to lose some of its vitality. Characterising the radio as 'a thief' and its emanations as 'noise', Udo berates those youths who turn away from traditional music and dance. When reminded that one radio programme – the weekly 'Idoma Magazine' – features traditional music and folklore, he responds bitterly: 'It is a thief! It robs our way of life!'[24]

The district councillor is a local leader, a man of considerable influence and prestige. As such, he tends to be immersed in the traditional life of the clan in general and, where he is an elected official, of the legal constituency in particular. Even those few councillors who manifest various attributes of the 'modern outlook' – for

---

[23]A fourth Region, the Mid-West, was soon after carved out of the eastern sector of the Western Region. The NCNC formed the government in the Mid-West Region, under the premiership of Chief Dennis Osadebay, an Ibo.

[24]Lerner (1965: 194, 325) has encountered a similar rejection of modern media among the Bedouin in Jordan.

example, Audu Entonu and, to a much lesser extent, Apochi Ichichi –
are deeply involved in traditional ways. It is the manner of the
involvement which distinguishes the councillors and which, in turn,
interests us here. In most cases, the stress is placed on what is readily
observable – the ritual and associational aspects of traditional life.
Udo Okwu and even the frustrated Apochi Ichichi reflect the essential styles of these local leaders. In exceptional cases, however, the
emphasis is placed on what may elude the casual observer – namely,
the feeling of 'Idoma-ness'. Viewed from this perspective, it is clear
that Audu Entonu's traditionality is illuminated by his modern ways,
not obscured by them. His marginality is not a guidepost to modernity, but a coming to terms with traditionality. Put differently, we
have encountered in rural Idoma what contemporary social science
has too often failed to sensitise us to expect: that in the mutual
adaptation of traditionality and modernity, in their reciprocal pen-
etration and transformation, the former may reign and the latter
serve (Rudolph and Rudolph 1969: 1ff.; Whitaker 1967: 415–57;
Gluckman 1968a: 1–27). In that situation it is misleading to speak of
the actor as 'modern' or 'transitional'. As a case in point, neither type
is found among the councillors. What we have discovered instead is a
group of local leaders whose individual differences call attention to
the rich variety of ways in which they give meaning to traditionality in
everyday life, and to changes gradually taking place against the background of persistence (Nisbet 1969: 270–1). It is these qualities, as we
shall see presently, which sharpen their debureaucratic hostility to
local government based on strong chieftaincy and centralised political
authority and which, in turn, make possible their election to office.

Chapter Five Accession politics and the office of district councillor: a study in institutional adaptation

The strongly conservative, parochial character of the Idoma has already been illuminated. In the rural districts – where a great majority of the population lived and worked in 1963 – human existence was still organised around the annual cycle of hoe agriculture, the earth and the ancestral cults, and secret societies, dance groups, and age groups. For most rural dwellers, everything else – including Christianity and the apparatus of modern government and political party, local, regional, and national – was superstructure, a mask.

To be sure, colonialism did penetrate and weaken the old order in Idoma. Yet in the process of strengthening a single institution – chieftaincy – and building a centralised local government organisation, colonial officials bent on doing so could not substitute the norm of efficiency for traditional political norms and patterns of behaviour. Modern institutions grafted on to Idoma were transformed along with facets of the host culture. But none of this involved a radical transformation in the style of political life. Alien institutions were generally assimilated into the norms and behavioural patterns which had long dominated politics in that society. As a case in point, the District Council system was organised in the mid-1950s in accordance with the English model of majoritarian local government. Provision was made for the designation of council officers, the establishment of committees, and record-keeping. Prior to the first triennial elections held in 1955, colonial officials toured the districts extolling political competition organised around democratic elections; rational debate over political issues; and the role of the citizen as public office-holder. All these things were alien to Idoma thinking.

Various reactions attended the District Council 'reform'. Some rural dwellers were understandably confused, indifferent, or both.

Others decried the scheme as yet another assault on Idoma constitutionalism. A third group was elated. Comprised mostly of educated youths in the IHRU, it viewed council democracy as a salutary break with prevailing patterns of authority – traditional as well as colonial. Still another group, the largest by far, reacted quite differently from the rest. It quickly construed and adapted the 'democratic' council system in terms of traditional political competition. This response was especially evident in the matter of recruitment. Most rural dwellers harnessed the accession process for the office of district councillor to the service of traditional ways, deepening the sense of continuity in Idoma life and reaffirming their own commitment to constitutionalism in the face of strong chieftaincy and Native Authority centralisation. The same phenomenon could be observed in the 1958 and 1962 elections. In this chapter I shall employ the latter elections to examine the institutional adaptation which took place in the arena of accession politics and its implications for bureaucratic–debureaucratic role conflict surrounding the councillors.

More than three years had elapsed since the twenty-two District Councils were last installed as agents of the Idoma Native Authority and as representatives of the district population. Their official mandate having recently expired, the councils were dissolved by the regional Minister for Local Government, thereby initiating the process for constituting new bodies in their place. In Idoma the outgoing General Purposes Committee in the Native Authority instructed one of its members, the portfolio councillor for local government, to prepare for the installation of a new council in every district. That official, in turn, apprised the district heads of procedures to be followed: on a specified date, usually several weeks after the old councils had been dissolved, the adult males in each constituency were to convene for the purpose of electing a single representative on the council. Voting for the elected members, who would form a majority on the council, was to take place openly before a returning officer. (The electors usually lined up behind the candidate of their choice. Occasionally their choice was indicated by acclamation or by a show of hands.)[1] Shortly thereafter the district head was to recommend to the central administration of the Native Authority those persons who would constitute the official minority on the council. Following the minority's appointment by the central administration, each council

[1] By the mid-1960s, secret balloting was mandatory in all Northern local government elections (Blitz, ed. 1965: 122).

was to meet to elect its representative councillor(s). (The twenty-eight representative councillors in Idoma Division would then convene in four groups representing the former intermediate areas. Each group would designate a portfolio councillor to serve both as a member of the newly constituted General Purposes Committee and as the head of a department in the Native Authority.)

The District Councils proceeded to communicate this information to tax collectors, elders, and other notables in their units for dissemination to the populace. Thus began the process of filling new political bottles with old political wines at the base of Idoma society.

The elected district councillor

Nominating a candidate

Because kinship was the single most important factor in Idoma political life, responsibility for designating a candidate for the office of district councillor rested with the *ojira* assembly in a particular sublineage unit. In most cases, the adult men in the sublineage responded to the official call for new elections by meeting and collectively nominating a member of the unit. The initiative was sometimes taken, however, by certain elements in the *ojira* – e.g., by an elder or a group of young men, the latter acting either in their own right or as representatives of an age group, secret society, or dance group. In that event the full assembly convened to evaluate the petition presented by such elements for support of a particular individual. Clan heads, district heads, and aspirants for the offices of representative councillor and portfolio councillor occasionally worked through 'agents' in the sublineage *ojira* to persuade it to designate a relative and/or political supporter as candidate for the office of district councillor. Aspirants rarely declared their own candidacy. Knowing that such behaviour would be widely regarded as boorish and offensive, they usually attempted to enlist support beforehand from influential members of the assembly.

Conflict among compound families and generational groups in the *ojira* assembly usually combined with the consensual democratic principle which governed its deliberative process to prevent any individual or faction from imposing a candidate on the full body. This is not to say that all who participated in the sublineage *ojira* spoke with equal voice. Individually and as a group, the elders wielded the greatest influence in choosing a candidate for the modern office of

87

district councillor. No aspirant could reasonably hope to be designated by the assembly without the support or acquiescence of its most senior members. And among the lineage elders, the 'owner' or 'father' of the earth and ancestral cults was the most influential. On at least one occasion, for example, the mere absence of that esteemed figure from a sublineage *ojira* which convened to consider the qualifications of a youthful aspirant was interpreted as tacit disapproval of his candidacy; the petition submitted on his behalf was quickly rejected as an affront to *olaje* (the 'owner' of the earth or land cult). The elders' considerable influence at the nominating stage, and in assembly deliberations generally, is reflected in these remarks by various councillors:

Long ago [in 1955] I wanted to stand for the council. *Adaalekwu* ['father of the dead,' title of the senior elder who 'owns' the ancestral cult] did not hear me. My people agreed that it was no place for a boy. The boy is a man now.

When two young men in the *ojira* said that my senior brother should stand for the council, the elders protested that Ochekpe [pseudonym] is a thief and a wife-chaser. Ochekpe shouted that he is not a thief. The *ojira* laughed when he said nothing of wife-chasing. Ochekpe was embarrassed. Then some young men said I should stand for the council. When the elders did not speak on the matter, I agreed to stand.

I asked my age-mates to support my candidacy. They said that they must first consult with the elders. When the *ojira* met, my age-mates spoke for me. Other young men spoke for the trader, Adeka [pseudonym], from another *ipooma* [sublineage]. The elders said that we were both good men, but that the father of Adeka is already the tax collector in this place. My age-mates said that my *ipooma* should provide the councillor. There was much debate. When Adeka finally said that he must sometimes travel far from this place to trade, I was hailed by the *ojira*.

When my brother said I would be a good councillor, the elders denounced me as a spy, a supporter of the old tyrant who is district head. I denied this. The *ojira* began to shout, '*Oche awanda!* ['one who brings big trouble'] We will not send a spy to the council!' Many still scorn me because I was later appointed to the council by the district head.

Also reflected in these remarks are the criteria which were most frequently employed in nominating candidates for the office of district councillor. Undoubtedly the most important criterion invoked by the *ojira* assembly was that of kinship. It will be recalled that in traditional Idoma appointments to various offices generally rotated between lineage and sublineage units and that, in theory at least, the eligible unit nominated its most senior member. But because social conflict usually arose when rival candidates claimed closer proximity to the founding ancestor, it was often necessary to downgrade the principle of seniority in order to restore harmony among the rivals and their supporting kin groups. As a result, the principle of rotation tended to prevail over the principle of seniority in filling traditional offices. A similar phenomenon could be observed in the case of the district councillorship.

The council constituency incorporated more than one traditional lineage or sublineage unit intact and/or parts of several units. Where the constituency was formed of more than one lineage intact,[2] every sublineage in the various lineages sought to enhance its prestige and influence *vis-à-vis* the rest by claiming the right to fill the office of district councillor. One group might contend that it had not filled the office on any previous occasion, another that a member of a rival group had recently been appointed clan head, district head, tax collector, or court member. An *ojira* assembly was convened in each lineage to adjudicate the political claims of rival groups of kin. After much acrimonious debate, sometimes accompanied by scuffling, the lineage assembly usually managed to reduce the intensity of conflict between groups by establishing a schedule of rotation. It was agreed – until the next election, at any rate – that a specified order of sublineages would provide the candidate on this and on subsequent occasions. (A new order usually had to be negotiated at each triennial election.)

A parallel arrangement generally obtained where the council constituency was organised along different lines – for example, where, in addition to more than one lineage intact or as an alternative to that pattern, the constituency incorporated parts of different lineages. Such cases illuminate the adaptation of the traditional principle of rotation to a disquieting political situation produced by various developments in contemporary Idoma: first, by an increasing preoccupation with modern office-holding at the base of the society, and second, by an administrative decision which threatened to weaken the traditional political moorings of numerous compound families, viz. the decision to organise many council constituencies around parts of sublineage and lineage units. Whereas the compound family had traditionally played only a secondary role in political

[2]One-fifth of the fifty-five constituencies in the study were organised around more than one traditional sublineage or lineage unit intact. The remainder included one lineage unit intact with parts of other units, or parts of more than one lineage or sublineage.

affairs, these two developments now conspired to intensify the politicisation of that social unit. Many Idoma reckoned that, if left unchecked, rivalry within and between compound families for the prestige and influence associated with the modern district councillorship would escalate in such constituencies and possibly spread throughout the society. Recalling the colonial legacy of instability and disunity engendered by disputes over chieftaincy, the most pessimistic Idoma foresaw intolerable political strain and divisiveness at the lowest rung of the social structure.[3] The principle of rotation was employed with considerable success to thwart this development. The *ojira* assembly in each sublineage usually responded to a fractious situation by establishing a schedule of rotation for the rivalrous compound families; and the *ojira* in each compound family usually specified the order of rotation for its own rivalrous groups.

The overall effectiveness of the *ojira* assembly in attempting to resolve differences between kin groups in this way is illuminated by the following data. Among the fifty-five district councillors who were elected to office in 1962, thirty-nine were opposed in the general election. Of the thirty-nine, all but four were members of sublineages whose right to nominate the candidate was originally challenged by rival groups of kin in the lineage *ojira*. Each challenge was defeated when the *ojira* eventually decided to invoke the principle of rotation. As a consequence of that arrangement, thirty-five candidates who took office in 1962 were opposed in the general election by men who represented another lineage altogether. The four remaining councillors were opposed by lineage mates representing rival sublineages. No councillor was required to stand against a member of his own sublineage in the general election. Finally, among the sixteen councillors who were unopposed that year, all but five were aided at the nominating stage by assembly arrangements based on the principle of rotation.[4]

Having been authorised to nominate the candidate, the *ojira* assembly of the eligible sublineage unit then convened secretly for that purpose. As in traditional Idoma, it was often necessary to forgo

[3]Older informants often expressed the fear that this development might conspire with the movement of married sons to outlying farm communities to destroy the compound family as such.

[4]Eleven district councillors ran unopposed when the *ojira* assemblies in constituencies organised around more than one lineage unit intact were able to settle on the eligible lineage. The assembly in that lineage then specified the sublineage which would nominate the single candidate in the general election.

strict application of the principle of seniority based on genealogy. Faced with conflicting claims regarding the most senior status in the *ojira*, that body was usually content to designate the candidate from among its more senior – and, coincidentally, older – members. This arrangement was sometimes facilitated by the unwillingness or inability of members of the most senior age group to occupy the office of district councillor. Quite often old and infirm, they were reluctant to attend lengthy council meetings and to travel on council business. Moreover, lack of interest in the minutiae of council affairs discouraged office-seeking. Finally, the most senior members of the *ojira* assembly usually preferred, as did elderly clan heads in traditional Idoma, to concentrate on cult activities. They tended to look upon modern office-holding and the competitiveness associated with it as an affront to their dignity as spiritual leaders. For all of these reasons, the most senior members of the *ojira* were generally satisfied just to prevent the candidacy of a 'boy', i.e., of a member of an age group with low seniority in the assembly.

While the ascriptive criterion of kinship embodied in the principles of rotation and seniority carried the greatest weight in nominating candidates, various criteria of achievement were also invoked at this stage of the process of recruitment. Because the assessment of personal attributes had long been a factor in the choice of leaders – along with lineage eligibility, candidates for clan head were judged for their intelligence, courage, and fair-mindedness – the eligible sublineage was constrained to designate a candidate who would be personally attractive to the electorate in the council constituency. Hoping to enhance its prestige and influence by producing the victor in the general election, the sublineage *ojira* was apt to settle on a relatively senior person with a reputation for integrity, courage, oratorical accomplishment, and generosity.

Excepting generosity (which I shall discuss in another context below), each of these attributes was also deemed essential if a candidate was to take his place on the District Council as an outspoken foe of strong chieftaincy and Native Authority centralisation. By 1962 the Idoma had witnessed for nearly a decade the steady erosion of political opposition to a powerful Native Authority organised at all levels around the institution of chieftaincy. As hostility to the second *Och'Idoma*, Ajene Ukpabi, increased in the division, many rural dwellers began to speak of the need to reverse the course of local affairs. Much of the discussion focused on the theme of Idoma constitutionalism. Some favoured restoring the constitutional system in its traditional form – i.e., without the Idoma Chieftaincy and its supporting administrative apparatus in the Native Authority. A still larger group emphasised the need to retain the office, albeit with a new incumbent constrained to operate within the framework of a strengthened constitutional system. The latter group included two elements, viz. those who viewed the office as a legitimate expression of the traditional ideology of proud and vigorous chieftaincy, and those who contended that it could not be eliminated in any case. It was widely assumed at the time that restoration of the traditional constitutional system – in whatever form – could only be achieved under the leadership of men who combined personal honesty and fearlessness with an exceptional ability to express opposition to the Native Authority in open forum.

The significance of these two considerations – pursuit of interests of groups of kin and opposition to strong chieftaincy and centralised political authority – at the nominating stage is reflected in the following data. Forty-nine of the fifty-five councillors who were elected to office in 1962 reported that they had originally agreed to become candidates because they shared the view of kinsmen that their victory would serve two key purposes: first, it would enhance the prestige and influence of their sublineage in the council constituency; and second, it would provide an opportunity to argue boldy in the council for restoration of the constitutional equilibrium rooted in principles of chieftaincy, gerontocracy, and democracy in the *ojira*. Of the forty-nine, all but eight ranked the second consideration as the more important of the two. Interestingly, only six councillors had regarded neither consideration as particularly important; each of these office-holders reported that his designation as candidate by the sublineage assembly had reflected its belief that he was best qualified to work for such amenities as better roads, pipe-borne water systems, and more Native Authority schools and scholarships.

Our examination of the nominating process for the office of district councillor has drawn attention to traditional issues and practices tending to dominate ostensibly modern institutional life at the base of Idoma society. As we shall see, a similar pattern also obtained at the next stage preceding the general election – the campaign.[5]

[5]As with the district councillorship in Idoma, Steiner (1955: 195) reports that discussion of political issues – especially party matters – was often avoided in local government elections in post-war Japan. Nominations were based mainly on family and personal

From candidate to councillor: the campaign

Upon receiving the nomination of his kin group – whether it be a sublineage or a compound family unit – a candidate for the office of district councillor was ready to take initiatives to achieve victory in the general election. Whereas such a posture would have been widely denounced as arrogant, unbridled ambition at the nominating stage, it was now regarded as basic to the campaign strategy.

The campaign was typically organised around two core objectives: that of mobilising sufficient support among male voters in the constituency to produce a victory in the general election; and concomitantly, that of preparing the ground for what Bowen (1964)[6] has termed a 'return to laughter' after a period of intense political conflict. In Idoma, prestige and influence usually accrued to the winning candidate and his followers as a function of both electoral success and their ability jointly to minimise rancour and divisiveness in the constituency. Discussing the candidate's need to temper the aspiration to victory with a concern for future peace and unity among the electorate, one district councillor observed:

A candidate and his people are scorned as 'boys' when victory brings anger and hatred. A councillor is a peacemaker. A candidate who sows trouble even before he takes office can never be esteemed as a man of peace.

This preoccupation with having to achieve a speedy 'return to laughter' following the election derived essentially from two sources: endogenously, from the traditional cosmology which laid stress upon unity as the highest ideal in political life; and exogenously, from the sobering effect of various developments associated with colonial rule, viz. the intensification of disputes over chieftaincy resulting from the decision taken in the inter-war period to make that institution the fulcrum for an efficient local government organisation, and the introduction of party strife into Idoma in the post-World War II period of nationalist ferment.

considerations in Japan; and in Idoma, on those two factors and the candidates' well-known opposition to the Native Authority *status quo*. These narrow foci gave their respective electoral processes a strikingly conservative hue. But as we shall see, the two systems of local government elections did differ in this important respect: campaigning was usually necessary only in Idoma, and balloting was often more than a mere formality in that society.

[6]E. S. Bowen is the *nom de plume* of Laura Bohannan, the wife of anthropologist Paul Bohannan. Her novel draws on their extensive fieldwork in Tivland, which borders Idoma on the east.

1. Historical backdrop to the campaign strategy

(a) Disputes over chieftaincy

It will be recalled that in the two decades following World War I the chief – in the person of the district head – capitalised on Administration sponsorship to achieve a position of primacy *vis-à-vis* the elders and the *ojira* assembly. As competition for the power, prestige, and emoluments associated with the district headship grew more fierce, political instability and disunity increased at all levels in the various districts – from the clan down to the compound family. Notwithstanding the ideal of unity in political life, the institution of chieftaincy quickly became the focal point for relentless conflict among ambitious individuals and social groups. Whereas the institution had traditionally symbolised the unity of several lineages around a common earth-shrine, under European auspices it came to represent privilege and a source of virulent conflict and division. The latter condition persisted in both colonial and post-colonial Idoma, even where the district headship was filled either by an *oche* (clan head) or by a prospective bearer of that traditional title.

The appointment of a new district head rarely brought the struggle over succession to a close, since that individual was usually incapable of inspiring unity around his person or his office. Unsuccessful aspirants and their disappointed followers generally conspired to deprive the incumbent of his office. District heads and their followers met their foes' provocations with an assortment of reprisals, including arson, beatings, and excessive tax levies. In most cases, reprisals merely strengthened the conspirators' resolve, thus closing the vicious circle which enveloped disputes over chieftaincy in Idoma. With the creation of an Idoma Chieftaincy in 1947, a similar 'game' was begun at a still higher level. Official reports affirm a kind of permanent political warfare surrounding the institution of chieftaincy in the period 1919–60. The testimony of numerous informants, together with my own observation of events precipitated by Ajene Ukpabi's appointment as *Och'Idoma* in the latter year, show that these convulsions did not abate with independence.[7] Reflecting on a general condition with special reference to a dispute raging around the recent

[7]Fortes (1948: 23 note 1) reports similiar agitation and instability surrounding the Ashanti institution of chieftaincy.

appointment of a clan head as district head, an elderly Idoma observed with bitterness and nostalgia:

When Oga [pseudonym] died long ago, my people struggled for the beads [worn on the wrist by the clan head as insignia of his office]. They were placed on the wrist of Adanu [pseudonym], from another *ipoopu* [lineage]. My people were bitter, but we agreed to hail Adanu as the new chief. We feasted through the night in his honour. All this has changed. The white man has brought dishonour to our chiefs by using them to spoil the land. Yes, we feast for the new chief today, but many still plot against Ondoma [pseudonym]. It will not end. The struggle between Ondoma and his enemies is worse than a swarm of locusts. Both spoil the land. But only the locusts leave this place.

(b) Party politics

(i) *Nigeria and Idoma*. Overlapping the chieftaincy issue as a persistent source of political discord was the initiation of party activity in Idoma Division following World War II. I have already observed that opposition to official conservatism in Nigeria was not confined to the nationalist organisations and their leaders working at the centre for change. As a case in point, members of minority groups in the 'Middle Belt'[8] were also organised as tribal unions to pressure the Administration to accelerate reform of Native Authorities along democratic lines (Magid 1971: 350–1, 360).

Many of these groups were eventually drawn into a tug-of-war between the three major political parties in Nigeria. While the NPC encouraged integration of the 'Middle Belt' with the Moslem North, both the AG and the NCNC promoted the creation of a separate Middle Belt Region as a means of preventing the political domination of Nigeria by traditionalists in the Northern Region. Throughout the 1950s it was clear that the organisation of an independent Nigeria and the relative power of the major parties within it would depend, in large measure, on developments in the 'Middle Belt'.

Among the 'Middle Belt' elements who participated in both the agitation for reform of local government and the conflict between the major parties were young men in the IHRU. At the close of World War II the IHRU began to press for democratic reform of, and a major policy role in, the Idoma Native Authority. In due course, it was drawn into the tug-of-war over the future of the 'Middle Belt' (Magid 1971: 350–1, 360–5).

[8]Before Nigeria's reorganisation in 1967, the 'Middle Belt' (or lower Northern Region) was said to include the provinces of Adamawa, Benue, Ilorin, Kabba, Niger, and Plateau, and the southern parts of Bauchi and Zaria Provinces.

The attempt by the IHRU to secure a major policy role in a Native Authority controlled by chiefly elements and its relationship with the party system were both set against the background of official conservatism in post-war Nigeria. The union's views on two issues, local reform and the future of the 'Middle Belt',[9] were generally at odds with the official commitment to gradual change. Responding to IHRU demands by instituting ostensibly democratic reforms in the Native Authority, the Administration simultaneously reaffirmed its commitment to gradualism by helping to lay the groundwork for the demise of the reformist tribal union, and by encouraging close ties between the IHRU's increasingly powerful adversary, the Native Authority, and the governing party in the Region, the NPC. After more than a decade of political confrontation, the IHRU finally dissolved in 1959 – thus affirming the political hegemony in Idoma of the conservative Native Authority–NPC alliance. The conflict had been waged at great cost, however; its legacy was deep resentment and distrust between victor and vanquished.

Even with the demise of the IHRU, party strife continued in the division without abatement. The AG, and the NCNC, waged aggressive, albeit unsuccessful, campaigns against the NPC in the federal parliamentary elections of 1959 and the Northern Assembly elections of 1961 (Post 1963: *passim*; Dudley 1968: *passim*). The history of the conflict between the IHRU and the Native Authority together with the frequently violent confrontations between branches of the AG, NCNC, and NPC in 1959 and 1961, left most Idoma – opposition elements included – profoundly hostile to modern party activity at the local level. Notwithstanding its reliance on electioneering and lobbying in the pursuit of political objectives, the IHRU had always proclaimed its non-political, non-party character as a tribal or cultural union. Its members tended to view political parties as essentially divisive instruments, destined inevitably to 'spoil the land' by engendering friction and bitterness. Whether or not most Idoma accepted the IHRU's definition of its own organisational character, it was quite evident in the early independence period that they were deeply divided and exhausted by years of party strife.

(ii) *The system of District Councils*. The backwardness which characterised party life in the Northern Region has frequently been

[9]The tribal union was briefly affiliated with the NCNC, a party which also espoused the cause of regional autonomy for the 'Middle Belt'.

contrasted with the situation prevailing in the rest of Nigeria (Blitz, ed. 1965: 143ff.; Cowan 1958: 221–32; Sklar 1963: 321–78). Prior to January 1966, when a military *coup* put an end to civil rule, the contrast was perhaps most striking in the relationship between party politics and local government (Cowan 1958: 226–32; Wraith 3 September 1955: 821–2).[10] Whereas local council affairs, including elections, were dominated by party considerations in the Eastern and Western Regions (Wraith has noted 'the insane grip which party politics exercise[d] upon [local] councillors' in those areas),[11] council life was usually nonpartisan within the framework of the North's Native Authority system.

Various reasons have been adduced to explain this state of affairs in Northern Nigeria. They include: (1) the social and political conditions obtaining in the North *vis-à-vis* the other Regions (e.g., a much lower literacy rate; less commercialisation; and less experience with the system of majoritarian local government, reflecting, among other things, sponsorship by the colonial power of traditional ruling groups organised in the Native Authority system and the governing NPC); (2) the reliance of the NPC on Native Authorities to restrict opposition parties (for example, by prohibiting public meetings in the guise of maintaining law and order; by intimidating political foes; and by violence); and (3) the organisational weakness of opposition parties in the North (e.g., the chronic financial distress of the United Middle Belt Congress and the Northern Elements Progressive Union, forcing them into uneasy alliances with the Western-based AG and the Eastern-based NCNC respectively; the narrow electoral base of the United Middle Belt Congress among the Tiv people in the 'Middle Belt'; and the inability of the secularist NEPU to cast off its reputation in the Moslem North as a heretic against the Islamic cosmology) (Sklar 1963: 355–65; Dudley 1968: 164–90; Cohen 1960: *passim*).

These explanations are useful – up to a point. To be sure, social conditions in the Northern Region did combine with the organisational weakness of opposition parties and the various legal and political handicaps under which they operated to limit their electoral effectiveness. Still it is doubtful that these factors were wholly responsible for the failure of a viable party system to take root in the North. At

[10]Military authorities continue to rule. Not surprisingly, public discussion of the future of local government is often conducted without referring to political parties (National Conference on Local Government 1969).

[11]Also see Akpan (1967: 124–8, 167–8).

least one other factor, illuminated by the preceding discussion of the impact of disputes over chieftaincy and party activity in Idoma, may have also contributed to that end, viz. popular antipathy to alien institutions regarded as having an essentially pernicious effect on political life. Its implications for the District Council system in Idoma merit particular attention.

As party strife escalated throughout the 1950s, most Idoma came to view modern party activity as inimical to the ideal of unity in political life. From their vantage point, the party system represented neither an aggregator of competing interests nor a fluid opportunity structure, but merely one more source of cleavage associated with colonial rule. Support for this view was readily available in the virulent conflict between the IHRU and the Native Authority; in the many public confrontations in Idoma between rival party leaders and their followers over remote ideologies, issues, and programmes; and in the partisan hostility which always survived the vigorously contested regional and federal elections. Having borne witness for nearly a decade to party strife, and for several decades more to similarly divisive disputes over chieftaincy, most rural dwellers were now experiencing weariness and impatience over the state of political affairs at the district level.

The District Council system was established in Idoma at a time when this mood was just beginning to crystallise. Fearful that council affairs organised around party considerations would only serve to exacerbate political discord in the districts, many Idoma were determined to eschew partisanship in the new system. Attempts by numerous candidates to inject party labels and programmes into the 1955 and 1958 election campaigns were generally checked by hostile public opinion, as was public debate over potentially divisive political issues. Most campaigns were conducted in secret fashion. By 1962, when the third triennial elections were held, the tradition of nonpartisanship was fairly well established in all spheres of council life – at the nominating stage, during the election campaign, and in council proceedings. The tradition was reinforced that year when most candidates tacitly agreed to refrain from campaigning on the issue which had loomed so large at the nominating stage, strong chieftaincy and Native Authority centralisation – lest they provoke open clashes in their constituencies between NPC supporters of the Native Authority and elements of the opposition parties. The spectre of bitter partisan conflict in the 1961 Northern Assembly elections still hung over Idoma.

The intense hostility with which most Idoma regarded partisanship in District Council affairs is reflected in this finding: when asked how he felt about candidates for his office campaigning as members or supporters of political parties, each of the seventy-one district councillors interviewed in the study objected strongly to the idea. Their feelings toward party politics in local affairs, widely shared in Idoma, are conveyed in these observations by three councillors:

Parties! *Oche awanda!* ['one who brings big trouble'] Have my people not suffered enough from parties?

Who will bring peace to this place when the parties make war?

The white man has brought us parties to spoil the land. He has brought sadness to this place.

2. Executing the campaign strategy

(a) Rules and procedures

Campaigning for the district councillorship was based on a series of meetings in the constituency between the candidate and the *ojira* assembly in each kin group; candidates always involved themselves in these meetings, whether or not they were opposed in the general election. The office-seeker usually took the initiative in arranging to meet secretly with the various kin groups. In a few cases, however, a third party – perhaps an influential elder in the constituency – was invited by the candidate to see to the arrangements or took it upon himself to do so. The usual procedure was for each kin group to gather once with the candidate, although a second meeting was sometimes convened at the behest of a sublineage or a compound family *ojira*.

Several informal rules were widely adopted to minimise rancour and divisiveness during the campaign and after the election. Contenders for a seat on the District Council were strongly encouraged to confine their electioneering to personal appearances before the assemblies of kin groups, at which they were expected to emphasise their own qualities rather than their opponents' shortcomings. Discussion of the candidates' views on political issues – especially party matters – was also to be studiously avoided at these meetings. Finally, debates between rival candidates were discouraged – both in the constituency at large and in the secret meetings of kin groups. This rule could be more easily applied in the latter context simply by refusing to permit joint appearances by office-seekers. Notwithstand-

ing, few candidates displayed any inclination to risk popular censure –
and defeat – by engaging their opponents in open debate elsewhere in
the constituency.

What tack the candidate chose to employ in secret meetings with
kin groups depended largely on the electoral situation which he
faced. Where the candidate was running unopposed, the primary
objective was to assure these groups that his own kinsmen had indeed
nominated a suitable person for the district councillorship. (Among
the fifty-five district councillors who were elected to office in 1962
sixteen fell into this category.) Failure to provide such assurance
might precipitate a low turnout of voters among kin groups other
than his own. In that event, the candidate and his supporters would
suffer an embarrassing loss of prestige and influence in the constituency – notwithstanding his election to the council.

Where the candidate in a contested election was nominated by a
kin group with a majority of the eligible voters in the constituency,
the main concern was to prevent defections to a rival candidate.
(Eight councillors fell into this category.) The candidate was particularly sensitive to the possibility that some elements, feeling wronged
by the schedule of rotation established at the nominating stage, might
now abandon him in the general election. If sufficiently large, such
defections would cause the candidate and his loyal kinsmen to lose
prestige and influence in the constituency – whether or not he was
victorious in the election. This situation could also be expected to
engender considerable political strain within the divided kin group
and perhaps in the constituency at large.

Finally, two objectives were paramount where the candidate in a
contested election was nominated by a kin group with a minority of
the eligible voters in the constituency: first, to prevent defections
from his own group, and second, to encourage defections from kin
groups disposed to support a rival candidate. (Thirty-one councillors
faced this situation.)[12] Considerable resourcefulness was needed here
in order simultaneously to achieve victory in the general election and
to promote a speedy 'return to laughter'.

---

[12]Twenty-six in this group faced at least three opponents in the general election. No
candidate in the twenty-six elections was nominated by a kin group with a majority of
the eligible voters in the constituency. In every case, the victor capitalised on defections from opposing kin groups plus the fact that some groups decided not to nominate
a candidate. That decision reflected the kin group's fear that it would make an embar-
rassingly poor showing and/or its desire to hold the 'swing' votes on election day.

In his personal appearance(s) before each kin group, the candidate appealed for electoral support by invoking the criteria which his own group had weighed at the nominating stage. Thus, he sought to demonstrate his singular attractiveness as a candidate by amplifying on such themes as seniority (*read*: maturity), integrity, courage, oratorical accomplishment, and generosity. Mixing old parables and personal reminiscences, solemnity and wit, he spoke at length of the need for a leader to possess these qualities and of the many occasions on which he himself had displayed them. His listeners interjected frequently, sometimes to express approval or to offer encouragement, at other times to ridicule the candidate's superficiality or to decry his prolixity. As the exchanges escalated in number and intensity, the meeting seemed to dissolve into a raucous free-for-all. The appearance was deceptive, however, for the gathering knew that what was ostensibly an appeal for electoral support had been transformed into an inquest – with the candidate always 'in the dock', as it were (Armstrong 1954: 1051–75).

In time, it became quite clear to all the participants that the candidate could rely neither on personal reputation nor self-adulation. The rivalries which traditionally existed between the various kin groups would conspire with the bruising treatment accorded him by the *ojira* assembly on these occasions to doom the appeal for support – unless the office-seeker could provide a tangible basis for certifying his praiseworthiness. As each meeting wore on the discussion turned increasingly on the theme of generosity.

(*b*) Generosity and corruption: two concepts

To understand the part generosity played in campaigns for the district councillorship, we must take note of its relationship to another matter with which it has sometimes been confused – namely, corruption (Cowan 1958: 274; Wraith and Simpkins 1963: 173ff.; Northern Nigeria 1954: 1–15). Social scientists have propounded numerous definitions of the word 'corruption'. Some of these centre on the public office, i.e., on deviance from norms and rules binding upon aspirants for, and incumbents of, public offices; others focus on the public interest, i.e., on violations of the common interest for special advantage in systems of public or civic order; and still others on market-like behaviour in public office-holding, i.e., on public officials who are encouraged by the nonexistence or weak emergence of norms and rules to try to maximise private gain (Heidenheimer, ed. 1970: 4–6).

Surveying political life in Idoma Division, one could find much evidence of corruption, especially as reflected in the public-office-centred and market-centred definitions of that concept:[13] 'kickbacks' paid to high officials in the Native Authority by individuals and firms doing business with the Native Authority; supplies stolen by low- and middle-level employees in the Native Authority departments; tax revenues embezzled by tax collectors and district heads; illegal fees (commonly known as 'dash' in Nigeria) paid to court presidents, court members, and district councillors;[14] 'dash' paid to Native Authority policemen by Ibo entrepreneurs and others in the division; and votes bought in Native Authority, regional, and federal elections.

Significantly, all of these practices, traceable directly to the colonial experience, were distinguished in the popular mind from such pre-colonial excesses as the levying of illegal fines against hapless victims by secret societies and dance groups in the *aiuta* constabulary; the illegal confiscation of goods by the *okpoju* or market-master; and the levying of extortionate fines against convicted violators of the customary criminal law by the clan head and his aides, the *aiigabo* or clan spokesmen. Despite their proscription in colonial and independent Nigeria, few Idoma attached the same stigma to modern forms of corruption rooted in vague, unfamiliar notions of the civic order, citizenship, and disinterested public service.[15] Except for the ubiquitous 'dash', which could work great hardship on subsistence farmers operating on the periphery of the cash economy, most Idoma viewed modern corruption either with indifference or as a complement to traditional practices which were still highly valued in the society. One such practice was the display of generosity. As we shall see presently, electoral corruption surrounding various high offices in the Native Authority was widely regarded as supportive of the tradition of generosity at a lower level in campaigns for the district councillorship.

The Idoma word *ijelaa* denotes the spirit of generosity in everyday

[13]See the series on corruption in the Idoma Native Authority published by the *Nigerian Citizen*, 19, 25, 28 January; 4, 15, 22, 25 February; 3, 17, 28, 31 March 1956.

[14]District councillors were occasionally 'dashed' in small amounts for mediating land disputes and for helping to fix the disposition of court cases.

[15]The reformist IHRU frequently requested an independent investigation of Native Authority corruption. The request was supported by opposition political parties, including the AG and its Northern ally, the United Middle Belt Congress. After a lengthy delay, the Administration advised the Native Authority to investigate its own Works Department (IHRU 2 June 1956; UMBC 12 May 1956; Idoma AG 22 June 1957; Idoma Division 6 August 1957).

life. *Ijelaa* could be expressed in many ways, on ordinary or on special occasions: for example, by gift-giving (in money and/or in kind); by extending a loan on liberal terms to an age-mate in distress; by preparing a feast for one's secret society or dance group; and by according hospitality to a visitor. Generosity was seen both as an admirable personal quality and as an important contributor to amity in social relations. As these comments by a district councillor and two other informants testify, the ungenerous person was widely regarded as boorish and as a disruptive influence in the community:

The district head is an old tyrant and a miser. He refuses to give us *buruktu* [beer] after the council meeting. He knows this angers the councillors and makes them even more opposed to his rule.

One young farmer has been in this place [an outlying farm settlement] for a long time, but he refuses to make a feast for his neighbours. The people are angered by his ways. We say that he is rude and a troublemaker.

Ekwo [pseudonym] is the tax collector and a strong farmer. But he is no longer a peacemaker. Ekwo buys drink for the Ibo man [a business associate] in Oturkpo Town, but he does not show money in this place. My people are bitter. They say that Ekwo is arrogant, that he thinks he is too big for this place.

Ijelaa also played an important part in the process of accession for various offices – both traditional and modern. For example, from time immemorial aspirants for the clan headship had sought to establish their bona fides by, among other things, preparing great feasts for the lineages over which they hoped to reign.[16] Similarly, most candidates for the office of district councillor presented token gifts of money to the elders in their constituencies and/or prepared feasts for the assemblies of kin groups whose support they hoped to enlist. While such practices could help pave the way for the candidates' election, in the popular mind they were separable from the corruption which was frequently associated with modern office-holding.

The distinction drawn between *ijelaa* and electoral corruption in the modern sense can best be illuminated with reference to vote-buying – an offence punishable under the Northern Region penal code and referred to in the division by the Idoma word *omichi* or the code-word 'tobacco'. *Omichi* was viewed by the Idoma as an essentially short-term transaction in which candidate and elector (the latter

[16] The *ojira* still bestows the title of *odejo* on men renowned for their generosity. Among the fifty-five elected district councillors interviewed in the study, seventeen bore the title. Three of the sixteen appointed councillors had been similarly honoured.

acting either on his own behalf or as representative of a group of electors) each sought to maximise his personal gain in concrete terms. Whereas the candidate was primarily motivated by a desire to obtain the pledge of a vote (or votes) at the lowest financial cost to himself, the elector made ready to exchange his vote(s) for the highest financial return. It should occasion no surprise that vote-buying often involved intensive bargaining, uncomplicated by considerations of personality and political stance, between the elector and one or more candidates for an office. The candidate sometimes persuaded the elector to swear a traditional oath, thus placing a mystical seal on their transaction. In that event, the elector who developed second thoughts about fulfilling his part of the bargain had to be formally released from the oath – lest his transgression on election day cause some great misfortune to befall him (see pp. 211–12). The candidate who gained the upper hand in this way was understandably loath to free the elector from his bond.

Ijelaa was viewed in an altogether different light by the Idoma – for reasons having nothing to do with the unlawfulness of vote-buying under the penal code. Whereas *omichi* was a short-term activity organised around the socially approved desire to maximise private gain, *ijelaa* represented the more highly valued spirit of generosity expressed over the long term. While that spirit could be discerned in individual activities – including the preparation of feasts for those whose support office-seekers hoped to enlist – *ijelaa* had to do with more than isolated displays of munificence. Where these were frequent over a long period of time, they were held to symbolise the essential praiseworthiness of a man as well as his commitment to promote amity in political matters and in social relations generally. A man was held in low esteem, indeed, if his fellows judged him to be lacking in *ijelaa*. In that event, sudden displays of munificence were apt to be met with scepticism or resentment. Various candidates for the district councillorship in 1962 learned that lesson as they went down in defeat.

(c) *Omichi* and *ijelaa*: the electoral alliance

Having illustrated the distinction in Idoma thinking between *ijelaa* (generosity) and electoral corruption in the form of *omichi* (vote-buying), we turn now to the matter of their complementarity in campaigns for the district councillorship. It will be recalled that following the installation of twenty-two District Councils in 1962, each of these bodies was to meet to elect its representative councillor(s). The twenty-eight representative councillors in the division were then to convene in four groups, each to designate a portfolio councillor to serve both as a member of the newly constituted General Purposes Committee and as the head of a department in the Native Authority. This system of direct and indirect elections at different levels of the Native Authority encouraged the building of electoral alliances as follows: A, seeking election to the District Council, would pledge his vote at a negotiated price to B, a candidate in his district for representative councillor, whereupon B would pledge his own vote at a negotiated price to C, a candidate for one of the portfolio councillor positions. Sometimes the process of alliance-building was reversed, however, commencing with a pact between B and C and culminating in a similar pact between A and B. The linch-pin in each vertical alliance thus formed was the candidate for representative councillor, A and C knowing of each other's involvement but having little or no direct contact. The strength of each three-way alliance was dependent, in the final analysis, on the outcome of the District Council and Representative Council elections. If A was defeated in the District Council election, then the candidate for representative councillor, B, would try to negotiate a new vote-buying pact with the victor, X – even where X's vote was already paid for by another candidate for the representative councillorship. Similarly, if B was defeated in the Representative Council election, then the candidate for portfolio councillor, C, would try to negotiate a new vote-buying pact with the victor, Y – even where Y's vote was already committed to another candidate for the portfolio councillorship.[17] Native Authority elections organised around these three-way alliances were free-wheeling affairs from beginning to end. Among the fifty-five district councillors who were elected to office in 1962, thirty-seven acknowledged participating in at least one electoral alliance as a candidate. Twenty-

[17]Candidates for representative councillor and portfolio councillor transacted vote-buying alliances before the District Council elections in the hope ultimately of minimising their investment in *omichi*. They assumed that their ally would be elected district councillor, whereupon he would vote straightaway for the ally seeking the representative councillorship. The strategy was a risky one. The ally who was elected district councillor might then demand a higher price for his vote from the candidate for representative councillor. Or if the ally lost the election, the victor (represented as X in the text) might then demand a very high price for his vote. Candidates for the portfolio councillorship faced similar risks *vis-à-vis* candidates for representative councillor.

two of the thirty-seven acknowledged receiving money in amounts ranging from £6·15 to £15·50.

Alliances were organised around the participants' short-term interest in maximising private gain – a motivation strengthened by their uncertainty as to the electoral outcome and/or their suspicion that, even if victorious, the arrangement would have little consequence after the elections. (As we shall see presently, candidates for district councillor were also motivated by the need to secure funds for campaigning among the assemblies of kin groups.) While a victorious candidate for the office of representative councillor might derive some long-term benefit from his association on the policy-making General Purposes Committee with an ally who had been elected portfolio councillor, and *vice versa*, neither could be sure that this would ultimately be the case. Indeed, the rule which stipulated that represesentative councillors would be chosen in rotation to sit on the Committee was seen by many as an obstacle to maintaining an effective alliance between those two officials after the election. The prospects were bleaker still for the victorious candidate for a seat on the District Council. Isolated from the decision-making centre at Oturkpo Town, he could expect to derive no long-term benefit from the alliance. No wonder, then, that each participant resolved to exploit the immediate electoral situation to the fullest extent possible. To do this, alliances were often formed across party lines, joining, however briefly, friend and foe alike.

In a typical case, a prominent member of an opposition party standing for the District Council pledged his vote to a candidate for representative councillor who was, coincidentally, a member of another opposition party and a close personal friend. The latter candidate, in turn, pledged his vote to a prominent member of the NPC, who was standing for the office of portfolio councillor. The candidates for district councillor and representative councillor were both bitter political foes of the NPC luminary.

Besides aiding individual candidacies, electoral alliances formed without regard to party affiliation and political conviction helped reduce the divisive influence of the party factor in local government affairs – an outcome which pleased the great majority in Idoma who, in 1962, were exhausted by years of party strife. With Idoma Division solidly in the NPC camp,[18] aspirants for offices in the Native Author-

[18]The NPC swept all the Idoma seats in the federal and regional legislative elections of 1959 and 1961 respectively.

ity and their supporters felt free to advance their own ambitions without concern for party labels, political issues, or remote ideologies (e.g., 'democratic socialism' and 'pan-Africanism', espoused by Chief Obafemi Awolowo and Dr Nnamdi Azikiwe respectively). The opportunism which prevailed in Native Authority elections is further illuminated by the part which one district head played in the cross-party alliance referred to in the preceding paragraph. An NPC member, he lent strong support to the opposition party member and the NPC luminary standing for representative councillor and portfolio councillor respectively; each candidate was provided with a substantial amount of money to use in vote-buying transactions. By helping to elect both men to offices which were represented on the General Purposes Committee, the district head hoped to enhance his own influence at the centre *vis-à-vis* the Chief of Idoma, titular head of the NPC in Idoma and President of the Committee.

While most assemblies of kin groups in each District Council constituency knew of these three-way electoral alliances, and even encouraged candidates to participate in them, few were privy to the financial details. As might be expected, some assembly members concluded on their own account that the candidate for district councillor had pledged his vote to the candidate for representative councillor at a very substantial price. Acting on that assumption, they would demand at the secret campaign meeting with the candidate for district councillor that he negotiate a similar pact with the kin group. The demand was sometimes met on the spot. Occasionally these members would represent the assembly in negotiations with the candidate. Such negotiations were usually initiated by the representative(s) and took place either before or after the candidate met the kin group to appeal for electoral support. To maximise the assembly's financial gain in this circumstance, bargaining was usually conducted with several office-seekers in the constituency. Finally, individual members of the various kin groups would sometimes attempt to meet with the candidate to arrange for the sale of their own votes. Here, too, bargaining nearly always involved more than one office-seeker.

Notwithstanding these incidents, however, *omichi* or 'tobacco' – the illegal buying of votes – was far less prevalent in campaigns for the district councillorship than in campaigns at higher levels for representative councillor and portfolio councillor. Several reasons can be adduced to explain this anomaly. First, most candidates for the district councillorship could argue that estimates of money received from the candidate for representative councillor were wildly exaggerated. Pointing both to their status as modest farmers and to the fact that the district councillor received no salary, they usually managed to assail the position that candidacy had produced a windfall and that office-holding held out the promise of great wealth. Some of the most covetous assemblies of kin groups and/or their representatives were won over by the candidates' eloquent claims of selflessness in seeking office.

Second, candidates for district councillor usually rebuffed individuals who tried to sell their own votes. Knowing that such an individual spoke for neither his kin group nor dissidents whose defection might be encouraged, the candidate was understandably reluctant to invest money in a solitary vote which would have little impact on the outcome of the election.

Third, *omichi* was unreliable. Individual electors and kin groups had been known to break their vote-buying pledges to office-seekers on previous occasions – in Native Authority, regional, and federal elections. Fearing duplicity in District Council elections, some candidates in 1962 resolved not to squander their own meagre resources and whatever financial gain they had already derived from three-way electoral alliances with candidates for representative councillor and portfolio councillor. Either they refused to engage in vote-buying in campaigns for the district councillorship or they invested little money in *omichi*.

Fourth, there was *ijelaa* or generosity – reputedly the most effective check on vote-buying in campaigns for district councillor. The considerable agreement which existed among rural dwellers as to the desirability of emphasising generosity over *omichi* in the 1962 council elections was rooted in considerations of principle and necessity. To begin with, most kin groups were concerned lest extensive vote-buying in these campaigns encouraged defections from their own candidates. This contingency aroused three fears: that the kin group experiencing numerous defections would lose much prestige and influence in the constituency; that there would be a weakening of the traditional rotation which had been employed so successfully at the nominating stage to minimise rancour and divisiveness;[19] and that the

[19]Older Idoma were especially fearful that the principle of rotation might be weakened as a regulatory device, just as it had been in chieftaincy affairs during the colonial period. The Tiv appear to have already experienced a weakening of that principle in contests for high political office (Wallace 1958: 66–7).

way would now be paved for an intensification of political strain in the divided kin group and in the constituency at large. The spectre of internecine conflict which had hung for so long over Idoma in chieftaincy and party matters strengthened the resolve at the base of the society to eschew any activities which might exacerbate political discord. As we have seen, partisan campaigning in local government elections was widely regarded as one such activity. Vote-buying in campaigns for the district councillorship, directed toward maximising private gain, was viewed as yet another. But *ijelaa* was quite a different matter. Symbolising a man's worth as an individual and his commitment to work for amity in social life, *ijelaa* was a more highly valued principle which seemed especially appropriate in those troubled times. Its vigorous application held out the hope that truly worthy candidates would be elected to office – men who, having given expression to their generosity before and during the campaign, would now possess sufficient prestige and influence as peacemakers to clear the way for a swift 'return to laughter' after the election. The importance of this consideration for a people weary of division and strife cannot be overestimated.

Barely distinguishable in other respects from the mass of the electorate in rural Idoma, most candidates for district councillor held similar views regarding *ijelaa*. The candidate sought to underscore his own potential for promoting amity as an office-holder by organising elaborate displays of generosity in campaign appearances before the various assembled kin groups – including his own. Thus, among the fifty-five councillors who were elected to office in 1962, all but three presented token gifts of money (rarely exceeding five shillings) to the elders and, most important, also prepared great feasts for the assemblies. The sums expended on these displays were considerable for Idoma farmers, ranging from £7·55 in one of the least populous constituencies to £19·25 in one of the most populous.

Probed for the source of this money, district councillors and other informants called attention to the way in which electoral corruption surrounding high offices in the Native Authority complemented generosity in campaigns for the district councillorship. Candidates were normally expected by the electorate to obtain the wherewithal for expressing generosity in the campaign by transacting vote-buying alliances with candidates for representative councillor and portfolio councillor. That expectation was usually fulfilled. Thus nineteen of the twenty-two district councillors who acknowledged receiving money from candidates for representative councillor affirmed that exhortations by kinsmen had contributed to their decision to negotiate vote-buying pacts; seventeen of the nineteen invested all the proceeds (as well as small amounts of money received from friends and relatives) in elaborate displays of generosity during the campaign. Fifteen district councillors, it will be recalled, refused to divulge the amount of money which they received for participating in an electoral alliance. Of these, all but four did affirm, however, that they lacked sufficient personal resources to make a proper investment in *ijelaa*.[20] It seems reasonable to conclude that here, too, the decision to participate in a vote-buying pact was motivated very largely by a combination of encouragement from kin and awareness of the need to obtain money quickly for essential displays of generosity in the campaign.

What emerges from the examination of vote-buying and generosity as practised in Native Authority elections is a picture of a people bent on muting the conflicts engendered by colonial rule – by whatever means were at their disposal. Indifferent to the unlawfulness of *omichi* – few Idoma believed that electoral corruption could or should be eliminated entirely – but nevertheless sensitive to its potential for fomenting discord, most resolved to prevent its domination of District Council elections. They sought to do this by stressing the importance of *ijelaa* in campaigns for the district councillorship as well as the part which vote-buying in other Native Authority elections might play in furthering this. Three-way alliances based on *omichi* were widely favoured as the principal source of the money which candidates for the council would use to organise displays of *ijelaa* – and, coincidentally, to promote amity in social life. In Idoma, as elsewhere, electoral corruption was regarded as something which could be manipulated to serve legitimate social ends.

The appointed district councillor

Shortly after the popular election of a majority on the District Council, its permanent chairman, the district head, provided the central administration of the Native Authority with the names of those he wished to have constitute the official minority. Almost without exception, the nominees were routinely appointed by the central adminis-

[20]This acknowledgment was made in response to some skilful questioning by my interpreter-informant. See pp. 79–80, 266–7.

tration to serve as 'Native Authority councillors'.

'Native Authority councillors' were nominated by the district head because of their past record of loyalty to that official. Either close relatives or long-time supporters of the district head and of strong chieftaincy generally, they could be counted on to defend his interests in District Council affairs. As a case in point, the five incumbents who lost in bids for re-election in 1962 were subsequently appointed to the council. Two were from the same sublineage as the district head; the other three owed their appointments as tax collectors some years before to that official. Moreover, all five had demonstrated their reliability while serving as elected councillors from 1958 to 1962. 'Native Authority councillors' could be expected to support the district head's choice for representative councillor and to vote his line in other matters before the council. Further evidence of the deference which the appointees paid to that figure can be found in their handling of *omichi*: even where 'Native Authority councillors' negotiated vote-buying pacts on their own with the candidate for representative councillor, they usually volunteered to turn over part of the proceeds to the district head. As we shall see, the strong ties which existed between the official minority and the district head tended to exacerbate bureaucratic–debureaucratic tension on the council.

In adapting the modern district councillorship in terms of traditional political competition – with its emphasis on rotation, seniority, personal integrity, courage, oratory, and generosity – the Idoma were not simply 'playing politics as in days of yore', as it were. To apprehend what more was involved in institutional adaptation in this case, it is necessary to underscore once again the clash between traditional ideals and colonial practices which served as a backdrop for the 1962 Native Authority elections – the first held in Idoma Division since independence nearly two years earlier. The process of accession surrounding the district councillorship in particular can be seen against this backdrop as an expression of two moods: on the one hand, there was the deepening sense of continuity in Idoma life felt by most members of the society, notwithstanding some five decades of European rule. And on the other, there was a renewed commitment to traditional principles in the face of what most Idoma had anathematised under that rule, viz. the imposition of a system of local government based on strong chieftaincy and centralised authority and the disruption caused by struggles over chieftaincy and by party strife.

Men in the middle

At the nominating stage, the assemblies of kin groups in each constituency tended to weigh the credentials of prospective candidates for district councillor with particular regard to their attitudes toward the Native Authority. Those nominated to stand in the general election were reputedly honest, fearless, and skilled as orators. In effect, this meant that they could usually be relied upon to argue boldly in the council for a restoration in some form of the constitutional equilibrium; and against Native Authority interference in village affairs. The emphasis placed on this qualification in nominating candidates for the district councillorship set the stage for the bureaucratic–debureaucratic role conflict which would face those who triumphed in the general election. Upon taking office, they could anticipate being subjected to conflicting role-expectations reflecting, on the one hand, their constituents' hostility toward strong chieftaincy and centralised political authority, and on the other, their superiors' defence of the *status quo* in local government affairs. As if this was not enough, they had also to consider the implications of *ijelaa* for their official performance. Having been judged sufficiently generous before and during the campaign to warrant election to office, they were now expected by their constituents to foster amity – an objective hardly compatible with the expectation that they be uncompromising foes of the Native Authority as then constituted. How the councillors dealt with their situation as 'men in the middle' will be examined in the next part of the study.

Part IV Role perceptions and role conflict: empirical analyses

Chapter Six Analysing role conflict: concepts and definitions

Systematic social inquiry presupposes an ability to employ language in a manner which will facilitate communication. As Stinchcombe (1968: 6) has so aptly observed, 'Social theorists should prefer to be wrong rather than misunderstood. Being misunderstood shows sloppy theoretical work.' With that caveat in mind, a conceptual language is outlined here for analysing role conflict (Magid 1970: 81–91). Nine concepts are explicated with illustrations from Idoma.

Position

Position denotes the location of an actor in a system of social relationships (Gross *et al.* 1958: 48; Kothari and Roy 1969: 36ff.).[1] For example, the offices of district councillor, district head, and tax collector are positions in the social and political systems of contemporary Idoma. In order to underscore my preoccupation with a particular actor – the councillor – his office is designated the *focal position* (Gross *et al*. 1958: 51–5); those with whom he interacts are said to occupy *non-focal positions*. Since position is an essentially locative concept, focal and non-focal ought not to be interpreted as indicating positional significance. The focal position may or may not be the most important position in a system under investigation.

Role

While most conceptualisations of 'role' incorporate the notion that 'individuals . . . in social locations [or positions] . . . behave . . . with reference to expectations' (*ibid*.: 17), there is considerable disagreement on specific meaning. Definitions of the role concept usually fall into at least one of three categories reflecting quite different emphases: normative culture patterns, behaviour of an individual,

---

[1]The concept *position* is preferred over *status* in order to avoid confusing the latter with such concepts as *prestige* and *esteem* (Linton 1936: 113–14; Thibaut and Kelley 1959: 222–38; Homans 1961: 336–58).

and orientation of the individual to a situation (*ibid*.: 11–18). In this study, *role is defined as a behavioural pattern expected of the occupant of a position*. Essentially normative, role is distinguished from an actual behavioural pattern which may or may not conform with expectations.

Having stipulated a definition for the concept of role, attention is directed to the distinction between *role-position* and *role-occupant*. That distinction is reflected in two concepts, *social role* and *personal role*. According to Jacobson *et al.* (1951: 9), a social role is

a set of expectations which others share of the behaviour associated with a position, without reference to the characteristics of the person who occupies the position.

In contrast, a personal role is

a set of expectations which others have of an individual's behaviour in a position, without regard to the social role.

An analogue can be found in Cottrell's conceptualisation (1942: 617) of *cultural role* and *unique role*.[2]

In order to ascertain the district councillors' perceptions of social role and personal role, I included these questions and alternative responses in a pre-test questionnaire:

Set I. *Social Role*
A. *Question*: Could you tell me how these people would feel about *councillors* campaigning for the governing NPC in the [1964 federal parliamentary] elections?
B. *Responses*: (1) they would expect *councillors* to campaign for the NPC; (2) they would expect *councillors* not to campaign for the NPC; or (3) they would have no expectation of *councillors* in this situation.

Set II *Personal Role*
A. *Question*: Could you tell me how these people would feel about *you as a councillor* campaigning for the NPC in the elections?
B. *Responses*: (1) they would expect *me as a councillor* to campaign for the NPC; (2) they would expect *me as a councillor* not to campaign for the NPC; or (3) they would have no expectation of *me as a councillor* in this situation.

Because the councillors tended to interpret *all* questions and responses in Set I and Set II in terms of personal roles, the questionnaire was revised to include only the format of personal role.

After noting one series of responses to a question in the revised instrument, however, future investigators may be encouraged to employ both concepts. Four district councillors (representing less

[2]Also see McMullan's distinction (1961: 194) between *subjective role* and *objective role*.

than 6 per cent of those interviewed) volunteered this distinction between social role and personal role: each perceived that high officials in the Native Authority would expect their subordinates, the councillors, to campaign for the governing NPC in the 1964 elections (social role); but each hastened to add that those officials would hold the opposite expectation for himself as a councillor (personal role). The four councillors explained their sensitivity to the distinction between social role and personal role in this situation by noting their well-publicised association with political parties which were opposed to the NPC.

Audience

Audiences are those 'by whom the [focal] actor sees his role [behaviour] observed and evaluated, and [to whose]... evaluations and expectations [he attends]' (Turner 1956: 328).[3] Audiences may be an individual or group occupying non-focal positions.

While audiences are often physically present to express expectations and/or to observe actual behaviour, this is not a prerequisite for meaningful role interaction. For example, the district councillor established role relationships with audiences which were physically present (e.g., fellow councillors); physically absent (e.g., Native Authority superiors in Oturkpo Town); and non-physically present (e.g., the ancestors, who are believed to be omnipresent members of the society). His symbolic role interaction with the ancestors reflected a continuing dialogue between past and present generations in Idoma – a dialogue sustained by the periodic intercession of elder-priests of the *alekwu* cult; by the offerings which each individual had to make to the ancestors on propitious occasions; and by the assistance which the ancestors were obliged to provide, in turn, to individual supplicants and to the society as a whole.

Role relationships were structured pyramidally between the district councillor and his audiences. (See Figure 1.) At the base, he interacted with three audiences which usually resided in the constituency: elders, young men, and tax collectors.[4] Ascending the pyramid, role relationships involved elected and appointed councillors, the representative councillor(s), and the district head (who was

[3]Also see Mead (1947: *passim*).

[4]Because tax collectors were widely viewed as a separate audience in the *ojira* assembly, they are treated as such in the study.

also permanent chairman of the District Council). Finally, the district councillor interacted at the apex with the Chief of Idoma and the other members of the policy-making General Purposes Committee. The decision to treat the Chief and the Committee as a single audience reflects the popular view of their relationship. From its inception in 1958, the Committee was widely regarded as dominated by, and

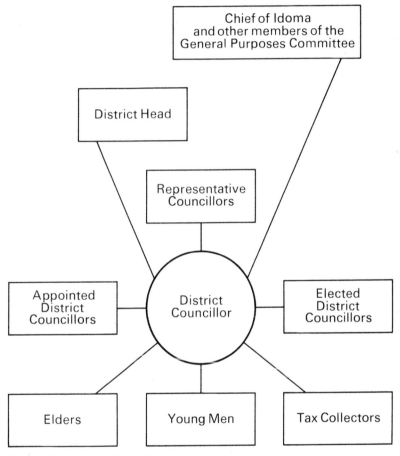

Fig. 1. Structure of role relationships between district councillor and audiences

indeed indistinguishable from, the *Och'Idoma* in matters of policy. This was reaffirmed in the pre-test of the questionnaire, when respondents indicated that they could not imagine portfolio council-

E

lors and representative councillors on the Committee holding views which differed from those of the *Och'Idoma*. As one respondent put it:

Ogiri Oko [the first Chief] cast a long shadow. Because Ajene Ukpabi [his successor] is a small man next to Oko, his shadow is not so long. But things have not really changed in the Native Authority. The shadow goes by the same name. It is still called 'the Committee'.

Drawing on both the pre-test and the testimony of informants, I decided to exclude these officials from the list of audiences: the District Officer (who represented the Northern Region Minister for Local Government in Idoma); Idoma members of the Federal Parliament and the Northern House of Assembly; and civil servants in the Federal, Regional, Provincial, and Native Authority establishments.[5] Preoccupied with policy matters at Oturkpo Town, by 1962 the District Officer had little contact with district councillors in rural Idoma. Legislators as well as government and Native Authority careerists were not known to the councillors and/or regarded by them as not involved in council affairs.

Also excluded from the list of audiences were women and such traditional office-holders as the clan head and the *aiigabo* or titled spokesmen of clans. The old prohibition against women participating in political life extended extralegally to District Council affairs and to Native Authority matters generally. Clan heads and clan spokesmen, usually old, infirm, and not interested in the minutiae of council life, were grouped by the district councillors with the audience designated as 'elders' in Figure 1 – regardless of where those traditional office-holders lived in the district.[6] Finally, it was not possible to specify the ancestors as an audience for the purpose of analysing role conflict. Because the *alekwu* exercises a mystical influence in Idoma life, it could not be treated as an audience in the conventional empirical sense. However, some light is shed on the councillor's role interaction with the ancestors by examining his evaluations of supernatural sanctions in perceived situations of role conflict (see pp. 211–12, 215).

[5] By 1962, when the field investigation began, changes had been made in the North's system of provincial administration. The old office of Resident had been eliminated, and many of its political and administrative responsibilities parcelled among the Provincial Commissioner (chief political officer in the province) and the Provincial Secretary (head of the provincial administrative service).

[6] Exceptions were made for district heads who also served as clan heads in three of the five districts on which the study concentrates. Those officials were classed with the district head audience.

Role conflict

The literature on role conflict reveals a confusing array of definitions. For example, various definitions of the concept emphasise expectations which are *antithetical, incompatible, inconsistent*, or *discrepant* (Burchard 1954: 528; Spiegel 1957: 2 note; Jacobson *et al*. 1951: 22–3; Getzels and Guba 1954: 165). Superficially, these terms apppear to be synonymous; but closer inspection reveals a significant difference. That difference can perhaps best be illuminated from the perspective of formal logic.

In formal logic, antithesis denotes terms in opposition. In contrast, incompatibility, inconsistency, and discrepancy subsume conflict which may be antithetical or non-antithetical. Clearly, then, definitions of role conflict require specification of antithetical and non-antithetical expectations. Unfortunately, such specification rarely appears in the literature. Rather, it tends to be replete with statements which merely imply that role conflict is analogous to antithesis in formal logic.

Pursuing this line of thought still further, it is observed that antithesis subsumes *contradiction* (where A is false, B must be true) and *contrariety* (where A and B can both be false, but never true together) (Eaton 1959: 83–5). Translated into the language for analysing role conflict, these two principles in formal logic point up the following analogy: contradictory and contrary role situations both involve opposing expectations which cannot be fulfilled together. But the two situations differ in one important respect. Whereas no expectation can be ignored by the actor confronting a contradictory role situation, all expectations can be ignored and yet another behavioural alternative selected by the actor confronting a contrary role situation; the latter is thus accorded greater freedom of action in the face of opposing expectations.[7] For the purpose of this study, I shall stipulate a definition of role conflict which incorporates the notion of contradiction in formal logic: *a situation of role conflict exists where there are contradictory expectations which cannot be fulfilled together. Men in the Middle* deals exclusively with role conflict (i.e., role contradiction) surrounding the district councillors.

[7] Ehrlich (1959: 7), too, distinguishes between role contradiction and role contrariety; he refers to the former as 'role conflict', the latter as 'role dilemma'. Also see the distinction which Gluckman (1965: 109; 1968b: 88–9; 1969: 338; 1971: 131–2) draws between conflict and contradiction.

Role conflict may arise *within* and/or *between* audiences and may reflect (1) consensus on a single, inherently contradictory role pattern; or (2) dissensus involving multiple role patterns. In the first case, for example, an audience may expect an impecunious district councillor to be honest, efficient, and a generous host to his constituents and kinsmen; in the second, one audience may expect him to be honest and efficient and another may expect him to be a generous host. This study focuses on dissensus involving multiple role patterns – the type of role conflict which, arising both within and between audiences, most often confronted the councillors.

Ambivalence

Before stipulating a definition of ambivalence, it is necessary to identify the three analytic elements in any situation of role conflict. They are (1) the objective conflict; (2) perception of the objective conflict; and (3) the subjective conflict (Getzels and Guba 1954: 166; Seeman 1953: 373; Kahn *et al.* 1964: 12).[8] The occupant of a focal position may fail to perceive an objective role conflict, i.e., he may not be aware that audiences hold contradictory expectations for his behaviour. His ability to perceive that situation is a necessary condition for experiencing subjective role conflict. It is important to add that subjective role conflict need not accompany perception of an objective conflict. *We shall know that the district councillor experiences subjective role conflict when he indicates ambivalence, i.e., when he indicates difficulty in choosing his behaviour from among given role alternatives* (Seeman 1953: 373).

Legitimacy, obligation, and sanction

While social scientists generally acknowledge the multi-dimensional character of role conflict, some fail to pursue its implications. For example, Parsons (1959: 280) defines role conflict as 'the exposure of the actor to conflicting sets of legitimised [i.e., rightful or proper] role-expectations such that complete fulfilment of both is realistically impossible'. His definition precludes situations involving (1) conflicting illegitimate expectations or (2) conflicting legitimate and illegiti-

[8]Analogues of these elements can be found in Parsons' concepts (1959: 7ff.) of *cognitive orientation* and *cathectic response*, and Thibaut and Kelley's distinction (1959: 67ff.) between *production of behaviour* and *perception of behaviour*.

mate expectations. Moreover, it apparently causes him to assume that deviance from role-expectations must result in punitive sanction (*ibid.*: 28off.). Parsons overlooks the fact that role conflict may involve expectations which, when unfulfilled, do not result in punishment of the actor. Various investigators in Africa manifest a similar preoccupation with legitimate, sanction-bearing expectations in role conflict (e.g., Fallers 1955: 303; 1965: 3, 246). A broader perspective may be adopted for analysing role conflict by treating its three dimensions – legitimacy, obligation, and sanction – as discrete concepts.

Legitimacy may be defined, after Dahl (1956: 46 note, 138), as belief in the rightness or propriety of decisions or decision-making processes. In this study, *the concept of legitimacy denotes belief in the rightness or propriety of specific expectations. Expectations which the district councillor feels an audience has a right to entertain are construed as legitimate. Conversely, expectations which he feels an audience does not have a right to entertain are construed as illegitimate.*

Two concepts, obligation and sanction, draw attention to a problem which confronts all social and political systems, that of maximising conformity between (1) expectations for the behaviour of members, and (2) their actual behaviour. System stability is in part a function of the degree of conformity between (1) and (2) (Goode 1960: 253). *A sanction is role-related behaviour of an essentially punitive or remunerative character* (Gross *et al.* 1958: 249–50). Since *punitive* and *remunerative sanction* may operate at both a *social* and *personal level*, I distinguish between four basic sanctional types: (1) *punitive–social* (sanction originating in others and directed toward the focal actor); (2) *punitive–personal* (sanction originating in and directed toward the focal actor); (3) *remunerative–social* (sanction originating in others and directed toward the focal actor); and (4) *remunerative–personal* (sanction originating in and directed toward the focal actor). This study deals exclusively with the first type of sanction. Accordingly, *an obligatory expectation is defined as one which, when not fulfilled in actual behaviour, is expected to result in punitive–social sanctioning; behavioural conformity with the expectation by definition precludes the imposition of such sanction. Conversely, an optional expectation is not expected to result in punitive–social sanctioning, regardless of conformity or nonconformity in actual behaviour.* These definitions underscore the fact that participants in a situation of role conflict may evaluate one or more expectations as legitimate-obligatory, legitimate-optional, illegitimate-obligatory, or illegitimate-optional.

Optional expectations do not constitute *prima facie* evidence of apathy. For example, an audience's decision not to punish a recalcitrant district councillor may reflect loyalty to a kinsman or willingness to pardon a generally responsive office-holder. Thus, the brother of a councillor reported that he would never punish the latter for failing to fulfil his expectations. And a councillor recently elected to a third term observed that those elders who were impressed with his past record would tend to overlook an occasional refusal to fulfil their expectations.

At this juncture, a caveat ought to be noted. *Men in the Middle* focuses on the evaluations which district councillors are wont to make of role-expectations which they perceive audiences as likely to hold for the councillors' behaviour in certain situations. The analysis does *not* inquire into the accuracy of the councillors' role perceptions or of their evaluations of role obligation and role sanction (see p. 184 note 1). Morever, the procedure which is employed for scoring their evaluations of role legitimacy (legitimate or illegitimate) and role obligation (obligatory or optional) does *not* assume a pattern for particular audiences within or between situations. For example, it is not assumed that the councillors will (or must) evaluate as legitimate and therefore obligatory in any or all situations role-expectations which are attributed by them to the audience of elders. Nor is it assumed that those officials will (or must) evaluate as illegitimate and therefore optional in any or all situations role-expectations which they perceive the Chief of Idoma and his colleagues on the General Purposes Committee as holding for the councillors' behaviour. Role-expectations which the councillors attribute to the elders may be evaluated by those officials as legitimate (or illegitimate) in one situation, illegitimate (or legitimate) in another; and as obligatory (or optional) in the former situation, optional (or obligatory) in the latter. The same may hold for the Native Authority leadership and for other audiences in the study. What pattern, if any, obtains here can only be determined, in the final analysis, by empirical investigation.

Resolution

Resolution denotes the behavioural response to a perceived situation of role conflict. Before taking up the matter of the district councillors' approach to resolution, the relationship between resolution and the objective, perceptual, and subjective elements in any situation of role conflict is elucidated. It has been observed above that perception of an objective conflict is a necessary, but not a sufficient, condition for experiencing subjective role conflict. The presence of the latter is ascertained when an actor indicates ambivalence, i.e., when he indicates difficulty in choosing his behaviour from among given role alternatives. Resolution is a response to a perceived conflict; it does not require the presence of ambivalence. Furthermore, resolution need not terminate objective role conflict. An objective conflict may persist, notwithstanding resolution at a personal level. In that event, an actor may either ignore it or attempt to persuade one or more audiences to renounce an expectation. On occasion resolution may even prolong an objective conflict. For example, two councillors reported that they had once responded to a situation of role conflict by publicly denouncing elders and the district head who held contradictory expectations for their behaviour. Upon realising that their response had prolonged and intensified the conflict, the councillors proceeded to apologise to both audiences. Neither audience reacted sympathetically; the objective conflict persisted for some time.

Despite the many procedures which are potentially available for resolving role conflict – compromise, aggression, withdrawal, etc. (Dollard *et al.* 1945: 1ff.; Wardwell 1955: 16–25; Spiegel 1957: 4ff.; Toby 1952: 324ff.; Getzels and Guba 1954: 173–5; Burchard 1954: 535; Goffman 1956: 83; Preiss and Ehrlich 1966: 96ff.; Wheeldon 1969: 140)[9] – the district councillors consistently voiced preference for a single alternative: the major role procedure. That is, faced with conflicting expectations, they tended to evaluate one expectation as the major role to be fulfilled.[10] This finding in the study raises a crucial question: What determines the evaluation of a major role among contradictory expectations? Merton (1957: 113–16; 1961: 371–6) has suggested three factors: (1) *involvement* (the extent to which others are perceived to be concerned with the role behaviour of the actor); (2) *power* (the extent to which others are perceived to be able to prevail upon the actor to do something he would not otherwise do);[11] and (3) *observability* (the extent to which others are

[9]Also see p. 15.

[10]Occasionally other procedures accompanied the evaluation of a major role; for example, verbal aggression in the form of denunciation and epithet.

[11]This definition is adapted from Dahl (1957: 202–3).

perceived tc be able to view the role behaviour of the actor). Focusing on involvement for purposes of illustration, it is hypothesised that the councillor will fulfil the expectation of those who are perceived to be most concerned with his role behaviour. (Similar hypotheses can be constructed for power and observability.) Other writers have suggested that personality may also affect the resolution of role conflict. For example, Ackerman (1951: 1–17) hypothesises that the actor will fulfil the expectation which is most compatible with his personality needs.[12]   Potentially relevant to the relationship between resolution, personality, and factors of social structure are two dimensions of role conflict, legitimacy and obligation. It is hypothesised that the district councillor who perceives a situation of role conflict will have a personal need to fulfil the expectation which he evaluates as more legitimate and/or more obligatory (Getzels and Guba 1954: 174–5). Moreover, we observe that the two dimensions cut across involvement, power, and observability. It is assumed that those who are perceived as holding legitimate and/or obligatory expectations for the actor will have some involvement in, power over, and observability of his role behaviour. Accordingly, it is expected that an actor's evaluations of role legitimacy and role obligation will be useful in predicting his resolutions. This is borne out with respect to the councillors.

In summary, the study of bureaucratic–debureaucratic role conflict surrounding the district councillors is organised around seven analytic variables and four main sets of hypotheses:

Analytic variables

(1) *Expectations perceived by the councillor.*

(2) *Perceived role conflict.* A situation of role conflict involves contradictory expectations which cannot be fulfilled together.

(3) *Experienced ambivalence.* A councillor experiences ambivalence (subjective role conflict) when he has difficulty choosing his behaviour from among given role alternatives.

(4) *Perceived legitimacy of expectations.* Expectations which the councillor feels an audience has a right to entertain are construed as legitimate; those which he feels an audience does not have a right to entertain are construed as illegitimate.

(5) *Perceived obligatoriness of expectations.* An obligatory expectation is one which, when not fulfilled by the councillor, is expected to result in punitive–social sanctioning; an optional expectation is not expected to result in

[12]Also see Kahn *et al.* (1964: 233ff.) and Parsons (1959: 32).

such sanction, regardless of conformity or nonconformity in actual behaviour.

(6) *Perceived sanction*. This refers to the specific punitive sanction(s) which the councillor expects to result from his failure to fulfil an audience's expectation.

(7) *Direction of resolution*. Resolution involves the councillor's behavioural response to a perceived situation of role conflict. 'Direction of resolution' refers to the major role which he chooses to fulfil in a situation involving contradictory expectations.

Hypotheses

(1) *There is a relationship between role legitimacy and role obligation*. The councillor who evaluates an audience expectation as legitimate will also evaluate it as obligatory. Conversely, the councillor who evaluates an audience expectation as illegitimate will also evaluate it as optional.[13]

(2) *There is a relationship between role legitimacy, role obligation, and ambivalence*. The degree to which the councillor experiences difficulty choosing his behaviour from among given role alternatives will vary directly with the number of conflicting expectations which he evaluates as legitimate and/or obligatory.

(3) *There is a relationship between role sanction and ambivalence*. The councillor will experience greater ambivalence when he perceives expectations to be supported by the same types of sanctions than when he perceives them to be supported by different types of sanctions.[14]

(4) *There is a relationship between role legitimacy, role obligation, and resolution of role conflict*. The councillor who perceives a situation of role

[13]Legitimacy and obligation are operationalised here as dichotomous variables: legitimate/illegitimate, obligatory/optional. Alternative hypotheses may be framed with two continuous variables: more or less legitimate, more or less obligatory. In that event, we would expect the evaluations of role legitimacy and role obligation to vary directly with each other.

[14]The focus here is upon punitive–social sanction. Alternative hypotheses need to be constructed for punitive–personal, remunerative–personal, and remunerative–social sanction. See pp. 121–2.

The relationship between sanction and ambivalence is hypothesised with respect to a *typology of punitive sanctions* (see pp. 209–14). No test is made in the study of the relationship between those two variables with respect to the *potency of individual sanctions*. Such a test could conceivably be organised around the following hypotheses: (1) Where the focal actor perceives no differences in the potency of audiences' sanctions, the degree to which he experiences ambivalence in resolving role conflict will vary directly with the potency of sanctions. (2) Where the focal actor perceives differences in the potency of audiences' sanctions, the degree to which he experiences ambivalence in resolving role conflict will vary inversely with the extent of the differences in the potency of sanctions.

conflict will fulfil the expectation which he evaluates as more legitimate and/or more obligatory.[15]

The analysis begins in Chapter Seven with a report on the councillors' perceptions of role-expectations in various situations reflecting bureaucratic–debureaucratic tension.

[15] A single resolution procedure is involved here, evaluation of the major role. Alternative hypotheses need to be constructed for other procedures.

Chapter Seven Confronting role conflict: case-studies

Following World War II, it will be recalled, the colonial Administration sought to meet the challenge of Nigerian nationalism by reaffirming its commitment to gradual, controlled change at all levels of the society. In Idoma, as elsewhere in the Northern Region, agitation by reformist elements combined with nationalist ferment throughout the country to produce ostensible 'democratic' reforms in the Native Authority; 'council democracy' commenced in 1955 with the establishment of the District Council system.

With few exceptions, the first generation of district councillors who took office that year were ignorant of, and uninterested in, the English model of majoritarian local government–on which, in theory at least, 'council democracy' was to be based. To remedy this situation, colonial officials encouraged the central administration of the Native Authority to provide quickly each of the twenty–two District Councils with a set of standing orders. These sketched the method of election in the new system, rules of procedure, and committee organisation and functions. During the next half decade, the standing orders were periodically modified to render the councils more efficient in operation and more professional in outlook.

The drive to professionalise the District Council system was accelerated after independence, ostensibly to enhance operational efficiency and to minimise partisanship in local affairs. (While favouring the end of party divisiveness, many Idoma suspected that the real motive was a desire to check the councils' ability to challenge strong chieftaincy and centralised political authority.) Reorganisation of the court system in Idoma provided the model for council reforms intended to achieve those objectives. In 1961, it will be recalled, the District and Central Courts were replaced by six Circuit Courts of first instance. The six court presidents received intensive training in substantive law and court procedure under the new penal code at the Institute for Administration in Zaria. A similar attempt to professionalise the council system was made in 1963, when the Ford Foundation and the Institute jointly sponsored two instructorships in Idoma in local government affairs. Each council participated in a two-week short-course at its headquarters site. The objective, as one instructor put it, was 'to flesh-out the standing orders and run some blood between the lines, so that the councillors could learn about modern local government and take pride in serving it'.

Lectures, discussions, and demonstrations covered such topics as financial management, committee procedures, record-keeping,[1] and the proper relationship between the council and its permanent chairman, the district head. The surbordinate status of the councils in Native Authority affairs was emphasised, along with their obligation to eschew partisan politics. While the two instructors and a handful of councillors were enthusiastic about the project, on the whole it appears to have had little impact on either the operations of the councils or the attitudes of their members. Sixty-two of the seventy-one councillors interviewed complained at length of the course's irrelevance to 'the ways of Idoma' and of its unfortunate reaffirmation of the political *status quo* in the division. Thirty-six of the complainants also drew attention to its interference with the farming and household routine during two weeks of daily attendance and to the inadequate compensation which they received.[2]

As with the process of accession surrounding the district councillorship, the performance of that official (in council meetings and in his constituency activities) usually reflected the norms and styles which had long shaped political life in Idoma. Because most Idoma viewed administrative efficiency and majoritarian local government as absurdly irrelevant to the traditional ways which they still preferred, these alien notions were more often ignored than opposed. Thus, the attempt to professionalise the District Councils was defeated neither by popular hostility nor by the antagonism of those officials whose behaviour it was intended to reshape; rather, it foundered on the rock of nearly universal indifference. What had trans-

[1] The District Council scribe kept its minutes. These records were periodically examined by the Native Authority Department of Local Government.

[2] The course had ended several months before, and thirty-nine district councillors (in three districts) had not yet received £2·50 each for participating. Of these, thirty-seven observed bitterly that corrupt district heads were conspiring with Native Authority officials in Oturkpo Town to deny them even this paltry sum. Various Native Authority officials in Town subsequently told me that inefficiency was to blame and that payment would eventually be made. Whatever the truth of the matter, the incident illuminates the deep distrust which existed among councillors *vis-à-vis* district heads and other Native Authority superiors.

pired is conveyed in this discourse by a district councillor who was serving his ninth year in office:

Only a fool or a child will describe himself as he describes another's garment. Who but a fool or a child will believe that the man who wears a Hausa robe must call himself a 'Hausa man' or even become a Hausa man some–day? The *ukansulu* ['District Council', after the English word 'council'] was the white man's garment. But only a fool or a child or even some white men will believe that the Idoma man who wears the garment of the councillor must call himself a 'white man' or even become a white man some-day. It is our garment now. The Idoma man will not describe himself as he describes another's garment.

Conceived elsewhere, the council system had been altered in its transplantation. The new 'garment' was an artifact of political life in Idoma.

At their inception the District Councils were assigned various tasks. While some of these were outlined fairly explicitly in the instruments which brought the new system formally into existence in the twilight of colonial rule, others were left ambiguous in the councils' mandate to operate as representatives of the district population and as statutory agents of the Native Authority (Benue Province May 1955: 1–2; Northern Nigeria 3 March 1958; 19 April 1962). The more precisely defined responsibilities included recommending to the General Purposes Committee the appointment of district heads and local tax collectors; levying taxes on individuals and village units; and authorising the expenditure of council funds. Five other responsibilities were assigned to the councils, albeit with less explicit delineation. These included supervising work for the regional government and the Native Authority in the district when required to do so; supervising the use of communal labour approved by the Committee; carrying out duties which might occasionally be delegated by the Committee; maintaining law and order within the district; and serving as popular representatives. Finally, the councils were informally instructed to assist both their Native Authority superiors and the local branches of the NPC in mobilising political support for the governing party in regional and federal elections.

The vagueness which characterised important aspects of their mandate together with the popular preference for traditional ways encouraged a rapid assimilation of District Council operations into established normative and behavioural patterns. Two examples will suffice:

(1) Authorised as agents of the Native Authority to maintain law and order within their respective jurisdictions, the District Councils were nevertheless provided with neither a definition of the scope of that responsibility nor the resources to execute it. Most councillors knew nothing of the penal code – or of local government ordinances and administrative rules and regulations which might bear upon that responsibility. What was their relationship with the Native Authority police based at Oturkpo Town, the Native Authority court system, and the district head (who, in addition to serving as council chairman, was chief administrative officer of the district)? Was the council an arm of the constabulary in rural Idoma? Could it legally detain suspected wrongdoers? If so, for whom? The Circuit Court? The district head? A touring contingent of Native Authority police? Could it legally compel the appearance of villagers, either as defendants or as witnesses, before the civil or criminal section of the court? Lacking reliable guidelines, and commanding no machinery of enforcement, the council as such largely abdicated its responsibility in this area. The obligation to maintain law and order devolved informally upon its members as individuals. Each elected councillor policed his own constituency as best he could, each appointed councillor his residential location. Occasionally several councillors co-operated in a particular effort at enforcing the law.

Most district councillors policed their areas with the aid of traditional associations which had long been active in enforcement of law. Secret societies and dance groups were called upon to assist in mediating family and land disputes, detecting malefactors, overseeing social gatherings, and collecting tax. The traditional associations served *de facto* as an adjunct of the District Council system. Maintenance of law and order under the councils' mandate was often synonymous with activities in enforcing law of the various secret societies and dance groups in each district.

(2) District Council meetings were conducted monthly[3] in the style of the *ojira* assembly. As in traditional Idoma, a consensual democratic principle governed the decision-making process; debate was usually not regulated by a formal agenda and rarely ended with a formal vote.[4] Women did not venture into the council hall unless they were

[3]Special meetings were sometimes convened to announce Native Authority policies, to receive visiting dignitaries, or to transact unfinished business.

[4]Even where a vote was taken, by show of hands, the recorded vote was often changed by the scribe, in collusion with the district head, to create the impression of harmony in

invited to testify on some matter before the body; and their testimony was rarely solicited.

Five functional committees (works, markets, roads, finance, and general purposes) were constituted after each triennial council election, but tended to remain inactive. Committee reports rarely materialised and council records were fragmentary and doctored for periodic transmission to Native Authority headquarters.

The legal obligation to represent the interests of the district population was interpreted by many district councillors as justification for their opposing strong chieftaincy and Native Authority centralisation. Accordingly, council meetings were usually lively affairs in which members took turns criticising particular local government policies and in espousing the cause of reorganisation based on the traditional constitutional equilibrium. The *status quo* in Native Authority affairs was often decried as an obstacle to unity – an objective which seemed always to elude definition as well as attainment. Party matters rarely commanded the attention of the meeting. The conferees' interest in concrete problems of rural development was ordinarily limited to petitioning Oturkpo Town for such amenities as pipe-borne water systems, postal facilities, and more Native Authority schools and scholarships. Self-help schemes were rarely initiated by the councils and money on deposit in their fund was expended only occasionally for development purposes.

The assimilation of District Council operations into deeply-rooted normative and behavioural patterns contrasted markedly with developments at higher levels of the Native Authority organisation: careerist district heads and employees of Native Authority departments, the portfolio councillors, and the *Och'Idoma* were all becoming more bureaucratic in both outlook and performance. As assimilation became more complete, the councils were increasingly regarded by villagers as a legitimate expression of traditional ways, and as the vanguard of popular resistance to chiefly power and rule from Oturkpo Town. Traditional titles of office were often bestowed on the district councillors as a mark of esteem. Moreover, they were usually hailed in public with repeated cries of *ejila!* or *okala!* – salutations traditionally reserved for distinguished leaders and men of outstanding reputation. Viewed from below as popular heroes and resis-

the council and support for the district head and for Native Authority policies. This study attempts analysis of role conflict in Idoma. Woe to the scholar who attempts analysis of roll-calls in that place!

tance leaders, and from above essentially as functionaries in the Native Authority, the councillors became caught up in the post-independence struggle over the character of local government in Idoma. Their most important legacy as 'men in the middle' was bureaucratic–debureaucratic role conflict – that is, cross-pressures reflecting, on the one hand, support for, and on the other, opposition to, the pattern of authority prevailing in Idoma Division.

Early in the field investigation, numerous instances of such conflict surrounding the district councillors were identified from three main sources:

(1) *discussions with informants in Idoma,* including the District Officer, the *Och'Idoma*, portfolio councillors, representative councillors, employees in the Native Authority departments, district heads, tax collectors, private citizens, European missionaries, and former as well as incumbent district councillors;

(2) *documentary materials*, including administrative reports prepared by the Native Authority departments, minutes of the General Purposes Committee (sometimes referred to as the 'Native Authority Executive'), and administrative and intelligence reports, memoranda, and touring notes available in the Divisional Office; and

(3)*participant observation*, including attendance at District Council meetings and surveillance of such day-to-day activities of the district councillors in their constituency units and residential areas as organising communal labour, helping to mediate family and land disputes, and investigating cases of praedial larceny.

Role conflict reflecting the competition between bureaucratic and debureaucratic values and interests was found to be highly diverse in origin, encompassing modern as well as traditional spheres of conciliar activity. Moreover, such conflict was found to involve activities of the full District Council in meetings at the headquarters site as well as day-to-day activities of individual district councillors in their own areas. From the numerous instances of role conflict which had been uncovered, six were eventually selected by me for analysis. Reflecting the diversity noted above, they involve contradictory role-expectations held for the councillor: (1) in the disbursement of council funds for a local project; (2) as a campaigner for the governing party in a federal parliamentary election; (3) as a participant in social and ritual activities of secret societies and dance groups; (4) as an agent of law enforcement having to cope with illicit activities of those associations; (5) as a participant in proceedings over succession to the district headship; and (6) as a participant in proceedings over succession to the traditional clan headship. The councillors' perceptions of bureaucratic and debureaucratic expectations held for their behaviour by audiences in each of the six situations are analysed below and in Chapter Eight.

Case 1. The District Council fund: 'fighting big over something small'

Under their legal mandate, the District Councils could make certain expenditures for development purposes. The projects which they were permitted to undertake in this regard included construction and repair of market stalls, wooden footbridges, recreational facilities, and meeting halls. Money for such projects was available in the District Council fund.

Every year each of the twenty-two District Councils in Idoma received a fixed portion of the poll tax collected by the Native Authority. For example, in the two fiscal years preceding the field investigation, 1961 and 1962, the Native Authority collected £1·75 and £2 respectively from every adult male in the division (excepting the elderly and infirm). The more affluent, constituting a very small percentage of the taxpaying population, paid an income tax of up to 50p in addition to the flat rate. In those two years each council received 7½p as its share of the poll tax collected from each adult male in the district. Upon receiving the annual tax revenues, the Native Treasury deposited the council shares in the District Council fund. By 1963, councils in the six most populous districts had built their accounts at the Treasury as high as £600–£800. The remaining accounts did not exceed £400.

Native Authority regulations provided that no District Council could expend more than £50 at a time for development purposes. (To the consternation of the district councillors and villagers generally, the ceiling had been progressively lowered from £150.) The normal procedure was for the council to debate the item of expenditure and then formally authorise its chairman, the district head, to sign a payment voucher in the specified amount for services to be rendered by a private contractor or for materials to be purchased from a similar source.[5] The central administration of the Native Authority, which was represented on these occasions by the portfolio councillor in charge of the relevant department at Oturkpo Town, a designated Treasury official, or the full General Purposes Committee, had then to assent to the release of money from an account in the District Council fund.[6] According to various informants in the Central administration, this procedure ensured that the councils undertook legitimate development projects without overdrawing their accounts.

The cumbersome process for appropriating moneys in the District Council fund produced great strain in Native Authority affairs. Suspecting that the restrictive ceiling on expenditures together with the management of the fund from Oturkpo Town was in fact intended to enhance the political leverage of Native Authority superiors, most district councillors were deeply resentful of the arrangement. In the words of one councillor,

Oturkpo Town believes it must prove its power by denying the councils an important part in development matters. The people lose. A powerless people must remain a backward people.

Exacerbating the problem were inefficiencies associated with the downgrading of the Native Treasury. In 1963, it will be recalled, the Native Authority was punished for its chronic tardiness in tax collection by having the status of the Treasury reduced from Grade 'B' to Grade 'C'. Concomitantly, the District Officer in Idoma was instructed by the regional Ministry for Local Government to take charge of that agency. Henceforth, he had personally to approve all Native Authority outlays exceeding £5. Not surprisingly, approval for District Council fund expenditures was slow in coming from that hard-pressed official. Only vaguely aware of the details of this development, and of its administrative implications, most district councillors concluded that Oturkpo Town was now intent on further limiting the councils' use of the fund, if not on eliminating it altogether.

Yet another factor contributing to strain in the administration of the District Council fund was the popular belief that corrupt Native Authority officials in Oturkpo Town were conspiring with private contractors to defraud the councils. In exceptional cases, the General

[5]Because most contractors in Idoma operated on a 'shoestring', they often required a substantial down payment or even full payment in advance. The Native Authority was usually accommodating.

[6]An exceptional procedure is noted below.

Purposes Committee could initiate relatively inexpensive development projects on behalf of the council without awaiting formal authorisation by the latter body. Expecting that their subordinates, the district councillors and the district head, would eventually authorise and sign the necessary payment vouchers, the Committee proceeded on these occasions to let contracts and to draw on the fund. That expectation was often frustrated, however, when distrustful councils refused to accede to these arrangements. The suspicion that the fund was being maladministered from above to defraud the councils usually gave rise to two interrelated situations of role conflict – one focusing on the councillors who were supposed to authorise the signing of vouchers by the district head, the other on the district head as signatory. Both situations are analysed here.[7]

Each of the seventy-one district councillors interviewed was provided with this backdrop to the two situations of role conflict:

Several weeks ago, I received a letter from my friend in Wukari Division. He told me about a problem involving a District Council there, and asked how the councillors and people of Idoma Division would deal with it. I wrote to him that I would ask the Idoma councillors how they would deal with such a problem in their own districts.[8]

The General Purposes Committee in the Native Authority made an agreement with an Ibo contractor who was to build a council hall.[9] The contractor agreed to build the hall for £450 and was paid the £450 immediately from the District Council fund. After completing the building, except for the roof and plastering, the contractor said he had incorrectly estimated the cost involved. He now told the Committee and the council that what he had so far built had cost him £500. He told the Committee that unless the council agreed to pay him £50 for work already completed, plus another £100 for the roof and plastering, he would not complete the building. In other words, he wanted £600 to build the hall rather than his original estimate of £450, which he had already been paid.

[7]The situations of role conflict listed on pp. 132–3 involve the district councillors as *focal actor*. The situation involving the district head as signatory (and *focal actor*) is added here because of its relevance generally to Case 1 and to the analysis of 'role buffering' on pp. 228–40.

[8]Virtually the same case had arisen shortly before in one of the five districts on which the study concentrates. The projective technique, directing attention to Wukari Division in Jukun country east of Idoma, was employed to dispel fears in some quarters that the study was part of an official investigation of Native Authority corruption.

[9]Many Idoma alleged that unscrupulous Ibos colluded with corrupt Native Authority officials.

The council told the district head he must not sign any payment vouchers. The General Purposes Committee then told the council that it must authorise the district head to sign the vouchers totaling £600. The Committee also said the district head must sign the vouchers, even if the council does not authorise him to do this.

Could you tell me what certain people would expect of you and your district head if your council faced this problem?

The district councillor was then asked to indicate verbally[10] the role alternative(s) that each audience would hold relevant to his authorising the district head to sign the payment vouchers (Situation *1a*) and to the district head as signatory (Situation *1b*).[11]

Situation *1a*	Situation *1b*
A. Expect me as a councillor to authorise the district head to sign the payment vouchers.	A. Expect the district head to sign the payment vouchers.

(Bureaucratic role-expectations)

B. Expect me as a councillor not to authorise the district head to sign the payment vouchers.	B. Expect the district head not to sign the payment vouchers.

(Debureaucratic role-expectations)

C. Have no expectation of me as a councillor in this situation.	C. Have no expectation of the district head in this situation.

A district councillor who indicated any alternative(s) other than *C* was subsequently probed for perceived legitimacy and obligatoriness of expectations.

Situation *1a*	Situation *1b*
Do you think that the (audience) has a right to expect you as a councillor (to authorise) (not to authorise) the district head to sign the payment vouchers?	Do you think that the (audience) has a right to expect the district head (to sign) (not to sign) the payment vouchers?
Yes	Yes

(Legitimate role-expectations)

[10]Widespread illiteracy among the seventy-one district councillors precluded my using a self-administered instrument.

[11]The analysis in Chapter Seven and Chapter Eight focuses on the district councillors' role perceptions in the various situations. Their evaluations of role legitimacy, obligation, and sanction are analysed in Chapter Nine and Chapter Ten along with data on ambivalence and resolution of role conflict.

Confronting role conflict

No
No
(Illegitimate role-expectations)

Why do you think that the (audience) (has a right) (does not have a right) to expect you to act this way?	Why do you think that the (audience) (has a right) (does not have a right) to expect the district head to act this way?
Would the (audience) insist that you (authorise) (not authorise) the district head to sign the payment vouchers? That is, would the (audience) punish you for not doing what they expected you to do?	Would the (audience) insist that the district head (sign) (not sign) the payment vouchers? That is, would the (audience) punish the district head for not doing what they expected him to do?

Yes
Yes
(Obligatory role-expectations)

No
No
(Optional role-expectations)

At this juncture, a district councillor who indicated *Yes* (*obligatory role-expectation*) in either or both situations was probed for anticipated punitive–social sanction.[12]

Situation 1a	*Situation 1b*
How would the (audience) punish you if you did not behave as expected?	How would the (audience) punish the district head if he did not behave as expected?

The entire procedure was repeated for each audience in Situation *1a* and Situation *1b*. Each district councillor was then asked to reaffirm his *perception* of *role conflict* or *role consensus* among audiences in the two situations. A councillor who perceived role conflict was subsequently questioned about ambivalence in resolving it.

Situation 1a	*Situation 1b*
Would this situation trouble you? That is, would you have difficulty deciding what to do?	Would this situation trouble the district head? That is, would he have difficulty deciding what to do?

[12]District councillors who indicated *Yes* (*obligatory role-expectation*) but who could not specify the punishment which an audience would employ to effect conformity had their responses changed to *No* (*optional role-expectation*). Of the more than 3,000 evaluations of role obligation reported by those officials, only twenty-seven (less than 1 per cent) required conversion of a *Yes* response to a *No*. See pp. 202–3.

Yes	Yes
No	No
If yes: How much difficulty would you have deciding what to do?	*If yes*: How much difficulty would the district head have deciding what to do?
Some	Some
Very much	Very much

Finally, a district councillor who perceived role conflict in either or both situations was probed for his and/or the district head's resolution procedure(s).

Situation 1a	*Situation 1b*
What would you do in this situation?	What would the district head do in this situation?

The district councillors' role perceptions

Having examined the administration of the district council fund, and its implications for bureaucratic–debureaucratic role conflict, we turn to the matter of the district councillors' role perceptions in the two situations.

Situation 1a. During the course of the field investigation, numerous informants stressed the persistence of tension and conflict in local government affairs – pointing, on the one hand, to a Native Authority leadership allegedly bent on enhancing its power (and, coincidentally, its perquisites) and, on the other, to the district population and its elected representatives seeking to check that impulse. That view-point, widely held in Idoma, is reflected in these comments by an elder, a young man, and a portfolio councillor, respectively:

The *Och'Idoma* makes us feel shame for our chiefs. First, Ogiri Oko; now Ajene Ukpabi. The *ojira* opposes this madness, it protests to the councillor. But we are weak. Will we become like our Hausa enemy? Will we be like the *talakawa* [Hausa: 'common people'], slaves to our Emir? This is not the way of the Idoma. But I fear this.

The *Och'Idoma* and the portfolio councillors are rich and powerful men. It does not offend me that they use this power to get money from the white man in Oturkpo Town [an allusion to kickbacks allegedly obtained from an Italian firm contracted to construct a Secretariat building for the Native Authority]. My people suffer only when the General Purposes Committee steals from the

District Council fund. It is as if they steal our yams and our guinea corn. The people and their councillors must resist this. It does not matter that there is little money in the fund, it does not matter that we are fighting big over something small.

We are a backward people in a backward country. We must change this, with education, scientific farming, and health schemes. But who will bring these things? The elders who think only of the *alekwu* [ancestors]? The farmers who bend over the hoe? No! Only those who understand the new ways, the educated men in the Native Authority offices and their leaders on the Committee. It cannot be otherwise in the struggle to change.[13]

That most of the district councillors held similar views about the hostile confrontation between apex and base in Idoma is borne out in Situation *1a*. Thus, we observe in Table 1 (*Total* column) that while 94 per cent of the councillors viewed the Native Authority leadership as expecting them to authorise the signing of the payment vouchers, only 13 per cent attributed the bureaucratic role-expectation to the elders and young men.[14] Moreover, we observe a relationship between the councillors' perceptions of that role-expectation and the location of audiences *vis-à-vis* the leadership. The percentage of councillors who perceived audiences as expecting them to heed the General Purposes Committee and authorise the district head to sign the vouchers increases steadily in the ascent from constituency unit or residential area (elders, 13 per cent; young men, 13 per cent) through low and intermediate levels of the Native Authority (tax collectors, 28 per cent; elected councillors, 30 per cent; appointed or 'Native Authority councillors', 43 per cent; representative councillor(s), 45 per cent; district head, 55 per cent) to the Committee headed by the *Och'Idoma* (94 per cent). As we shall see in Chapter Ten, this relationship between the councillors' role perceptions and the location of audiences *vis-à-vis* the Native Authority pinnacle had important consequences for resolution of role conflict.

[13]While changes were apt to be initiated by the regional government, not the Native Authority, the quotation does illuminate the view which many Native Authority officials in Oturkpo Town had of their own part in the development process. Their claims were often challenged by dissidents, especially the IHRU.

[14]Chi-square tests were executed on rotated district pairings in Situation 1a (Table 1) and in the other situations analysed in Chapter Seven and Chapter Eight (Tables 2–7). These revealed differences which are significant at the 0·05 level. Accordingly, the district variable is examined in the various situations.

Table 1. Councillor perceptions of audience expectations: the district councillor and the council hall (percentages) [a]

Audience	Expectation	District [b]					
		One	Two	Three	Four	Five	Total
Elders	To authorise	23	–	10	–	25	13
	Not to authorise	50	7	10	85	33	39
	To/not to authorise	9	50	60	15	42	31
	No expectation	18	43	20	–	–	17
	Number of councillors	(22)	(14)	(10)	(13)	(12)	(71)
Young	To authorise	14	7	10	–	33	13
men	Not to authorise	50	–	10	85	33	38
	To/not to authorise	27	50	70	15	33	36
	No expectation	9	43	10	–	–	13
	Number of councillors	(22)	(14)	(10)	(13)	(12)	(71)
Tax	To authorise	27	36	30	–	50	28
collectors	Not to authorise	50	–	10	85	42	39
	To/not to authorise	14	28	50	15	8	22
	No expectation	9	36	10	–	–	11
	Number of councillors	(22)	(14)	(10)	(13)	(12)	(71)
Elected	To authorise	32	57	20	–	33	30
district	Not to authorise	59	21	10	46	50	41
councillors	To/not to authorise	9	21	70	54	17	29
	No expectation	–	–	–	–	–	–
	Number of councillors	(22)	(14)	(10)	(13)	(12)	(71)
Appointed	To authorise	36	71	60	8	50	43
district	Not to authorise	59	21	20	54	50	44
councillors	To/not to authorise	5	7	20	38	–	13
	No expectation	–	–	–	–	–	–
	Number of councillors	(22)	(14)	(10)	(13)	(12)	(71)
Representative	To authorise	41	79	60	–	50	45
councillor(s)	Not to authorise	59	21	40	100	42	53
	To/not to authorise	–	–	–	–	–	–
	No expectation	–	–	–	–	8	1
	Number of councillors	(22)	(14)	(10)	(13)	(12)	(71)
District	To authorise	41	57	80	69	42	55
head	Not to authorise	59	43	20	31	58	45
	To/not to authorise	–	–	–	–	–	–
	No expectation	–	–	–	–	–	–
	Number of councillors	(22)	(14)	(10)	(13)	(12)	(71)
Chief of	To authorise	95	93	100	100	83	94
Idoma and	Not to authorise	5	7	–	–	17	6
General	To/not to authorise	–	–	–	–	–	–
Purposes	No expectation	–	–	–	–	–	–
Committee	Number of councillors	(22)	(14)	(10)	(13)	(12)	(71)

Confronting role conflict

Disagreement regarding the district councillors' behaviour in Situation 1*a* was not limited to the confrontation between apex and base. Individual audiences were also seen as dividing over the matter. Thus, 31 per cent of the councillors perceived bureaucratic–debureaucratic role conflict among the elders; 36 per cent among the young men; 22 per cent among the tax collectors; 29 per cent among elected colleagues on the District Council; and 13 per cent among the 'Native Authority councillors'. Addressing both the source of such conflict and its consequences, one councillor observed:

Two elders in my place believe that I must be loyal to the Native Authority. They fear that the *Och'Idoma* will be vengeful if I displease the Native Authority. It is difficult for me when all my people disagree with the *Och'Idoma* over whether I must serve Oturkpo Town. But it is even more difficult when my own people disagree about this matter. *Oche awanda!* ['It brings big trouble!']

Follow-up probes of the councillors who perceived role conflict among the elders, young men, and elected colleagues revealed that only a small minority within each audience was viewed as holding the bureaucratic role-expectation. Strikingly different responses were obtained, however, from the councillors who perceived role conflict among the tax collectors and 'Native Authority councillors': every respondent estimated that a substantial majority within both audiences would expect him to authorise the district head to sign the payment vouchers.

This contrast between the two groups of audiences together with the earlier analysis of the district councillors' perceptions of the bureaucratic role-expectation call attention to the popular view of tax collectors and 'Native Authority councillors' in Idoma. Appointed by the central administration of the Native Authority upon the recommendation of the district head, those officials were widely regarded as supporters of strong chieftaincy and centralised political authority;

many were denounced as Native Authority spies and *agents provocateurs*. But there were exceptions. For example, in District Four, where the elderly district head relied on his son, a prominent member of an opposition party, to make the recommendations, fairly independent-minded persons were often appointed as tax collectors and 'Native Authority councillors'. Excepting District Four, then, the data in Table 1 illuminate the profound distrust which existed between the district population and its elected representatives, on the one hand, and the Native Authority appointees, on the other.

Situation 1b. Notwithstanding the resentment which they sometimes felt towards superiors in Oturkpo Town, most district heads owed their primary allegiance to their employer, the Native Authority. Responsible for overall administration in the districts, and for the District Councils' operations as permanent chairmen of those bodies, the district heads were, in the words of one of their number, 'Native Authority men from head to toe'. And as they saw themselves, so were they seen by others. For example, by an elder:

Otache [pseudonym] was clan head, the father of his people, even before he became *och'mbeke* ['chief of the white man', district head]. But now he must serve his master, not his people.

By another elder:

Long ago, our chief heard the ancestors and the *ojira*. The white man has changed this. *Och'mbeke* does not hear the *ojira* now. He only pretends to hear the ancestors. Our chief hears the Native Authority. I have seen him tremble before the *Och'Idoma*.

And by a tax collector:

The Native Authority is my father, and the father of Ochoche [pseudonym], the 'Native Authority councillor' in this place, and Adeka [pseudonym], the district head. The Native Authority knows that its sons are loyal and obedient.

This view of the district heads is also reflected in Situation 1b. In Table 2 (*Total* column) we observe that the percentage of district councillors who perceived audiences as expecting the district head to follow the General Purposes Committee directive and sign the payment vouchers ranges from 28 per cent (the elders and young men) to 100 per cent (the *Och'Idoma* and the Committee). With one minor exception, the elected councillor audience, we encounter the same relationship as in Situation *1a* between the councillors' perceptions of

Table 2. Councillor perceptions of audience expectations: the district head and the council hall (percentages) [a]

Audience	Expectation	District One	Two	Three	Four	Five	Total
Elders	To sign	32	28	50	–	33	28
	Not to sign	50	–	–	54	17	28
	To/not to sign	9	28	40	46	50	31
	No expectation	9	43	10	–	–	13
	Number of councillors	(22)	(14)	(10)	(13)	(12)	(71)
Young	To sign	32	28	50	–	33	28
men	Not to sign	50	–	–	54	17	28
	To/not to sign	18	28	40	46	50	34
	No expectation	–	43	10	–	–	10
	Number of councillors	(22)	(14)	(10)	(13)	(12)	(71)
Tax	To sign	45	43	80	8	58	45
collectors	Not to sign	50	–	–	54	17	28
	To/not to sign	5	21	10	38	25	19
	No expectation	–	36	10	–	–	8
	Number of councillors	(22)	(14)	(10)	(13)	(12)	(71)
Elected	To sign	27	79	90	–	33	42
district	Not to sign	59	7	–	54	58	39
councillors	To/not to sign	14	14	10	46	8	18
	No expectation	–	–	–	–	–	–
	Number of councillors	(22)	(14)	(10)	(13)	(12)	(71)
Appointed	To sign	45	86	90	8	67	52
district	Not to sign	59	7	–	54	33	35
councillors	To/not to sign	9	7	10	38	–	13
	No expectation	–	–	–	–	–	–
	Number of councillors	(22)	(14)	(10)	(13)	(12)	(71)
Represen-	To sign	41	93	90	–	67	55
tative	Not to sign	59	7	10	100	33	45
councillor(s)	To/not to sign	–	–	–	–	–	–
	No expectation	–	–	–	–	–	–
	Number of councillors	(22)	(14)	(10)	(13)	(12)	(71)
Chief of	To sign	100	100	100	100	100	100
Idoma and	Not to sign	–	–	–	–	–	–
General	To/not to sign	–	–	–	–	–	–
Purposes	No expectation	–	–	–	–	–	–
Committee	Number of councillors	(22)	(14)	(10)	(13)	(12)	(71)

Note
[a] The table reports the proportion of district councillors who perceived audiences as expecting district head to act bureaucratically, i.e., to sign payment vouchers; or to act debureaucratically, i.e., not to sign vouchers. The table also includes councillor's perception of role conflict *within* audience (to/not to sign vouchers); and councillor's perception that audience holds no expectation for district head's behaviour.

the bureaucratic role-expectation and the location of audiences *vis-à-vis* the Native Authority leadership, i.e., the percentage of councillors who perceived audiences as expecting the district head to sign the vouchers steadily increases in the ascent from rural base to Native Authority pinnacle. By itself, this finding appears to assail the popular view of the district heads as 'Native Authority men'. Taken together with other data in the table, however, it can be seen as reinforcing that stereotype.

The district councillors who perceived role conflict *within* any of five audiences – the elders, young men, tax collectors, elected councillors, and 'Native Authority councillors' – were subsequently probed for their estimates of the number in each group who would expect the district head to sign the payment vouchers: every respondent estimated that nearly all the tax collectors and 'Native Authority councillors' would, as Native Authority appointees, expect the district head to sign the vouchers, and that a sizeable minority of the elders and young men would join with a handful of elected councillors in expecting that official to act bureaucratically in Situation *1b*. Probed as to the motives of those elders, young men, and elected councillors, the respondents usually noted their timidity in the face of Native Authority power or their fear that Oturkpo Town would retaliate against rural dwellers who encouraged the district head to disobey its directive, or both.

The report on the district councillors' perceptions of the debureaucratic role-expectation in Situation *1b* can be interpreted in the same vein. In Table 2 we observe that a substantially higher percentage of the councillors in Districts One, Four, and Five than in Districts Two and Three perceived all but one audience, the Chief of Idoma and the General Purposes Committee, as expecting the district head not to sign the payment vouchers. Follow-up probes of these councillors in the five districts revealed that they, too, regarded the district heads as Native Authority loyalists. This characterisation of the district heads appeared anomalous, in view of the councillors' earlier attribution of the debureaucratic role-expectation to six audiences. On being asked to clarify the matter, the respondents took note of this important contrast: while the district heads in Districts One and Five were widely respected for their honesty in personal and local government affairs, those in Districts Two and Three were renowned for their venality. With this in mind, the councillors in Districts One and Five opined that the Ibo contractor's demand for more money in the council hall case disguised a conspiracy to defraud the council; and that the six audiences would expect the honest district heads to recognise this and thereupon refuse to sign the vouchers. According to the councillors in District Four, those audiences would expect the elderly district head to be influenced by his reform-minded son, and his son's political allies on the council, and also refuse to sign the vouchers. Significantly, the councillors in Districts One, Four, and Five all emphasized that had their district head's predecessor and probable successor been involved in Situation *1b*, the six audiences would have expected those office-holders to heed the Committee directive and sign the vouchers. The atypicality of that situation for the incumbent district heads in these three districts is illuminated by one of their admirers, a representative councillor:

There are honest soldiers like Enyogaji and Okwu [pseudonyms] who would not let their loyalty to the Native Authority blind them to cheating in Oturkpo Town. Relatives and friends can sometimes make an old soldier like Agabi [pseudonym] forget his loyalty to the Native Authority. Enyogaji and Okwu would quickly sign the vouchers if they thought it was an honest affair. And Agabi would not always bow to his people. They are usually good soldiers. But sometimes they are good men.

Comparing the district councillors' role perceptions in Situation *1a* and Situation *1b*, we observe the following: while those officials tended to see themselves as being widely expected to act debureaucratically in the council hall case, they also tended to see many audiences as expecting the district head to act bureaucratically. Put differently, most councillors believed that the district head was widely expected to ignore their strictures in the face of opposition from his superiors. This finding, and the high probability that the district head would defy the councillors and sign the payment vouchers (see p. 263), point up the main source of councillor feelings of inefficacy and frustration *vis-à-vis* their supporters, on the one hand, and the district head and Native Authority leadership, on the other. The councillors' pursuit of an opposition line in local government affairs could generate much short-term support, but inspire little hope. The desire for change among rural dwellers was bound up with a deep sense of futility. As we shall see, this mixing of aspiration and despair sometimes gave rise to scapegoating behaviour in the form of 'role buffering'.

Case 2. Political parties: 'the land is spoiled'

Organised political activity commenced during World War II in Idoma Division with the founding of the IHRU. Born of the discontent of Idoma youth (mostly primary school leavers), and fortified by nationalist ferment, the IHRU sought a major policy role in a democratised Native Authority organisation (Magid 1971:342–66). It failed for several reasons to achieve that objective.

First, persistent internecine conflict prevented the IHRU from uniting against its main adversary, the Native Authority. Rivalry between the branch organisations combined with unresolved differences over the political character of the IHRU and its position on the issue of regional minorities to limit organisational effectiveness. Some members preferred to operate as a political party, others as a nonpartisan tribal or cultural union; the membership also divided over whether a separate 'Middle Belt' Region ought to be carved out of the Moslem-dominated Northern Region. An increasingly powerful Native Authority, led by a politically astute *Och'Idoma*, Ogiri Oko, managed to exacerbate those deliberating conflicts.

Second, the IHRU was weakened by its chronic inability to produce a dynamic leader round whom the disputatious factions might unite.

Third, many Idoma were deeply suspicious of the motives of the would-be reformers. Only three of the seventy-one district councillors interviewed had been members of the tribal union. Forty-eight councillors recalled their doubts about its commitment to traditional ways, including a restoration in some form of the constitutional equilibrium rooted in principles of chieftaincy, gerontocracy, and democracy in the *ojira*.

Fourth, the IHRU was weakened by the Administration's post-war commitment to gradual, controlled change. The commitment encouraged an inexorable increase in Native Authority power at the expense of all the opposition forces in Idoma. By early 1959 that power had paved the way for the demise of the IHRU. Later that year, the Native Authority had occasion to demonstrate its political invincibility in the division when it led three candidates of the conservative NPC to easy victories in federal parliamentary elections. By 1960, when Nigeria became independent, Idoma Division was firmly aligned with the NPC, the political party which controlled governments in Kaduna and Lagos.

The failure of the IHRU to make deep inroads in the division may thus be attributed to three principal factors: organisational debility, insufficient popular appeal, and the sustained opposition of colonial and regional officialdom and the Native Authority. Beset by the same pressures, the AG and the NCNC were nevertheless able to survive the colonial period. While more durable than the IHRU, the nationalist parties were hardly more effectual in the division after independence. The AG and the NCNC were routed once again in Idoma in the 1961 Northern legislative elections.

The relationship between the Native Authority and the NPC illuminates the organisation of political power in Idoma and in Northern Nigeria generally. Moreover, as we shall see, it draws attention to bureaucratic–debureaucratic role conflict involving the district councillors. But before turning to the matter of role conflict, we must examine more fully the political and organisational ties which existed between the NPC and the Native Authority.

At the divisional level, the *Och'Idoma*, who was 'patron' of the NPC organisation in Idoma, and the portfolio councillors exercised control over the party headquarters in Oturkpo Town; further down the Native Authority hierarchy, the district heads usually kept close check on the branch organisations in their administrative units. And within each district, tax collectors and district councillors were mobilised every five years by their Native Authority superiors and by NPC branch officials to campaign for the governing party in regional and federal elections. Often criticised by opposition elements for obscuring the lines in the North between party and local government, regional officials usually countered that Native Authority personnel were free to engage in partisan activities during election campaigns if they wished to do so (Northern House of Assembly 5 August 1958; 10 December 1958).

Allegiance to the governing party helped strengthen the hold of local government personnel on their offices. Moreover, notables and former notables in the Idoma Native Authority were occasionally rewarded with regional and federal sinecures.[15]

[15]At the time of the study, a portfolio councillor and a district head were members of the Northern House of Assembly; regional legislators received at least £1,000 yearly in salaries, allowances, and other emoluments in addition to their Native Authority salaries and perquisites. A former high official in the Native Authority was also a member of the Assembly and Minister of State for Kaduna Affairs in the Northern Government (see pp 55–6). Another former Native Authority official was Minister of State in the Federal Prime Minister's Office; government ministers received at least £3,000 yearly in salaries, allowances, and emoluments. In addition to his regular Native Authority salary and perquisites – together these exceeded £1,000 yearly – the *Och'Idoma* received at least £1,000 yearly as a member of the Northern House of Chiefs.

While some in Idoma personally benefited from the fusion of ruling party and local government organisation, others were greatly disturbed by the arrangement. It will be recalled that popular hostility to party politics had escalated rapidly on the eve of independence and in its aftermath. Not surprisingly, that hostility was directed also at persons whose party activities appeared to exacerbate political strife in Idoma. Having been called upon in 1959 and 1961 to campaign for the NPC in important legislative elections, the district councillors were among those who felt the popular wrath. These bitter reminiscences by an elder and a young farmer in two council constituencies evoke the mood of many rural dwellers during the 1961 regional elections:

My people were angered when Umolo [pseudonym] said we must vote for the NPC man. They did not want to know parties. When one young man said to Umolo that the land is spoiled by bloodshed [an allusion to a pitched battle fought between AG, NCNC, and NPC partisans in the 1959 federal elections], Umolo said we must obey him. I, too, rebuked Umolo.

I have always been a poor farmer, but the [1961] election made me even poorer. When Ekwo [pseudonym], the councillor, told me that I must vote for the NPC, I said that parties bring hatred and that I hate all parties. Ekwo shouted that I love the Ibo man [an allusion to the Ibo-dominated NCNC]. My storehouse was destroyed by fire in the night. The next morning Ekwo asked me if I still love the Ibo man. I told Ekwo that I hate him and the Ibo man as I hate all parties.

At the same time, however, there were Idoma who, either fearing or favouring the NPC and its Native Authority ally, openly supported councillors who did campaign for the governing party. The following observations, obtained from fellow villagers along with the foregoing reminiscences, point up the conflict in the two constituencies over the role of the councillor:

It is true that parties spoil the land. But would it help my people if Umolo refused to campaign for the NPC? We would have suffered for this. The Native Authority is vengeful. Umolo was a wise councillor. I rebuked the fools who rebuked Umolo.

I voted for the NPC because it opposed the NCNC. Look at Agala and Ulayi [districts in southern Idoma bordering on Iboland]. The Ibo man and his NCNC steal our land [an allusion to the many Ibos who have settled in southern Idoma]. The Ibo traders in Oturkpo Town steal our money and crops. The NPC promised to stop this. Oisi [pseudonym for the young farmer in the second reminiscence] is a foolish boy. Did he not see that Ekwo campaigned for the NPC because it promised to help the Idoma man?

Similar reports of role conflict, which I gathered throughout Idoma, led me to analyse a situation involving the councillor as campaigner for the NPC.

Each district councillor was provided with the following backdrop to Situation 2:

Some people have told me that the NPC is the party of the Sardauna [of Sokoto, then Premier of Northern Nigeria and head of the NPC] and that the Sardauna protects the Idoma man from his enemies. They say that the NPC is our father and that the councillor must be a good son and campaign for the NPC in the [1964 federal parliamentary] election. Other people say that parties spoil the land, but that a wise councillor must campaign for the NPC. They say the *Och'Idoma* will be vengeful if he does not do this. But some people have told me that the councillor must not campaign for the Sardauna. They say that the people do not want to hear of parties, that parties spoil the land with strife and bloodshed. They say that the councillor must love his people, not the Sardauna.

Can you tell me what certain people would expect of you in this matter?

Situation 2

A. Expect me as a councillor to campaign for the NPC in the next election.

(*Bureaucratic role-expectation*)

B. Expect me as a councillor not to campaign for the NPC in the next election.

(*Debureaucratic role-expectation*)

C. Have no expectation of me as a councillor in this situation.

The district councillors' role perceptions

Comparing the district councillors' role perceptions in Situation *1a* and Situation *2*, we observe this difference: whereas the councillors tended to see themselves as being widely expected to act debureaucratically in the hypothetical case of the council hall, by refusing to authorise the district head to sign the payment vouchers, they tended to see audiences as expecting them to act bureaucratically with regard to party campaigning (see Table 3, *Total* column). Excluding the audience of elected councillors in Situation *2*, the percentage of councillors who perceived audiences as expecting them to campaign for the NPC in the forthcoming federal parliamentary elections ranges from 45 per cent (the elders and young men) to 99 per cent (the *Och'Idoma* and the General Purposes Committee). No more

F

Table 3. Councillor perceptions of audience expectations: the district councillor and party campaigning (percentages) [a]

Audience	Expectation	District One	Two	Three	Four	Five	Total
Elders	To campaign	41	71	40	8	67	45
	Not to campaign	–	–	10	–	8	3
	To/not to campaign	14	–	10	23	8	11
	No expectation	45	29	40	69	17	41
	Number of councillors	(22)	(14)	(10)	(13)	(12)	(71)
Young	To campaign	59	43	40	15	58	45
men	Not to campaign	–	–	10	–	–	1
	To/not to campaign	18	50	40	31	25	31
	No expectation	23	7	10	54	71	23
	Number of councillors	(22)	(14)	(10)	(13)	(12)	(71)
Tax	To campaign	73	93	90	46	83	76
collectors	Not to campaign	–	–	–	–	–	–
	To/not to campaign	4	–	–	8	17	6
	No expectation	23	7	10	46	–	18
	Number of councillors	(22)	(14)	(10)	(13)	(12)	(71)
Elected	To campaign	–	–	–	–	–	–
district	Not to campaign	82	100	100	38	92	82
councillors	To/not to campaign	–	–	–	–	8	1
	No expectation	18	–	–	62	–	17
	Number of councillors	(22)	(14)	(10)	(13)	(12)	(71)
Appointed	To campaign	82	100	100	31	100	82
district	Not to campaign	–	–	–	–	–	–
councillors	To/not to campaign	–	–	–	–	–	–
	No expectation	18	–	–	69	–	18
	Number of councillors	(22)	(14)	(10)	(13)	(12)	(71)
Representative	To campaign	77	100	100	38	100	82
councillor(s)	Not to campaign	–	–	–	–	–	–
	To/not to campaign	–	–	–	–	–	–
	No expectation	23	–	–	62	–	18
	Number of councillors	(22)	(14)	(10)	(13)	(12)	(71)
District	To campaign	95	100	100	31	100	86
head	Not to campaign	–	–	–	–	–	–
	To/not to campaign	–	–	–	–	–	–
	No expectation	5	–	–	69	–	14
	Number of councillors	(22)	(14)	(10)	(13)	(12)	(71)
Chief of	To campaign	95	100	100	100	100	99
Idoma and	Not to campaign	–	–	–	–	–	–
General	To/not to campaign	–	–	–	–	–	–
Purposes	No expectation	5	–	–	–	–	1
Committee	Number of councillors	(22)	(14)	(10)	(13)	(12)	(71)

than 3 per cent of the councillors viewed any audience other than the elected representatives as expecting them to refrain from campaigning for the governing party in 1964 (see Table 3, *Total* column, *elders*). And follow-up probes of those who perceived role conflict among the elders and young men revealed that only a small minority within each audience was seen as holding the debureaucratic role-expectation.

Given the widespread antipathy in Idoma to the divisiveness which had long been associated with strong chieftaincy and centralised political authority, and correlatively, with party politics, the contrast between Situation *1a* and Situation *2* is particularly striking. How to account for the contrast? The district councillors were questioned about the matter, along with many other informants in Idoma Division.

Explanations why the district councillors tended to perceive audiences as expecting them to campaign for the NPC in the next election usually focused on two considerations – loyalty to the NPC and fear of Native Authority reprisals. Predictably, informants with a strong vested interest in the local government *status quo* – tax collectors, representative councillors, district heads, and portfolio councillors – stressed that, despite popular hostility to partisan politics, most Idoma realistically expected the councillors to be NPC loyalists and hence campaigners for that party. Some of these informants noted that the governing party and its Native Authority ally were defenders of Idoma values and institutions against opposition parties identified with 'radical youth' in the division and with the encroaching Ibos. Others emphasised the sanctions which were readily available to the Native Authority leadership to ensure the councillors' loyalty in Situation *2*. In this vein, a portfolio councillor observed that

the Native Authority is strong – with its courts, police, and the power to tax. The councillors know that the election is not like the matter of the District Council fund. A vote is more important than a payment voucher. The Native Authority is the NPC and the NPC is the Native Authority. The councillors know that their people will expect them to campaign for the NPC. Native Authority vengeance can be more fierce than party strife. The councillors know they must obey their people and the Native Authority and campaign for the NPC.

The same considerations were also attributed by the district councillors to the elders and young men who were seen as expecting them to campaign for the NPC – albeit with an important difference among the respondents. Nearly all the elected councillors, whether or not they were NPC members or supporters,[16] emphasised their constituents' outright fear of Native Authority reprisals should the elected councillors refuse to campaign for the governing party. Various 'Native Authority councillors' noted that such fear could also be found in their own localities. But as might be expected, these officials laid far greater stress on the part which loyalty to the NPC, rooted in the enlightened self-interest of the Idoma, would play in shaping the two audiences' bureaucratic role-expectations in Situation 2.

Finally, we turn to the district councillors' role perceptions with regard to the audience of elected councillors. Here we encounter a departure from the dominant pattern in Situation 2: as many as 82 per cent of the councillors (n=58) viewed their elected colleagues as expecting them to act debureaucratically in the next election, and to refuse to campaign for the NPC. Among the fifty-eight, the fifty-five who were elected representatives had their own reasons for attributing the debureaucratic role-expectation to the audience of elected councillors. Seven (13 per cent) reported that as members of opposition parties they were expected not to campaign for the NPC. Interestingly, after acknowledging that most of the elected councillors would prefer them to refrain from party campaigning altogether, all seven proclaimed their intention to work openly for their parties in the 1964 elections. More than three-quarters of the fifty-five elected councillors (n=42) opined that colleagues who had avoided injecting the divisive party factor into their own election campaigns were generally hostile to partisanship in Idoma political life. It was observed that these councillors might soon press for a nonpartisan strategy in campaigns for higher political office. Among the forty-two councillors who speculated thus thirty-six expressed great sympathy for such an approach – both as a means of minimising party strife in the districts and as a way of registering their

[16]Only four of the sixty-three 'NPC men' among the district councillors regarded themselves as strongly committed to the governing party.

hostility to the main source of NPC power in Idoma, strong chieftaincy and Native Authority centralisation. Most of those who favoured a nonpartisan strategy in the next election were hopeful that its adoption would not arouse the ire of the local government organisation. Needless to say, their perspective was not shared by the councillors who were members of opposition parties. Asked to comment on the proposal, the seven oppositionists evinced incredulity and a sense of resignation.

Chapter Eight
Confronting role conflict: case-studies (continued)

Case 3. Secret societies and dance groups: 'the policeman is sometimes an outlaw'

In Idoma, as elsewhere in West Africa, associational life long revolved around secret societies and dance groups (Magid 1972: 289–304).[1] But Idoma differed from many of its neighbours in one important respect. Whereas a single association held sway among numerous peoples in West Africa – e.g., the Poro society in Mende (Little 1965 and 1966: 349–65, 62–71), Ogboni in Yoruba (Morton-Williams 1960: 362–74), and the Leopard society in Banyang (Ruel 1969: 1ff.) – no association ever permanently dominated Idoma or any of its clan, lineage, or sublineage units. Nevertheless, collectively they had a considerable impact on the society. Secret societies and dance groups reinforced status relationships between the sexes, organised recreation, and executed important administrative and judicial responsibilities (both as members of the *aiuta* constabulary and in their own right). Concomitantly, they served as agents of socialisation.

Cognisant of their real power, headstrong young men in the associations periodically challenged the secular authority of the clan head, *aiigabo* or clan spokesmen, and the market-master and hamlet heads in the *aiuta* constabulary. Constituting themselves a sovereign tribunal, secret societies and dance group sometimes 'tried' non-members in kangaroo courts. Illegal fines were then levied against the hapless

[1]It is necessary to distinguish here between the two types of associations in Idoma. Men's secret societies (*aiowa*) traditionally excluded non-members and women from their social and ritual activities (neither of which involved dancing). Contrastingly, dance groups (*aiije*) were either open or, in Armstrong's words (1955: 98), 'semi-secret', combining open and secret activities. In contemporary Idoma, secret societies often resemble dance groups with their open and secret activities. Nevertheless, because the Idoma generally insist on distinguishing between *aiowa* and *aiije*, and because the former usually forbid dancing, the traditional distinction is still a useful one.

The few women's secret societies and mixed dance groups in pre-colonial Idoma were unimportant politically; the latter associations continue to operate.

victims. When collecting legal fines on behalf of the clan head and the *aiigabo,* the associations often proceeded to extort additional sums from convicted wrongdoers. Beatings were also administered to non-members in the name of justice, and arbitration proceedings in inter-family disputes were sometimes rigged by the associations to benefit themselves. Finally, various secret societies and dance groups occasionally usurped the administrative prerogatives of hamlet heads in the sublineage units. Whenever they acted *ultra vires,* the associations provoked inter-generational discord and intensified political strains on the traditional constitutional system. As we shall see, the combination of anti-social behaviour and legitimate administrative and judicial practices in associational life caused the colonial Administration to be ambivalent about the role of secret societies and dance groups in modern local government.

Bent on imposing the *pax britannica* and paving the way for more intensive civilising efforts under missionary auspices, the first generation of European officers sought to destroy or drive underground those institutions which seemed to them to embody the worst qualities of the Idoma (see p. 42 note 6). The decision taken in those early years not to rehabilitate the *aiuta* reflected their awareness that the associations had always dominated the constabulary. Familiar with the tradition of reckless abandon and headhunting in associational life (Temple and Temple 1922: 143–4), officials were alert to the threat which secret societies and dance groups posed to the new order.[2]

The Oglinye dance group was proscribed during World War I (Nigeria 1917), as subsequently were other headhunting associations. During the next fifteen years the Administration employed fear and example – including numerous executions of convicted offenders – to drive home the lesson that headhunting was illegal and immoral. Most secret societies and dance groups were compelled to retreat underground. An uneasy peace was thus achieved by the early 1930s, broken only by the sporadic recrudescence of the associations' various anti-social activities.

Various developments soon encouraged a shift in the official policy towards the associations. The commitment recently made by the Administration to downgrade the role of chieftaincy in indirect rule led it to seek other traditional bases for modern local government.

[2]The Administration feared bloody uprisings by the associations similar to those by the Long Juju and AroChuku cults in Southern Nigeria.

Moreover, evidence was accumulating that the secret societies and dance groups had managed to flourish despite official repression – albeit clandestinely, and usually without resuming headhunting activities. Their influence had not been curtailed.[3] Finally some officials were openly sceptical that district administration could be effective without help from the associations (Wright 1934).

The decision was taken to co-opt various associations into local government at the district level. They assisted in detecting criminal offenders, making arrests, and collecting tax, and were remunerated *ad hoc* for services rendered (Heath *c.* 1940: 77–83). A combination of factors prevented this scheme from being institutionalised throughout Idoma. First, most colonial officials in the division were ambivalent about the plan, conceding its potential usefulness but at the same time pointing to the tradition of youthful rebellion and illegal activity in associational life. These officials generally preferred the less hazardous course, viz. Native Authority reorganisation based on strong chieftaincy and centralisation. Second, having decided in the late 1930s to strengthen chieftaincy at the district level, the Administration was faced with the district heads' demand that secret societies and dance groups not be accorded official recognition. The district heads viewed such recognition as a threat to their own authority and perquisites (Idoma Division 1939; Idoma Native Authority April–May 1940). Fearing alienation of those officials, the Administration eventually agreed to treat the associations as social and recreational clubs instead. Third, the skeletal European staff which was serving in Idoma during World War II had neither the resources nor the disposition to cultivate the associations' role in the Native Authority. Finally, the original plan to adapt secret societies and dance groups to the increasingly complex needs of modern local government failed to take note of the associations' essentially spontaneous character. From time immemorial, they had come and gone in Idoma, behaving constructively on some occasions and anti-socially on others. The notion of organising spontaneity in this way was bold but impractical. For all of these reasons, the scheme was destined to fail – and indeed it did.

Following World War II, the associations continued to serve as a focal point for social and recreational activities in rural Idoma, as a vehicle for asserting male superiority and dominance, and as unofficial assistants of various district officials in local government matters.

[3] The Christian missions were still too weak to counter that influence.

Secret societies and dance groups also convened periodically to plot larceny, to pillage, and to harass non-members (Idoma Native Authority *c.* 1950).

Having made their own adaptation to colonial rule, the associations had managed to survive as part of the leadership in rural Idoma. In the aftermath of independence they played an important, albeit unofficial, role in local politics and administration. The associations were also active in electoral politics, helping various candidates campaign for the Northern House of Assembly elections in 1961 and for District Council seats in 1962. Finally, many district officials continued to solicit their assistance in local administration and adjudication.

Significantly, the combination of negative and positive elements in associational life which had engendered official ambivalence before World War II could also be found in post-colonial Idoma. On the one hand, there was the tradition of anti-social behaviour; kangaroo courts, illicit exactions, thievery, and harassment of non-members were still regular features of associational life. On the other, there was the recognition by most Idoma that the associations could perform useful functions in local government affairs. For example:

(1) Following reorganisation of the court system in 1961, many district heads and district councillors were even more disposed than before to encourage the unofficial involvement of secret societies and dance groups in local adjudication. With no permanent court presence in each of the twenty-two districts, the associations frequently acted either jointly with those officials or on their behalf in mediating family and land disputes. Since such disputes were ubiquitous in Idoma, the arrangement helped ease the burden of the new Circuit Courts. But reorganisation was only one factor in this development. Knowing the courts' reputation for venality, rural dwellers often preferred to have the associations adjudicate their differences. At the same time, many district heads and councillors viewed competition between the associations and the courts as a means of checking judicial power. In this way, they hoped to enhance their own power and perquisites at the district level.

(2) Numerous tax collectors also turned to the associations for assistance.[4] The methods employed by the latter in tax collection ranged from outright coercion to ingenious application of traditional

---

[4] Acting alone or together with tax collectors and associations, district councillors sometimes extorted 'tax' from persons not listed in the official tax registry.

sanctions. In one case, a farmer's refusal to pay income tax moved the tax collector to invite the intervention of a secret society, Akpantla. Upon being assured that it would be remunerated by the tax collector with drink, the society agreed to station a masked figure outside the farmer's wife's hut. Wishing to leave the hut to urinate but fearful that seeing the ritual mask would cause her to become barren, the wife pleaded with her husband to end his intransigence. He refused. Eventually the wife's physical pain combined with her fear of barrenness to bring on hysteria. Hearing her screams, the farmer relented. The tax collector was summoned to receive the tax, whereupon the masked figure withdrew into the bush. Reviewing the case for me, the tax collector observed that

because there are no *dogarai* [Native Authority police] here, Akpantla must be a policeman. Does it surprise you that the policeman is sometimes an outlaw?

Inevitably, great tension was engendered by the 'policeman/outlaw' mix in associational life. Generally impressed with the associations' contributions to local government within the district, rural dwellers were nevertheless outraged by their frequent excesses in the guise of justice or recreation. Much was heard in the early independence period of the need to check the associations' anti-social behaviour, and pleas to that effect were usually directed to the district councillor, who was responsible for maintaining law and order in the locality. The councillor was repeatedly admonished by villagers and Native Authority superiors alike to execute his responsibility without fear or favour *vis-à-vis* lawbreaking associations of which he was a member and on whose assistance he relied. Aggrieved villagers would even urge the councillor to invite intervention by the Native Authority against the associations; advising him, in effect, temporarily to cease operating as a buffer against interference by his superiors in village affairs. His varied relationships with a controversial secret society or dance group often involved that official in role conflict reflecting support for, and opposition to, bureaucratic values and interests.

Such conflict usually centred on the district councillors' posture in quarrels between lawbreaking associations and their victims. Would active membership in secret societies and dance groups compromise the councillors' impartiality as peacemakers in the face of such quarrels? Would those officials try to prevent the associations' illicit and disruptive activities? Would they as law enforcers report these activities to Native Authority superiors, knowing that this could pave the way for prosecution of the lawbreakers? Numerous situations of role conflict developed around those questions. The two situations which were reported on most frequently by informants and which were also observed by me are analysed here.

Each district councillor was provided with this backdrop to Situation *3a*:

Different people have told me that secret societies and dance groups often steal yams and chickens in the night, and that this angers the victims and causes quarrels in the village. It is also said that the councillor who is active in the secret society or dance group often finds it difficult to be an impartial peacemaker in these quarrels or to convince others that he is a peacemaker. Some say that such a councillor can only be an impartial peacemaker or convince others that he is a peacemaker by becoming inactive, by showing that he is the father of all in his place.[5] Others say 'No!', that the councillor must remain active, or he will be rebuked by his fellows for his betrayal.

This is very confusing to me. Can you help me to understand the ways of Idoma in this matter? Can you tell me what certain people would expect of you if you faced this problem?

Situation 3a

A.   Expect me as a councillor not to remain active in the secret society or dance group.
(Bureaucratic role-expectation)

B.   Expect me as a councillor to remain active in the secret society or dance group.
(Debureaucratic role-expectation)

C.   Have no expectation of me as a councillor in this situation.

Each district councillor was then provided with the backdrop to Situation *3b*:

Yesterday a councillor told me that his dance group, Odumu, has been stealing chickens and guinea corn. Because he cannot stop this, the victims and their relatives demand that the councillor report the matter to the district head or the Native Authority police. They threaten to burn the compounds of Odumu members if he does not obey them. But other villagers have told him that he must not do this, that he must not follow the white man. They say that he must be true to the ways of Idoma.

Could you tell me what certain people would expect of you if you faced this problem?

[5]Informants universally rejected the idea of resignation, holding that the associations were simply too important in rural Idoma to make this a realistic alternative.

Table 4. Councillor perceptions of audience expectations:
the district councillor and activism in secret societies
and dance groups (percentages) [a]

Audience	Expectation	District					
		One	Two	Three	Four	Five	Total
Elders	To remain active	41	21	50	23	42	35
	Not to remain active	4	–	–	8	–	3
	To/not to remain active	50	79	40	61	50	56
	No expectation	4	–	10	8	8	6
	Number of councillors	(22)	(14)	(10)	(13)	(12)	(71)
Young	To remain active	50	29	50	61	25	44
men	Not to remain active	9	–	–	8	–	4
	To/not to remain active	36	71	50	31	67	49
	No expectation	5	–	–	–	8	3
	Number of councillors	(22)	(14)	(10)	(13)	(12)	(71)
Tax	To remain active	55	29	90	61	50	55
collectors	Not to remain active	9	7	–	8	–	6
	To/not to remain active	31	64	10	23	42	35
	No expectation	5	–	–	8	8	4
	Number of councillors	(22)	(14)	(10)	(13)	(12)	(71)
Secret	To remain active	45	36	50	69	33	46
society	Not to remain active	9	–	–	8	–	4
members[b]	To/not to remain active	32	43	40	23	58	38
	No expectation	14	21	10	–	8	11
	Number of councillors	(22)	(14)	(10)	(13)	(12)	(71)
Dance	To remain active	45	43	50	69	25	46
group	Not to remain active	9	–	–	8	–	4
members [b]	To/not to remain active	27	43	50	23	58	38
	No expectation	19	14	–	–	16	11
	Number of councillors	(22)	(14)	(10)	(13)	(12)	(71)
Elected	To remain active	14	–	30	46	25	21
district	Not to remain active	9	–	–	8	–	4
councillors	To/not to remain active	–	–	–	–	–	–
	No expectation	77	100	70	46	75	75
	Number of councillors	(22)	(14)	(10)	(13)	(12)	(71)
Appointed	To remain active	14	–	20	46	25	20
district	Not to remain active	9	–	–	8	–	4
councillors	To/not to remain active	–	–	–	–	–	–
	No expectation	77	100	80	46	75	76
	Number of councillors	(22)	(14)	(10)	(13)	(12)	(71)

Table 4 *continued*

Audience	Expectation	District					Total
		One	Two	Three	Four	Five	
Representa-	To remain active	18	–	–	31	25	15
tive	Not to remain active	9	–	–	–	–	3
councillor(s)	To/not to remain active	–	–	–	–	–	–
	No expectation	73	100	100	69	75	82
	Number of councillors	(22)	(14)	(10)	(13)	(12)	(71)
District	To remain active	14	–	–	38	58	21
head	Not to remain active	9	–	–	8	–	4
	To/not to remain active	–	–	–	–	–	–
	No expectation	77	100	100	54	42	75
	Number of councillors	(22)	(14)	(10)	(13)	(12)	(71)
Chief of	To remain active	4	–	–	15	17	7
Idoma and	Not to remain active	4	–	–	8	–	3
General	To/not to remain active	–	–	–	–	–	–
Purposes	No expectation	91	100	100	77	83	90
Committee	Number of councillors	(22)	(14)	(10)	(13)	(12)	(71)

Notes

[a] The table reports the proportion of district councillors who perceived audiences as expecting councillor to act debureaucratically, i.e., to remain active in secret society or dance group; or to act bureaucratically, i.e., not to remain active. The table also includes councillor's perception of role conflict *within* audience (to/not to remain active); and councillor's perception that audience holds no expectation for his behaviour.

[b] Because secret society and dance group members were widely viewed as separate audiences in situations involving associational activities, they are treated as such in the study.

Situation 3b
A.   Expect me as a councillor to report the thefts to the district head or Native Authority police.
(Bureaucratic role-expectation)

B.   Expect me as a councillor not to report the thefts to the district head or Native Authority police.
(Debureaucratic role-expectation)

C.   Have no expectation of me as a councillor in this situation.

The district councillors' role perceptions

Situation 3a. Perhaps the most striking finding in this situation pertains to the scope of the involvement of audiences. In Table 4

(*Total* column), we observe that between 75 per cent and 90 per cent of the district councillors perceived audiences as being uninvolved in Situation *3a* by virtue of their having no role-expectation(s) attributed to them. Put differently, the councillors tended to regard their own activism in the associations as a matter within the purview of local elements – the elders, young men, tax collectors, and members of secret societies and dance groups. The following comments by various informants call attention to the fact that that viewpoint was shared by most Idoma.

An elder:

The *Och'Idoma* will never tell our councillor that he must not dance in Odumu. *Oche awanda!* ['It would bring big trouble!']

A young man:

Our councillor, Okwuli [pseudonym], is chairman of Ichahoho. Will the white man [an allusion to the Native Authority] say that he must not be chairman? Only my people can say this to Okwuli.

A district head:

If I say that the councillor must not dance in Echi . . . *Oche awanda!* There is already too much anger in this place. It is a matter for Echi and the people.

A portfolio councillor:

Does your President decide who will belong to a club? It is not a Native Authority problem.

We also observe in Table 4 that relatively few district councillors perceived any of the five local audiences as expecting them to act bureaucratically in Situation *3a*. The percentage of councillors who viewed local audiences as expecting them not to remain active in the secret society or dance group, in order that they might better serve as impartial peacemakers in quarrels provoked by the associations' transgressions, did not exceed 6 per cent (see *Total* column); in no district did the percentage exceed 9 per cent. In the same vein, the councillors who perceived role conflict within local audiences reported that, notwithstanding any difficulties which they might encounter in trying to adjudicate such quarrels, a substantial majority of the elders, young men, tax collectors, and members of secret societies and dance groups would expect them to act debureaucratically in Situation *3a*, i.e., remain active in associational affairs.

The tendency of the district councillors to view local audiences as expecting them to remain active in the secret society or dance group, even where their impartiality as peacemakers might be compromised or impugned, directs attention to the significance of associational life in Idoma. Following independence, the associations continued to execute important social, recreational, ritual, and, unofficially, politico-governmental functions. Despite their periodic excesses, against which outraged rural dwellers protested and sometimes retaliated, they were still highly esteemed – both as functional organisations and as symbols of traditional vitality in the face of social and political change.

By actively involving themselves with groups such as Odumu, Akpantla, and Ichahoho, the district councillors helped impart vigour to associational life. This was accomplished in several ways. First, their active membership underscored the associations' traditional status as leaders in local affairs. Second, where the councillors were functionaries in secret societies or dance groups, their services were especially important to the associations. For example, a councillor who was the singer in Odumu might cause the dance group to cease operating if he chose not to remain active in its affairs. In sum, the interests of the councillor and the local populace were such as to encourage the former to remain active in associational life – even where this strained his ability to serve as peacemaker between an offending association and its victims.

Situation 3b. The district councillors' perceptions in Situation *3b* differ from those in Situation *3a* in several important respects. The first pertains to the scope of the involvement of audiences. It will be recalled that the councillors' activism in associational life was widely regarded as a matter within the narrow purview of local audiences. It mattered little that active membership in secret societies and dance groups often impaired the councillors' ability to pacify local quarrels resulting from the associations' transgressions – and that their responsibility for effecting such pacification was a corollary of their obligation, as agents of the Native Authority, jointly to maintain law and order in the district. The question of the councillors' active membership in the traditional associations tended to be regarded by those officials – and indeed by most Idoma – as beyond the brief of council colleagues and superiors in the Native Authority.

But the scope of the involvement of audiences is considerably wider in Situation *3b*. In Table 5 (*Total* column), we observe that no more than 11 per cent of the district councillors perceived audiences at the middle and upper levels of the Native Authority as not being involved in Situation *3b* by virtue of their having no role-expectation(s) attributed to them. These comments by various informants illustrate the essential difference between the two situations with respect to involvement of audiences.

Table 5. Councillor perceptions of audience expectations: the district councillor, law enforcement, and secret societies and dance groups (percentages) [*a*]

Audience	Expectation	District					Total
		One	Two	Three	Four	Five	
Elders	To report thefts	–	21	–	8	25	10
	Not to report thefts	91	79	100	62	50	77
	To/not to report thefts	9	–	–	31	25	13
	No expectation	–	–	–	–	–	–
	Number of councillors	(22)	(14)	(10)	(13)	(12)	(71)
Young men	To report thefts	14	21	20	8	17	15
	Not to report thefts	73	79	80	77	83	77
	To/not to report thefts	14	–	–	15	–	7
	No expectation	–	–	–	–	–	–
	Number of councillors	(22)	(14)	(10)	(13)	(12)	(71)
Tax collectors	To report thefts	41	57	70	8	75	48
	Not to report thefts	23	43	10	77	25	35
	To/not to report thefts	36	–	20	15	–	17
	No expectation	–	–	–	–	–	–
	Number of councillors	(22)	(14)	(10)	(13)	(12)	(71)
Secret society members[b]	To report thefts	–	–	–	–	–	–
	Not to report thefts	100	100	100	100	100	100
	To/not to report thefts	–	–	–	–	–	–
	No expectation	–	–	–	–	–	–
	Number of councillors	(22)	(14)	(10)	(13)	(12)	(71)
Dance group members[b]	To report thefts	–	–	–	–	–	–
	Not to report thefts	100	100	100	100	100	100
	To/not to report thefts	–	–	–	–	–	–
	No expectation	–	–	–	–	–	–
	Number of councillors	(22)	(14)	(10)	(13)	(12)	(71)
Elected district councillors	To reports thefts	9	21	20	15	25	17
	Not to report thefts	77	64	70	69	58	69
	To/not to report thefts	–	7	–	–	8	3
	No expectation	14	7	10	15	8	11
	Number of councillors	(22)	(14)	(10)	(13)	(12)	(71)

Table 5 *continued*

Audience	Expectation	District One	Two	Three	Four	Five	Total
Appointed	To report thefts	64	100	50	31	50	61
district	Not to report thefts	23	–	–	38	25	18
councillors	To/not to report thefts	–	–	30	23	–	8
	No expectation	14	–	20	8	25	13
	Number of councillors	(22)	(14)	(10)	(13)	(12)	(71)
Representa-	To report thefts	73	71	80	62	83	73
tive	Not to report thefts	27	29	20	23	17	24
councillor(s)	To/not to report thefts	–	–	–	15	–	3
	No expectation	–	–	–	–	–	–
	Number of councillors	(22)	(14)	(10)	(13)	(12)	(71)
District	To report thefts	82	86	80	85	100	86
head	Not to report thefts	–	7	10	15	–	6
	To/not to report thefts	–	–	–	–	–	–
	No expectation	18	7	10	–	–	8
	Number of councillors	(22)	(14)	(10)	(13)	(12)	(71)
Chief of	To report thefts	91	86	100	85	100	91
Idoma and	Not to report thefts	–	14	–	–	–	3
General	To/not to report thefts	–	–	–	–	–	–
Purposes	No expectation	9	–	–	15	–	6
Committee	Number of councillors	(22)	(14)	(10)	(13)	(12)	(71)

Notes

[a] The table reports the proportion of district councillors who perceived audiences as expecting councillor to act bureaucratically, i.e., to report thefts to district head or National Authority police; or to act debureaucratically, i.e., not to report thefts. The table also includes councillor's perception of role conflict *within* audience (to/not to report thefts); and councillor's perception that audience holds no expectation for his behaviour.

[b] See Table 4, note [b].

An elder:

The Native Authority, not Odumu, is the white man's child. Only the people can tell the Idoma man how to act in Odumu. But the *Och'Idoma* can say to Akpachi [pseudonym], the councillor, that because he is an official of the Native Authority he must inform the district head whenever Odumu steals chickens and destroys crops. The Native Authority can tell Akpachi to uphold the white man's law. But I will not tell Akpachi to do this thing.

A youthful member of Akpantla:

We speak of different things here. The councillor, Ogbludu [pseudonym], is my brother in Akpantla. Who will say that brothers may not feast and play

together? The Native Authority will only say that because Ogbludu has
sworn to uphold the law, he must report Akpantla's mischief to his superiors.
But will one brother betray another to the Native Authority?

A district head:

It is not a Native Authority matter if the councillors dance and feast in Echi.
But I am responsible for the administration of the district, and I cannot do
this work alone. The councillors must tell me when the law is broken. It is a
Native Authority matter when Echi loots and burns.

A portfolio councillor:

Theft is a Native Authority matter. The councillors must report it to their
superiors, even where the culprits are their fellows in Ichahoho. The councillors may feast and play with their fellows. But they must also uphold the law.
They have sworn to do this without fear or favour.

Reflected in these comments is the propensity of most Idoma to
distinguish between activities which the district councillors pursued as
members of traditional associations and their responsibilities as functionaries of local government. The tendency to admit the involvement of higher authorities in Situation 3b, but not in Situation 3a, is
rooted in that distinction.

The district councillors' role perceptions in the two situations also
differ regarding role conflict within local audiences. Whereas the percentage of councillors who attributed conflicting role-expectations to
the elders, young men, tax collectors, and members of secret societies
and dance groups ranged between 35 per cent and 56 per cent in Situation 3a, no more than 17 per cent viewed any of those audiences as
holding conflicting expectations in Situation 3b. (See Table 5, *Total*
column, *Tax collectors.*) In sum, many more councillors perceived
local audiences as clashing internally over the former's activism in
associational life than over the question of whether those officials
should report their associations' flagrant larceny to their superiors.
Probed as to the reason(s) for this disparity, the councillors and other
informants drew attention once again to the antipathy which most
Idoma felt toward strong chieftaincy and Native Authority centralisation.

Nearly all respondents opined that local audiences were apt to see
Situation 3b as involving a basic clash of interests between Oturkpo
Town and the rural population. According to this view, a district
councillor who reported his association's transgressions to the district
head or Native Authority police would be inviting their intervention
(and, directly or indirectly, also that of the Native Authority leader-

ship) in the affairs of the locality. The power of the Native Authority to prosecute offending associations in the courts, or levy harsh administrative fines against them, recalled an earlier era – when colonial officials employed these and even more draconian measures to suppress organisations around which social, recreational, and, to a lesser extent, ritual life revolved. It was widely believed that the 'peace' which obtained between officialdom and the associations after independence reflected the inability of government and the Native Authority either to destroy those groups or sharply to reduce their influence – and not a genuine change of heart in any quarter. Despite the informal participation of secret societies and dance groups in district administration and adjudication, rural dwellers tended still to be deeply suspicious of the official attitude toward the associations. As these comments by the chairman of a dance group show, confidence was lacking in 1963 that a permanent detente would evolve from the marriage of convenience between hitherto implacable foes:

My people know that the district head is jealous of the power of Oglinye, and that the *Och'Idoma* tries to dominate the Idoma man. Because Oglinye is powerful it is useful to the Native Authority. And the Native Authority is useful to Oglinye. But the district head and the *Och'Idoma* grow more powerful and bolder each day. My people will not say that Oglinye will forever dance and play in peace with the Native Authority.

That which the chairman seemed only vaguely to foresee was anticipated more clearly by others in Idoma. For example, when asked why more Native Authority policemen were not posted in the districts, a thoughtful member of the policy-making General Purposes Committee responded at length:

I could say that we have no money to do this. But that is only part of the truth. I used to believe that we should have a permanent constabulary in every district. I no longer believe this. We choose to rely on district heads and councillors to maintain law and order and they, in turn, rely on Odumu and Akpantla. Unofficially, of course, since Odumu and Akpantla are troublemakers and must sometimes be punished themselves. But it is enough for now. The young hotheads who go to school do not stay long in the village to make trouble. They come to Oturkpo Town, to Kaduna, to Kano. Now we tax the districts. When we build in Oturkpo Town, we shall have more money to build in the districts. Then the young men will return home and make trouble, too. It will be time to post more policemen in the districts.

Desiring a restoration of the traditional constitutional system in some form, but faced with an inexorable increase in the power of the

Native Authority, the mass of disaffected rural dwellers could do little more than try to limit its encroachment on the local scene. The tendency of the district councillors and other informants to view local audiences as not clashing internally in Situation *3b* and, excepting the tax collectors, as opposing a bureaucratic move by the councillors to report their associations' excesses to higher authorities, reflects the popular resistance to intervention by the Native Authority in associational life and in local affairs generally; the percentage of councillors who attributed the expectation that they should play the debureaucratic role in that situation to the elders, young men, and members of secret societies and dance groups ranges between 77 per cent and 100 per cent. (See Table 5, *Total* column.) (Respondents tended to view the absence of a generalised Native Authority adversary in Situation *3a*, against which local audiences might unite, as the main reason why many more councillors perceived those audiences as clashing internally over the councillors' activism in associational life than over the central issue in Situation *3b*.)[6] Fearing suppression of traditional organisations whose positive contributions seemed usually to outweigh their predatoriness, most rural dwellers preferred not to enlist the aid of officials other than trusted councillors in combating the associations' anti-social proclivities.[7] Predictably, the Native Authority leadership in Oturkpo Town, and the district heads, representative councillors, 'Native Authority councillors', and tax collectors who were generally beholden to it, were widely viewed as expecting the district councillors to report acts of larceny committed by their associations to the district head or Native Authority police; the percentage of councillors who attributed the expectation of fulfilment of a bureaucratic role to those audiences ranges between 48 per cent and 91 per cent.[8] Excepting the elected councillors, who were widely seen as aligning with local audiences, and the tax collectors, who were often seen as identifying with their local government superiors, the

[6]The part such an adversary might play in uniting local audiences is illuminated by sociological theories of the dyad and triad (Wolff, ed. and trans. 1964: 137–69).

[7]Most informants observed that the associations' predatoriness was often surpassed by that of local government officials. As with villagers elsewhere (Rowley 1965: 85), they stressed that their elected officials must know what not to report to superiors.

[8]The relatively high percentage of district councillors who attributed the expectation of fulfilment of a bureaucratic role to the tax collectors in Situation *3b* reflects the popular view of those officials as 'Native Authority loyalists'. In District Four, where most councillors attributed the debureaucratic expectation to that audience, the tax collectors were regarded as fairly independent-minded (see pp. 141–2).

councillors' role perceptions in Situation *3b* point up the confrontation between rural base and Native Authority pinnacle in Idoma over attempts by the latter to encroach, directly or indirectly, on what was traditionally the domain of the former. We shall have occasion to pursue that theme again presently.

Case 4.
The clan head and the district head: 'to make a chief is to make war'

Early in the colonial period, as we have seen, the Administration resolved to establish the institution of chieftaincy as the cornerstone of local government in Idoma. The drive to strengthen chieftaincy at the district level was accelerated with each unsuccessful attempt to incorporate still other institutions – the *ojira* assembly, secret societies, and dance groups – into the Native Authority. 'Democratisation' of local government after World War II did not abate that drive; it was carried forward until independence under the vigorous leadership of the first Chief of Idoma, Ogiri Oko. In the early years of the administration of Oko's successor, Ajene Ukpabi, the prestige and power which had been associated with the Idoma Chieftaincy for more than a decade diminished somewhat. Nevertheless, the institution remained a vital force, as did chieftaincy at the district level. Nearly five decades after its rehabilitation under colonial auspices, the institution of chieftaincy was clearly in the ascendant in Idoma.

Accompanying the drive to strengthen chieftaincy was a progressive erosion of the various traditional checks on that institution: ritual, the principles of rotation and seniority, and public opinion in the *ojira* assembly. As these constitutional mechanisms became weaker, competition for positions of *och'mbeke* (chief of the white man) grew fiercer, causing political instability and disunity to increase in the society. These developments were given impetus by the strategy which the colonial Administration employed to foster strong chieftaincy. Rehabilitation of the traditional *oche* (clan head) and *aiigabo* (clan spokesmen) titles before World War I brought officialdom actively into the process of recruitment surrounding chieftaincy. Thereafter, colonial officials frequently intervened in the process, seeking to ensure (1) that appointments to district headships of clan heads and clan spokesmen were ratified by the *ojira* assembly, ostensibly in accordance with native law and custom (e.g. the principle of rotation); and (2) that appointments to district headships of persons without traditional office or title were further legitimised by their subsequently acquiring the *oche* title.

Official intervention in chieftaincy affairs extended also to the retirement of office-holders. Unsatisfactory performance – often vaguely defined – was cause for the summary dismissal of district heads; where a person filled the clan headship and the district headship simultaneously, dismissal from the latter position sometimes precipitated extralegal manoeuvres to deprive him of his traditional office (Idoma Division 1935–50).[9] The practice of higher authorities manipulating chieftaincy affairs was firmly rooted in Idoma in the inter-war years.

Upon assuming the office of *Och'Idoma* in 1947, Ogiri Oko indicated unequivocally his intention to continue that practice. Shortly before, Oko had renounced the district headship of Adoka, a single-clan unit, but had retained the clan headship. In order to consolidate his political base in Adoka, and to underscore his intent to become the dispenser of chiefly patronage in Idoma, the Chief quickly arranged for his brother to return from military service to succeed him as district head. Acting without regard to the principle of rotation in succession to chieftaincy, Oko precipitated a bitter conflict between rival kin groups which was to endure for more than a decade and culminate in a High Court challenge to his brother's district headship.[10] Oko's action in the Adoka case and the hostile response which it evoked were an augury of his controversial role in chieftaincy affairs during a thirteen year reign as *Och'Idoma*.

Hoping to attract the support of traditionalists in the campaign for 'democratisation' of the Native Authority, young men in the IHRU canvassed for reform in chieftaincy affairs. In the early 1950s the IHRU began to press for an end to manipulation from above in the succession. To forestall an alliance between traditionalists and the fading tribal union around this issue, the Native Authority eventually agreed to regularise succession to district headships, ostensibly in accordance with traditional practices and modern democratic norms

[9]There were no dismissals in the early independence period. District heads who were minimally efficient, and politically loyal to the Native Authority and the NPC, could reasonably expect to continue in office.

[10]On Oko's death in 1960, the clan headship passed to another kin group. Contending that he should also be the district head in a single-clan unit, the new clan head sought to have Oko's brother removed from office. A judicial decision was pending at the time of the study (Benue High Court 1962).

Confronting role conflict (continued)

(Idoma Native Authority 7 November 1957). It promulgated this formula: the district *ojira* would decide which clan was entitled to fill the office; whereupon the clan would specify which kindred had the right to convene alone to designate the district head. (Both decisions were to be based on the principle of rotation.) The district councillor(s) in the eligible clan and kindred would participate fully in the proceedings, and these would be witnessed by two members of the Native Authority Executive Council (later renamed the General Purposes Committee). The appointment of a district head recommended by the district *ojira* was subject to approval of the full council (including the *Och'Idoma*) and the Resident in charge of Benue Province.[11]

Little changed. The formal removal of the *Och'Idoma* from proceedings of the district *ojira* – a move which was hailed at the time as 'a good step towards democracy' (*ibid.*) – did not diminish his influence in chieftaincy affairs. Armed with the veto power, and still able to operate through the Executive Council and his supporters in the *ojira* assembly, Oko continued to manipulate the selection of district heads and clan heads. Moreover, the stipulation that eligible units alone would henceforth designate the district head merely served to exacerbate clan and kindred rivalries in the districts. The *Och'Idoma* was usually available on these occasions to mediate conflict between groups and to influence the proceedings.

Ironically, the apparent turnabout by the Native Authority in 1957 aroused fears of even greater manipulation from above in succession to chieftaincy. A primary source of anxiety was the stipulation that the district councillors, who were statutory agents of the Native Authority as well as district representatives, should participate in the proceedings. The District Councils had been established less than two years before and there was still suspicion about their allegiance. Some Idoma went so far as to insist that the *ojira* assemblies which chose the clan head and recommended the appointment of a district head be closed to all office-holders in the local government organisation.[12]

[11]Ogiri Oko was usually supported on these occasions by both the District Officer in Idoma and the Resident.
[12]In single-clan districts, the clan *ojira* designates the person who will serve as clan head and district head. It usually convenes twice, first to choose the clan head and then to recommend to the District Council his appointment as district head. In the multi-clan districts, each clan chooses its own clan head; the district *ojira*, comprising representatives from the various clans, recommends the appointment of a district head. The District Council communicates the recommendation *pro forma* to the General Purposes Committee (see pp. 58, 129).

171

Following independence, popular reliance on the councillors to lead the opposition to strong chieftaincy and Native Authority centralisation was accompanied by anxiety in some quarters over their role in succession.[13] That anxiety was the basis for two situations of bureaucratic–debureaucratic role conflict involving the councillors.

Each of the seventy-one district councillors was provided with this backdrop to the first situation:

When I travel to southern Idoma, to Agala, Igumale, and Ijigbam, I often hear that the councillors are expected to take part in the *ojira* which recommends the appointment of the district head. But when I travel to western Idoma, to Okwoga, Orokram, and Otukpa, I often hear that the councillors are expected not to take part. I am told that this is a matter for the *ojira*, for the people and the elders, not for the councillors and others who hold office in the Native Authority.

How is it in your place? Can you tell me what certain people would expect of you regarding your district head?

Situation 4a

A. Expect me as a councillor to take part in the *ojira* which recommends the appointment of the district head.

(Bureaucratic role-expectation)

B. Expect me as a councillor not to take part in the *ojira* which recommends the appointment of the district head.

(Debureaucratic role-expectation)

C. Have no expectation of me as a councillor in this situation.

Each district councillor was then provided with the backdrop to Situation *4b*:

When I travel to Agala, Igumale, and Ijigbam, I also hear that the councillors are expected to take part in the *ojira* which chooses the clan head. But when I travel to Okwoga, Orokram, and Otukpa, I often hear that the councillors are expected not to take part. I am told that this is also a matter for the *ojira*, for the people and the elders, not for the councillors and others who hold office in the Native Authority.

How is it in your place? Can you tell me what certain people would expect of you regarding your clan head?

Situation 4b

A. Expect me as a councillor to take part in the *ojira* which chooses the clan head.

(Bureaucratic role-expectation)

[13]Similar ambivalence toward local leaders has been reported among the Mayo Indians of Mexico (Erasmus 1952: 168–78) and the Tiv (Wallace 1958: 66–7).

B. Expect me as a councillor not to take part in the *ojira* which chooses the clan head.

(*Debureaucratic role-expectation*)

C. Have no expectation of me as a councillor in this situation.

The district councillors' role perceptions

Throughout the field investigation informants continually stressed the need to distinguish in chieftaincy affairs between the traditional clan headship and the district headship created and nurtured under European auspices. It did not seem to matter to the Idoma that the decision taken by the colonial Administration early in the century to revive the *oche* (clan head) and *aiigabo* (clan spokesmen) titles was motivated by a desire to endow the new district headships with a measure of traditional legitimacy. Nor did it appear to matter that appointments to district headships *and* clan headships were often manipulated from above by colonial officials, as was the establishment of the Idoma Chieftaincy after World War II and the installation of Ogiri Oko as *Och'Idoma*. Buoyed by an ideology of proud and vigorous chieftaincy, the Idoma managed to sort out its traditional and modern elements.[14] Referring to the district head as *och'mbeke,* the chief of the white man, they affirmed the essentially modern character of that office in the Native Authority. In the popular view, only the individual who had received the insignia of chiefly office in accordance with certain prescribed rituals could be esteemed as *oche*, the traditional clan head. As these comments by an elder and a district Councillor show, the distinction between the two offices was emphasised even where the clan headship and the district headship were occupied simultaneously by the same individual:

The elders decided that Aleichenu [pseudonym] should be *oche.* Aleichenu is also *och'mbeke,* the district head. But that is another matter. Our clan head wears the beaded wrist band, not our district head.

When Ogiri Oko became *Och'Idoma,* he had to resign his office as district head in Adoka. But my people generally agreed that Oko should continue to wear the wrist band of a traditional clan head.

The distinction in Idoma between traditional and modern chieftaincies bears significantly upon the two situations analysed here.

[14]A parallel distinction can be found in the Ashanti institution of chieftaincy. Thus, Fortes (1948: 27ff.) reports that efforts by the Gold Coast Administration to increase its control over chieftaincy affairs served to strengthen the popular view of that institution as 'a fundamental element in Ashanti political organisation' (p. 29). The elders were expected to see that the chiefs abided by custom.

Table 6. Councillor perceptions of audience expectations: the district councillor and district head succession (percentages) [a]

Audience [b]	Expectation	District One	Two	Three	Four	Five	Total
Elders	To take part	45	64	50	23	83	52
	Not to take part	9	–	–	8	–	4
	To/not to take part	41	36	50	61	8	39
	No expectation	5	–	–	8	8	4
	Number of councillors	(22)	(14)	(10)	(13)	(12)	(71)
Young	To take part	59	100	60	61	92	73
men	Not to take part	4	–	–	–	–	1
	To/not to take part	32	–	40	31	–	21
	No expectation	4	–	–	8	8	4
	Number of councillors	(22)	(14)	(10)	(13)	(12)	(71)
Tax	To take part	82	100	90	77	92	87
collectors	Not to take part	9	–	–	–	–	3
	To/not to take part	4	–	10	15	–	6
	No expectation	4	–	–	8	8	4
	Number of councillors	(22)	(14)	(10)	(13)	(12)	(71)
Elected	To take part	91	86	90	100	100	90
district	Not to take part	9	–	–	–	–	3
councillors	To/not to take part	–	14	10	–	–	7
	No expectation	–	–	–	–	–	–
	Number of councillors	(22)	(14)	(10)	(13)	(12)	(71)
Appointed	To take part	91	100	90	100	100	96
district	Not to take part	9	–	–	–	–	3
councillors	To/not to take part	–	–	10	–	–	1
	No expectation	–	–	–	–	–	–
	Number of councillors	(22)	(14)	(10)	(13)	(12)	(71)
Representa-	To take part	91	100	100	100	100	97
tive	Not to take part	9	–	–	–	–	3
councillor(s)	To/not to take part	–	–	–	–	–	–
	No expectation	–	–	–	–	–	–
	Number of councillors	(22)	(14)	(10)	(13)	(12)	(71)
Chief of	To take part	95	100	100	100	100	99
Idoma and	Not to take part	5	–	–	–	–	1
General	To/not to take part	–	–	–	–	–	–
Purposes	No expectation	–	–	–	–	–	–
Committee	Number of councillors	(22)	(14)	(10)	(13)	(12)	(71)

Notes

[a] The table reports the proportion of district councillors who perceived audiences as expecting councillor to act bureaucratically, i.e., to take part in *ojira* assembly which recommends appointment of district head; or to act debureaucratically, i.e., not to take part. The table also includes councillor's perception of role conflict *within* audience (to/not to take part); and councillor's perception that audience holds no expectation for his behaviour.

[b] Because the district headship would be vacated upon incumbent's death, that office is not included here as an audience (see p. 170, note 9).

Situation 4a. As might be expected, the district councillor was widely viewed by informants as having a part to play in the *ojira* assembly which recommends the appointment of his immediate superior in the Native Authority, the district head. That viewpoint is reflected also in the role-expectations which the councillors attributed to various audiences in Situation *4a*. Thus, we observe in Table 6 (*Total* column) that the percentage of those officials who perceived audiences as expecting them to act bureaucratically, participating in proceedings over succession to the district headship, ranges between 52 per cent (the elders) and 99 per cent (the General Purposes Committee under the presidency of the Chief of Idoma). Here again we also observe a relationship between the councillors' perceptions of the expectation of fulfilment of the bureaucratic role and the location of audiences *vis–à–vis* the Native Authority leadership: the percentage of councillors who perceived audiences as expecting them to participate in the succession proceedings steadily increases in the ascent from rural base (elders, 52 per cent; young men, 73 per cent; tax collectors, 87 per cent) through intermediate levels of the Native Authority (elected councillors, 90 per cent; appointed or 'Native Authority councillors', 96 per cent; representative councillor(s), 97 per cent) to the Committee (99 per cent).

But there were dissenters from this viewpoint. Thus, a small minority of the district councillors attributed the expectation of debureaucratic role to audiences which were seen as opposing the participation of those officials in proceedings over succession to the district headship. (See Table 6, *Total* column.) The dissenting audiences were viewed as falling into three groups. In the first were elements who based their opposition essentially on principle, contending without regard to the distinction between district headship and clan headship that chieftaincy *per se* should be treated as a traditional matter beyond the brief of officialdom in the modern Native Authority.The second and third groups were of a more pragmatic mind. One group of 'pragmatists' opined that the councillors' participation in the *ojira* which recommends the appointment of the district head would encourage the participation of councillors and other Native Authority officials in proceedings over succession to the traditional clan headship. They were apprehensive lest such a development blur the distinction between the two chiefly offices. Not surprisingly, these elements tended to be concentrated in single-clan districts where both chieftaincies were ordinarily filled by the same individual. Another

175

group of 'pragmatists' was comprised of elders who feared that a diminution of their own influence in chieftaincy affairs would attend the councillors' participation in proceedings over succession – whether for the district headship or the clan headship.

Additional evidence of similar dissent is available in the district councillors' perceptions of role conflict within various local audiences. Among the twenty-eight councillors who perceived the elders as holding role-expectations conflicting in Situation *4a*, twenty reported that nearly all the members of that audience would expect those officials not to take part in proceedings over succession to the district headship. Interestingly, eighteen of the twenty were from Districts One, Four, and Five – where a single individual had usually filled the clan headship and the district headship[15] and where, according to many informants, the elders had been working strenuously to maintain their influence in chieftaincy affairs.[16] Among the fifteen councillors who perceived the young men as holding role-expectations conflicting in Situation *4a*, five reported that nearly all the members of that audience would expect those officials not to participate in the *ojira* which recommends the appointment of the district head. The remaining ten councillors reported that nearly all the young men would rather expect them to participate in the proceedings; follow-up probes of the former elicited the opinion that the young men preferred that those officials participate as a means of circumscribing the elders' influence in chieftaincy affairs. As one respondent put it, 'the young men are true to the ways of Idoma. They do not oppose the tyranny of the chief and Oturkpo Town so that they can live under the tyranny of the elders in the *ojira* assembly'. Other responses in the same vein also drew attention both to the persistence of inter-generational discord in Idoma and to the widespread desire for a restoration of the traditional constitutional equilibrium rooted in principles of chieftaincy, gerontocracy, and democracy in the *ojira*.

[15]Districts One and Four are single-clan units with combined chieftaincy institutions. District Five has four clans. One of the clan heads in District Five has been district head for nearly three decades.

[16]Where one individual filled the clan headship and the district headship (Districts One and Four), the district head was apt to be more responsive to Native Authority superiors than to the elders. The problem of declining influence was compounded in District Four, where a relatively well-educated and politically sophisticated population was often reluctant to defer to gerontocratic authority. In District Five, the elders' influence in chieftaincy affairs was circumscribed during the long tenure of an autocratic district head.

Confronting role conflict (continued)

Situation 4b. Again as might be expected, district councillors and other local government officials were widely viewed as having little or no voice in the *ojira* assembly which chooses the traditional clan head. A similar attitude is reflected in the role-expectations which the councillors attributed to various audiences in Situation *4b*. (See Table 7, *Total* column.) The percentage of those officials who perceived

Table 7. Councillor perceptions of audience expectations: the district councillor and clan head succession (percentages) [a]

Audience	Expectation	District					Total
		One	Two	Three	Four	Five	
Elders	To take part	45	–	–	8	–	16
	Not to take part	9	79	60	54	83	51
	To/not to take part	41	21	40	38	17	32
	No expectation	5	–	–	–	–	1
	Number of councillors	(22)	(14)	(10)	(13)	(12)	(71)
Young	To take part	59	21	–	23	–	27
men	Not to take part	4	7	–	54	17	16
	To/not to take part	32	71	100	23	83	56
	No expectation	4	–	–	–	–	1
	Number of councillors	(22)	(14)	(10)	(13)	(12)	(71)
Tax	To take part	82	21	10	38	–	38
collectors	Not to take part	9	43	40	62	83	42
	To/not to take part	4	36	50	–	17	18
	No expectation	4	–	–	–	–	1
	Number of councillors	(22)	(14)	(10)	(13)	(12)	(71)
Elected	To take part	91	21	30	38	17	46
district	Not to take part	9	64	50	54	83	46
councillors	To/not to take part	–	7	20	8	–	6
	No expectation	–	7	–	–	–	1
	Number of councillors	(22)	(14)	(10)	(13)	(12)	(71)
Appointed	To take part	91	21	40	38	17	48
district	Not to take part	9	64	50	62	83	48
councillors	To/not to take part	–	7	10	–	–	3
	No expectation	–	7	–	–	–	1
	Number of councillors	(22)	(14)	(10)	(13)	(12)	(71)
Representa-	To take part	91	21	40	38	17	48
tive	Not to take part	9	71	60	62	83	51
councillor(s)	To/not to take part	–	–	–	–	–	–
	No expectation	–	7	–	–	–	1
	Number of councillors	(22)	(14)	(10)	(13)	(12)	(71)

Table 7 *(cont.)*

Audience	Expectation	District One	Two	Three	Four	Five	Total
District	To take part	–	21	40	–	8	11
head	Not to take part	–	71	60	–	67	34
	To/not to take part	–	–	–	–	–	–
	No expectation	–	7	–	–	–	1
	Not applicable [b]	100	–	–	100	25	53
	Number of councillors	(22)	(14)	(10)	(13)	(12)	(71)
Chief of	To take part	95	21	40	38	17	49
Idoma and	Not to take part	5	71	60	62	83	49
General	To/not to take part	–	–	–	–	–	–
Purposes	No expectation	–	7	–	–	–	1
Committee	Number of councillors	(22)	(14)	(10)	(13)	(12)	(71)

Notes

[a] The table reports the proportion of district councillors who perceived audiences as expecting councillor to act bureaucratically, i.e., to take part in *ojira* assembly which chooses clan head: or to act debureaucratically, i.e., not to take part. The table also includes councillor's perception of role conflict *within* audience (to/not to take part); and councillor's perception that audience holds no expectation for his behaviour.

[b] The same person occupied clan headship and district headship in single-clan Districts One and Four. Because his death would leave both offices vacant, the district head could not be an audience in those districts. The clan head in one of four clans in District Five was also district head. Because his death would leave both offices vacant, the district head could not be an audience for three district councillors (25 per cent) from that clan.

audiences as expecting them to act bureaucratically in that situation, by participating in proceedings over succession to the clan headship, is substantially lower than in Situation *4a*, ranging between 11 per cent and 49 per cent in the former and, it will be recalled, between 52 per cent and 99 per cent in the latter. Follow-up probes were made of the councillors who viewed audiences as expecting them to act bureaucratically in Situation *4b* in order to ascertain what part they felt they were expected to play in choosing the clan head. Their responses underscore the contrast between the two situations.

Those district councillors who viewed audiences as expecting them to participate in the *ojira* assembly which chooses the clan head usually opined that as officials responsible for maintaining law and order in the district they were expected merely to help police a large and potentially disruptive gathering. The single exception here involves the Chief of Idoma and the General Purposes Committee. Among the thirty-five councillors who attributed the expectation of bureaucratic role to that audience in Situation 4b, only three felt that the Native Authority leaders wished them merely to police the assembly. Thirty-two councillors viewed the Chief and the Committee as rather expecting them to participate fully in the deliberations. As we shall see presently, the majority view was associated with fears of manipulation from above in succession to clan head.

But proceedings over succession to the district headship were quite another matter. In accordance with the formula adopted in 1957, the district councillors were widely expected to participate fully in the *ojira* assembly which recommends the appointment of the district head. Acting either in his own right or as spokesman for a kin group or a traditional association, the councillor was expected to be among those who would nominate a candidate early in the deliberations and then lobby strenuously on his behalf. As with the process of accession surrounding the district councillorship, the deliberations were seldom speedy or calm; acrimonious debate was apt to continue for some time, occasionally punctuated by scuffling. The councillor was often expected eventually to join with other influential men in urging the *ojira* to settle upon a candidate who would be acceptable to most, if not all, of the participants.

Succession to district head usually accorded the district councillor an opportunity to mobilise a wide range of political resources (e.g., personal reputation, bargaining style, oratorical skill, family size and influence) in pursuit of his own (and presumably his supporters') political interests. Succession to clan head rarely accorded him the same opportunity. The most noteworthy exceptions occurred when the *ojira* in single-clan districts decided to meet once to choose the individual who would serve both as clan head and district head. Often on these occasions heated controversy surrounded the councillor's participation in the process of deliberation.

The essential difference between the district councillors' bureaucratic behaviour in Situation 4a and Situation 4b is illustrated in the following observations by an elder and a representative councillor:

To make a chief is to make war. As a Native Authority official, the councillor must try to keep peace in the *ojira*. But the Native Authority cannot tell us who should be the clan head, or how we must choose him. It is different with the district head, *och'mbeke* ['chief of the white man']. The councillor can help us make a choice here. It is the way in Idoma.

Before I was elected representative councillor, I was the district councillor here. Adenyi [pseudonym, as are the other personal and lineage names in this passage] was clan head and district head then. Adenyi died during my term as councillor. When the *ojira* met to choose a new clan head, my people said I could attend only to keep order. As a Native Authority official, I could speak only if a disturbance occurred. Omepa, from *AiNobi* lineage, was chosen clan head. Three days later, the *ojira* met again to choose the district head. This time I joined the deliberations. A small lineage, *AiOloja*, claimed the office. My lineage, *AiOkpachu*, said that we are one clan in the district and must have one ruler. The stranger lineage, *AiAmla,* joined the debate (see p. 32). I helped persuade the *ojira* that while Omepa and Ija, the *AiOloja* candidate, are both just men, we must have one ruler. *AiAmla* agreed. *AiNobi* did not speak. *AiOloja* then rose to challenge the strangers. A portfolio councillor who was present to observe the proceedings persuaded *AiOloja* to return to its place. I was too busy in the *ojira* to help restore order. *AiOloja* finally agreed to have Omepa as district head, but it swore vengeance against *AiAmla*. The *ojira* ended with bitterness.

Additional evidence of the stress placed upon the norm that district councillors have little or no voice in succession to clan head is available in their perceptions of role conflict within local audiences. Among the twenty-three councillors who perceived the elders as holding conflicting expectations in Situation *4b*, twenty-two reported that nearly all the members of that audience would expect those officials to absent themselves from the *ojira* assembly which chooses the clan head. Essentially the same report was made by twenty-three of the forty councillors who viewed the young men as holding conflicting expectations in Situation *4b*; and eleven of the thirteen councillors who perceived role conflict among the tax collectors. Interestingly, among the seventeen councillors who attributed the expectation of bureaucratic role to nearly all the young men in their areas, ten opined that they were expected by them merely to help police the *ojira*. The remaining seven were from single-clan units, Districts One and Four. Two councillors in the former reported that nearly all the young men would expect them to participate in the deliberations only if succession to clan head and district head were fused into a single process. Contrastingly, five councillors in District Four reported that young men bent on reducing the elders' influence in chieftaincy affairs would overwhelmingly expect them to participate in choice of a new clan head, whether or not the *ojira* met separately to fill that office and the district headship (see note 16).

The tendency in Idoma to emphasise the distinction between clan headship and district headship points up the nostalgia for traditional institutions and values in the face of changes wrought under European rule. As gerontocratic authority weakened *vis-à-vis* district headship in the period between the world wars, along with the principle of democracy in the *ojira*, the Idoma fell back upon their traditional ideology of proud and vigorous chieftaincy. In the process, they came to view district headship as separate from, and inferior to, the office of clan head – even where the two were filled by a single individual. The emergence of strong chieftaincy in the Native Authority seemed to heighten the emotional commitment to clan headship – a political institution which, as we have already seen, existed sporadically in the past and achieved only symbolic greatness.

Following World War II, the colonial Administration exploited that ideology as it moved to create an institution without precedent in Idoma, the divisional chieftaincy. Subsequently, Ogiri Oko used the ideology and the nostalgia associated with it as a rationale for centralising power in Oturkpo Town – all the while claiming that his office was a bulwark against would-be reformers assailing the institution of chieftaincy, and a spearhead for restoring the traditional constitutional system. Oko's cynicism was matched by popular scepticism on the eve of independence, and hostility to strong chieftaincy and Native Authority centralisation increased sharply.

After independence, rural resistance to the *status quo* in local government affairs was organised around the district councillors. But since they were basically suspicious of all officialdom, the Idoma generally tried to insulate traditional chieftaincy affairs, including succession to clan head, from interference by the Native Authority. The councillors and their superiors were either discouraged from attending the *ojira* assembly which chooses the clan head or encouraged to participate merely to enforce the law. By subscribing to Native Authority regulations which in any case required that certain officials participate in proceedings over succession to the district headship, the Idoma reaffirmed the distinction between that office and the clan headship. Still, they were vigilant lest higher officials gain complete control over traditional chieftaincy affairs. The mere suspicion that the Chief of Idoma and the General Purposes Committee might attempt to manipulate succession to clan head through the councillors was sufficient to make most rural dwellers uneasy. For example, follow-up probes of the thirty-two councillors who reported that the Chief and the Committee would expect them to participate

G

fully in the deliberations usually elicited the worried opinion that Oturkpo Town was bent on manipulating succession to clan head through its subordinates. Similar opinions were furnished by many other informants, along with a treasure chest of anecdotal evidence – both real and imagined. In chieftaincy affairs, as in other matters previously analysed, bureaucratic–debureaucratric role conflict surrounding the councillors underscored a preoccupation in Idoma with the confrontation between rural base and Native Authority pinnacle.

Chapter Nine Internalising role conflict: perception, ambivalence, and resolution among the district councillors

The basis for analysing role conflict surrounding the district councillors in different situations has been laid in the two preceding chapters. Now we address these questions: With what frequency do the councillors perceive such conflict? What is the relationship between their perceptions of role conflict and ambivalence, i.e., to what extent do they experience difficulty in resolving it? How do those officials ultimately resolve bureaucratic–debureaucratic role conflict? And what implications does ambivalence carry for the way they choose to effect resolution? In the next chapter we shall shift our focus from the 'how' in resolution to the 'why', first examining the relationship between the councillors' evaluations of role legitimacy, role obligation, and role sanction and the way they seek to cope with role conflict, and then the consequences of their efforts at interrelated personal and societal levels.

Objective and perceived role conflict

When presenting a conceptual language for analysis of role conflict in Chapter Six, I stressed the need to distinguish between the three analytic elements in any situation of role conflict. They are, it will be recalled, the objective conflict; perception of the objective conflict; and subjective role conflict or ambivalence. The relationship between the first and second elements is analysed in this section; the following section analyses the relationship between those two elements and ambivalence.

Because it cannot be assumed that the occupant of a focal position will always perceive an objective role conflict, it is important at the outset to determine whether he is even aware that audiences hold contradictory expectations for his behaviour in particular situations.[1] The following procedure was adopted to establish the extent to which seventy-one district councillors perceived such conflict: after being provided with the backdrop to an objective conflict reportedly surrounding those officials, each councillor was asked to indicate, first, the role-expectation(s) individual audiences would hold for his behaviour in that situation, and second, his evaluation of the legitimacy and obligatoriness of the expectation(s). Each councillor was then asked to reaffirm his *perception* of *role conflict* or *role consensus* among audiences involved in the situation. The entire procedure was repeated for each situation analysed in the study. Table 8 reports the percentage of councillors who perceived audiences as holding contradictory expectations in six objective situations of conflict.

At this juncture, it is necessary to specify the implications for our analysis of the relationship between the proportionate incidence of role conflict perceived by the district councillors and the situational and district variables. To assess the relative significance of the two variables for perceived role conflict, these null hypotheses were subjected to a Kruskal–Wallis one-way analysis of variance (or H) test (Siegel 1956: 184–94): (1) There is no difference between situations in the proportionate incidence of perceived role conflict. (2) There is no difference between districts in the proportionate incidence of perceived role conflict. Utilising the 0.05 level of significance, the first hypothesis is rejected ($p > 0.001$) and the second accepted ($p < 0.50$).[2] Because significant differences are limited to the situational variable in this context, the *situation* is treated as an independent variable. The analysis which follows encompasses that variable alone.

---

[1]Various perceptual problems may confront the focal actor. He may be wholly unaware of role conflict surrounding his behaviour. Or he may perceive role conflict where objectively it does not exist. And finally, he may correctly perceive the existence of role conflict, but misperceive which audiences hold conflicting expectations for his behaviour. This study concentrates on the first problem. Needless to say, the accuracy of the focal actor's perceptions (and of his evaluations of role obligation and role sanction) cannot be confirmed without consulting or observing the audiences themselves. This was partly accomplished for the district head audience (see pp. 261–5).

[2]The proportionate incidence of perceived role conflict was computed for six situations in each of the five districts. Thirty proportions were then ranked from thirty to one. The situational hypothesis was tested by constructing a table of ranks with situational columns and district rows. (H = 18·17, uncorrected for ties; $df = 5$.) The district hypothesis was tested by constructing a table of ranks with district columns and situational rows. (H = 4·08, uncorrected for ties; $df = 4$.) The unranked situational and district proportions are reported in Table 8.

Table 8. Councillors who perceived objective role conflict (percentages)

Case and conflict situation	District					
	One	Two	Three	Four	Five	Total
Case 1. The District Council fund						
Situation *1a*. The district councillor and the council hall	82	86	100	100	75	87
Number of councillors	(22)	(14)	(10)	(13)	(12)	(71)
Case 2. Political parties						
Situation *2*. The district councillor and party campaigning	23	50	60	38	33	38
Number of councillors	(22)	(14)	(10)	(13)	(12)	(71)
Case 3. Secret societies and dance groups						
Situation *3a*. The district councillor and activism in secret societies and dance groups	50	86	70	62	75	66
Number of councillors	(22)	(14)	(10)	(13)	(12)	(71)
Situation *3b*. The district councillor, law enforcement, and secret societies and dance groups	91	79	100	85	100	90
Number of councillors	(22)	(14)	(10)	(13)	(12)	(71)
Case 4. The clan head and the district head						
Situation *4a*. The district councillor and district head succession	50	50	70	69	25	52
Number of councillors	(22)	(14)	(10)	(13)	(12)	(71)
Situation *4b*. The district councillor and clan head succession	50	93	100	54	83	72
Number of councillors	(22)	(14)	(10)	(13)	(12)	(71)

Reflected in Table 8 (*Total* column) is less than universal perception of role conflict in each situation. Evident also is a wide range of differences between totalled responses. Whereas 90 per cent of the district councillors perceived role conflict in Situation *3b* – pertaining to whether they should report the transgressions of secret societies and dance groups to higher authorities – only 38 per cent perceived conflict in Situation 2 – pertaining to whether they should campaign for the governing party. Moreover, there is considerable variation even between related situations. While 66 per cent of the councillors perceived role conflict in Situation 3a – pertaining to whether their activism in associational life is compatible with their responsibility for local peacemaking – 90 per cent perceived conflict in Situation 3b. Similarly, while 52 per cent of the councillors perceived role conflict regarding their participation in proceedings over succession to the district headship (Situation 4a), 72 per cent perceived conflict over their role in succession to the clan headship (Situation 4b).

Yet another view of the extent of incongruence between objective and perceived role conflict may be gleaned from these data: whereas only one district councillor (1 per cent) perceived *role consensus* in all six situations, only four councillors (6 per cent) perceived *role conflict* in every situation. Ranging between those extremes, seven councillors (10 per cent) perceived role conflict in one situation, thirteen (18 per cent) in two situations, thirteen (18 per cent) in three situations, twenty-four (34 per cent) in four situations, and nine (13 per cent) in five situations. Finally, among the 426 observations analysed (seventy-one councillors multiplied by six situations), only 288 (68 per cent) indicate that role conflict was perceived by the councillors.

Since objective role conflict may arise *within* and/or *between* audiences, we must consider also the extent to which the district councillors perceived one type or another. First, however, some clarification of the basic typology is required. Role conflict can be said to obtain *between* audiences where, for example, all the elders expect the councillor to act bureaucratically in a particular situation and all the young men expect him to act debureaucratically. It can be said to obtain *within* audiences where some elders expect that official to act bureaucratically and other elders expect him to act debureaucratically. Finally, role conflict can be said to obtain simultaneously *within and between* audiences where some elders and some young men expect the councillor to act bureaucratically and other elders and other young men expect him to act debureaucratically. Since the councillor effects role relationships with no fewer than seven audiences in any situation, his perceptions of role conflict *within* audiences are apt to involve also perceptions of role conflict *between* audiences. For example, elders viewed by the councillor as holding conflicting expectations among themselves are usually viewed at the same time as holding conflicting expectations *vis-à-vis* all or some young men, tax collectors, representative councillors, etc. The single exception may occur where the district councillor perceives one audience as dividing internally in a particular situation and all the other audiences as holding no expectations for his behaviour. In that event, it can be said that role conflict is perceived *within* an audience, but not simultaneously *between* audiences.

Table 9 reports the percentage of district councillors in each situation who perceived role conflict *within* and/or *between* audiences. Their perceptions were either of role conflict *between* audiences or simultaneously *within and between* audiences; the exception noted above, role conflict perceived *within* an audience, but not simultaneously *between* audiences, was never encountered in the study.

Also evident in Table 9 is the relatively high incidence of role conflict perceived simultaneously *within and between* audiences; that category subsumes 216 (75 per cent) of the district councillors' 288 perceptions of role conflict. The percentage of those officials who viewed at least one audience as dividing internally, and its members as also holding conflicting expectations *vis-à-vis* other audiences, ranges between 66 per cent and 100 per cent in five situations. The exception is Situation 3b where, as we have seen, local audiences were widely viewed as unifying against a generalised Native Authority foe.

Table 9. Councillors who perceived role conflict within and between audiences (percentages)

Case and conflict situation	Within audiences	Within/between audiences	Between audiences
Case 1. The District Council fund			
Situation *1a*.The district councillor and the council hall	—	66	34
Number of councillors		(62)	
Case 2. Political parties			
Situation *2*. The district councillor and party campaigning	—	96	4
Number of councillors		(27)	

Table 9 *continued*

Case and conflict situation	Type of role conflict		
	Within audiences	Within/between audiences	Between audiences
Case 3. Secret societies and dance groups			
Situation *3a*. The district councillor and activism in secret societies and dance groups	—	100	—
Number of councillors		(47)	
Situation *3b*. The district councillor, law enforcement, and secret societies and dance groups	—	25	75
Number of councillors		(64)	
Case 4. The clan head and the district head			
Situation *4a*. The district councillor and district head succession	—	95	5
Number of councillors		(37)	
Situation *4b*. The district councillor and clan head succession	—	98	2
Number of councillors		(51)	
Total [a]	—	75	25
		(288)	

Note

[a] Among the seventy-one district councillors interviewed, sixty-two perceived role conflict in Situation *1a*, twenty-seven in Situation *2*, etc. Each perception of role conflict in the six situations is an 'observation' for purposes of analysis. There are 288 observations in all.

Significantly, while the Chief of Idoma and his colleagues on the General Purposes Committee were widely regarded as cohesive at the apex of the Native Authority, the opposite view was held of local audiences. Among the 216 instances of role conflict perceived simultaneously *within and between* audiences, 186 (86 per cent) draw attention to conflict among the elders and young men. Despite their widely shared hostility to strong chieftaincy and Native Authority centralisation, each group was seen as divided internally and against the other. While the latter conflicts are, of course, endemic in Idoma, some informants emphasised that their virulence had increased sharply under colonial rule. One elder observed, for example, that 'young men who return from the white man's town sometimes doubt the elders' wisdom in local affairs'. In a similar vein, two primary school leavers insisted that 'only the educated young men can make changes in the village'. An illiterate youth, in turn, deplored his educated brethren 'who have little regard for the *alekwu* ['the ways of the ancestors']'.

Lest the reader distort the meaning of such occurrences, confusing the scope of inter-generational discord resulting from urbanisation and Western education with its intensity, the following should also be noted: among the 186 instances of role conflict perceived simultaneously within and between audiences, all but thirteen (7 per cent) were seen by the councillors as pitting a very small, vocal minority of the young men in the *ojira* assembly against their generational peers and the elders. Needless to say, that Western-educated, urban-travelled minority is apt to grow in the future. But in 1963, at least, its size and influence were still quite restricted in rural Idoma. Accordingly, the data on the district councillors' perceptions of role conflict, when examined by type, should be interpreted as revealing two cleavages in Idoma – one extant (and perhaps widening) at the base of the society within the *ojira* assembly, the other undoubtedly widening between that institution and the Native Authority organisation.

Perceived role conflict and ambivalence

Having pursued the relationship between the objective and perceptual elements in analysis of role conflict, we turn next to their relationship with the third, or subjective, element. The ability of the focal actor to perceive objective role conflict is a necessary condition for his experiencing subjective role conflict. It must be emphasised here that subjective role conflict need not accompany the perception of an objective conflict situation. The focal actor is said to experience the former only when he manifests ambivalence, i.e., when he has difficulty in choosing his behaviour from among given role alternatives.

The following procedure was adopted to establish the extent to which the district councillors experienced subjective role conflict. Each councillor who perceived role conflict among audiences in a particular situation was asked, 'Would this situation trouble you? That is, would you have difficulty deciding what to do?' Those who responded affirmatively were then probed for the degree of difficulty they would experience in choosing from among given role alternatives: 'How much difficulty would you have deciding what to do? Some? Very much?' A three-point ambivalence scale was constructed for the alternative responses: *no difficulty, some difficulty, very much difficulty.*

Here, too, it is necessary to consider the implications for our analysis of the situational and district variables. To assess their relative significance for the degree of ambivalence experienced by the district councillors, these null hypotheses were subjected to the H-test:(1)There is no difference between situations in the degree of ambivalence experienced by the councillors.(2)There is no difference between districts in the degree of ambivalence experienced by the councillors. The first hypothesis is rejected ($p > 0.01$) and the second accepted ($p < 0.50$).[3] Because significant differences are again limited to the situational variable, the role conflict *situation* is treated as an independent variable in analysing ambivalence.

Table 10 reports the percentage of district councillors who experienced ambivalence in perceived situations of role conflict. Reflected in the *Total* column is the fact that in every situation ambivalence was experienced by substantially fewer than the number of councillors who perceived role conflict. Evident, too, is a wide range of differences between totalled responses. Whereas 66 per cent of the councillors experienced difficulty choosing between bureaucratic and debureaucratic role alternatives in Situation *3a*, such difficulty was experienced by only 20 per cent of the officials who perceived role conflict in Situation *3b*. There is also considerable variation between

[3]Mean scores of ambivalence were computed for six situations in each of the five districts. Thirty scores were then ranked from thirty to one. The situational hypothesis was tested by constructing a table of ranks with situational columns and district rows. (H = 14.43, uncorrected for ties; $df = 5$.) The district hypothesis was tested by constructing a table of ranks with district columns and situational rows. (H = 3.74, uncorrected for ties; $df = 4$.) The unranked situational and district scores are reported in Table 11.

Table 10. Councillors who experienced ambivalence in perceived situations of role conflict (percentages)

Case and conflict situation	District					Total
	One	Two	Three	Four	Five	
Case 1. The District Council fund						
Situation *1a*. The district councillor and the council hall	39	42	50	31	44	40
Number of councillors	(18)	(12)	(10)	(13)	(9)	(62)
Case 2. Political parties						
Situation *2*. The district councillor and party campaigning	20	29	33	20	25	26
Number of councillors	(5)	(7)	(6)	(5)	(4)	(27)
Case 3. Secret societies and dance groups						
Situation *3a*. The district councillor and activism in secret societies and dance groups	73	50	71	63	78	66
Number of councillors	(11)	(12)	(7)	(8)	(9)	(47)
Situation *3b*. The district councillor, law enforcement, and secret societies and dance groups	15	36	20	–	40	20
Number of councillors	(20)	(11)	(10)	(11)	(10)	(64)
Case 4. The clan head and the district head						
Situation *4a*. The district councillor and district head succession	73	86	71	33	67	65
Number of councillors	(11)	(7)	(7)	(9)	(3)	(37)
Situation *4b*. The district councillor and clan head succession	73	31	30	57	10	39
Number of councillors	(11)	(13)	(10)	(7)	(10)	(51)

related situations. While 66 per cent of the councillors who perceived role conflict in Situation *3a* had difficulty in deciding what to do, only 20 per cent of those who perceived role conflict in Situation *3b* experienced a similar problem. Moreover, while ambivalence was experienced by 65 per cent of the councillors who perceived conflict over their role in proceedings over succession to the district headship (Situation *4a*), that problem beset only 39 per cent of those who perceived conflict over their role in succession to the clan headship (Situation *4b*).

Another view of the extent of incongruence between perceived and subjective role conflict may be gleaned from these data: seventeen (24 per cent) of the seventy district councillors who perceived at least one situation of role conflict never experienced difficulty in choosing between bureaucratic and debureaucratic role alternatives. Sixty-two councillors (89 per cent) experienced ambivalence in fewer than the number of situations of role conflict which they perceived. Only eight councillors (11 per cent) experienced ambivalence in every situation of conflict which they perceived. And among the 288 perceptions of role conflict by those officials, only 132 (46 per cent) were accompanied by subjective role conflict.

Table 11. Mean scores of ambivalence for councillors who perceived situations of role conflict [a]

Case and conflict situation	District					Situational means
	One	Two	Three	Four	Five	
Case 1. The District Council fund Situation *1a*. The district councillor and the council hall	1·55	1·67	1·70	1·38	1·44	1·55
Case 2. Political parties Situation *2*. The district councillor and party campaigning	1·20	1·43	1·33	1·20	1·25	1·29
Case 3. Secret societies and dance groups Situation *3a*. The district councillor and activism in secret societies and dance groups	1·73	1·67	2·00	1·88	1·89	1·80
Situation *3b*. The district councillor, law enforcement, and secret societies and dance groups	1·40	1·36	1·80	1·64	1·50	1·52
Case 4. The clan head and the district head Situation *4a*. The district councillor and district head succession	2·00	1·57	1·71	1·67	1·33	1·73
Situation *4b*. The district councillor and clan head succession	2·00	1·46	1·50	1·57	1·30	1·57
District means	1·64	1·53	1·68	1·56	1·49	—

Note
[a] 1·00 = no ambivalence; 2·00 = some ambivalence; 3·00 = very much ambivalence.

Still another view of the considerable incongruence between the perceptual and subjective elements is obtained by examining the *degree* of ambivalence which the district councillors experienced. Among the 132 reports of difficulty experienced in choosing between bureaucratic and debureaucratic role alternatives, ninety-five (72 per cent) involve *some ambivalence*; only thirty-seven (28 per cent) involve *very much ambivalence*. The two categories, *some ambivalence* and *very much ambivalence,* subsume 33 per cent and 13 per cent respectively of the 288 perceptions of role conflict by the councillors. Underlining the ease with which most of those officials resolved role conflict are the mean scores of ambivalence reported in Table 11. These consistently fall within the lower range (1·00–2·00) of the three-point ambivalence scale.

An opportunity to reaffirm the general direction of the findings presented in this section was suggested quite by accident. Comparing the last columns in Table 8 and Table 11, it was discovered that the lowest proportionate incidence of perceived role conflict *and* the lowest mean score of ambivalence were reported in Situation 2 – suggesting a possible correlation between the two variables. To assess the extent of association between them, a Spearman rank correlation coefficient (Siegel 1956: 202–13) was computed from those columns. A rho of −0·08 was obtained, indicating no association between the two variables – and pointing up the fact that ambivalence need not accompany the perception of objective role conflict.[4]

Resolution of role conflict

To ascertain how the district councillors would resolve bureaucratic–debureaucratic role conflict, all those who perceived such conflict were subsequently asked, 'What would you do in this situation?' Among the many procedures of resolution which are potentially available to an actor, one was adopted universally by the councillors in 288 perceived situations of conflict: evaluation of a major role, i.e., selection by the 'men in the middle' of either the bureaucratic or the debureaucratic expectation as the major role to be fulfilled. Occasionally, it will be recalled, that procedure was accompanied by verbal aggression in the form of denunciation and epithet. For example, while they were resolving role conflict debureaucratically in Situation 2, four councillors bitterly denounced their district head and the Chief of Idoma and his colleagues on the General Purposes Committee for allegedly conspiring to 'spoil the land' with party strife 'and disunity. According to the councillors, Native Authority superiors hoped to promote the victory of 'official' candidates by expecting the councillors to act bureaucratically in that situation, i.e., by expecting them to campaign for the NPC in the next parliamentary elections. Debureaucratic resolution appeared to have little, if anything, to do here with attitudes toward the governing party in particular. Rather, it seemed to reflect those councillors' avowed preference for a non-partisan strategy in campaigns for higher political office, both as a

---

[4]Notwithstanding problems obviously associated with correlating ranked aggregate data, the obtained rho does lend general support to the earlier findings. It seems reasonable to expect that where role conflict is widely perceived, considerable ambivalence will be experienced in resolving it. Clearly this is not borne out with the Idoma data.

means of limiting party strife at the local level and as a way of registering their opposition to the main source of NPC power in Idoma Division, strong chieftaincy and Native Authority centralisation.[5]

Table 12. Councillors who resolved role conflict bureaucratically and debureaucratically (percentages)

Case and conflict situation	Direction of resolution		
	Bureaucratic		Debureaucratic
Case 1. The district council fund			
Situation 1a. The district councillor and the council hall	29		71
Number of councillors		(62)	
Case 2. Political parties			
Situation 2. The district councillor and party campaigning	48		52
Number of councillors		(27)	
Case 3. Secret societies and dance groups			
Situation 3a. The district councillor and activism in secret societies and dance groups	36		64
Number of councillors		(47)	
Situation 3b. The district councillor, law enforcement, and secret societies and dance groups	19		81
Number of councillors		(64)	
Case 4. The clan head and the district head			
Situation 4a. The district councillor and district head succession	95		5
Number of councillors		(37)	
Situation 4b. The district councillor and clan head succession	41		59
Number of councillors		(51)	
Total [a]	40		60
		(288)	

Note
[a] See Table 9, note [a].

Reported in Table 12 is the percentage of district councillors in each situation who were disposed to resolve role conflict bureaucratically or debureaucratically. Clearly, debureaucratic resolution was more widely preferred among those officials – as evidenced both by the totalled responses (bottom row in the table) and the fact that that alternative predominates in all but one situation, *4a*. At the same

[5]Viewing party politics as an even greater evil than the *status quo* in Idoma, those district councillors could not entertain campaigning either openly or clandestinely for the AG or the NCNC.

time, however, we observe a wide range of differences between situations. Whereas 81 per cent of the councillors would resolve role conflict debureaucratically in Situation *3b* (choosing not to report to higher authorities the theft of farm produce by a secret society or dance group), only 5 per cent would effect debureaucratic resolution in Situation *4a* (electing not to participate in the *ojira* assembly which chooses the district head). There is considerable variation also between related situations. While 64 per cent of the councillors were disposed to resolve role conflict debureaucratically in Situation *3a* (electing to remain active in a secret society or dance group, despite difficulty in attempting to serve as impartial peacemaker between an offending association and its angry victims), 81 per cent would effect debureaucratic resolution in Situation *3b*. Moreover, while only 5 per cent of the councillors who perceived role conflict in Situation *4a* would elect not to participate in proceedings over succession to the district headship, 59 per cent would effect the same debureaucratic resolution when faced with conflict over their role in succession to the clan headship (Situation *4b*).

Especially striking in Table 12 is the relatively high percentage of district councillors who would resolve role conflict debureaucratically in Situation *1a* and Situation *3b* and bureaucratically in Situation *4a*. In the first two, it will be recalled, those officials were inclined to perceive a hostile confrontation between apex and base in Idoma. Whereas the Native Authority leadership and its appointees were widely viewed as expecting the councillors to act bureaucratically in the case of the council hall (authorising the district head to sign the payment vouchers), local audiences tended to be seen as expecting the councillors to act debureaucratically (withholding such authorisation). In Situation *3b*, the Chief of Idoma, his colleagues on the General Purposes Committee, and their appointees were widely viewed as expecting the councillors to act bureaucratically (reporting theft by a secret society or dance group to higher authorities), while local audiences tended to be seen as holding the opposite expectation. The great majority of those councillors who saw role conflict as involving polarisation between apex and base were disposed to favour the latter and resolve it debureaucratically. It should occasion no surprise that nearly all the councillors who perceived role conflict in Situation *4a* resolved it as they did. Alert to the distinction in the popular mind between the modern district headship and the traditional clan headship, and having perceived audiences at all levels as

195

widely expecting them to participate in proceedings over succession to the former office, they were disposed to effect bureaucratic resolution. Interestingly, a substantial minority of the councillors who perceived role conflict in Situation *4b* were fully prepared to ignore the distinction between chiefly offices. They would also resolve role conflict bureaucratically in succession to the clan headship. Most of these officials were from Districts One and Four, single-clan units in

Table 13. Type of councillor and direction of role conflict resolution (percentages)

Case and conflict situation	Elected councillors' resolutions		Appointed councillors' resolutions	
	Bureau-cratic	Debureau-cratic	Bureau-cratic	Debureau-cratic
Case 1. The District Council fund Situation *1a*. The district councillor and the council hall	9	91	78	22
Number of councillors	(53)		(9)	
Case 2. Political parties Situation *2*. The district councillor and party campaigning	27	73	92	8
Number of councillors	(15)		(12)	
Case 3. Secret societies and dance groups Situation *3a*. The district councillor and activism in secret societies and dance groups	5	95	20	80
Number of councillors	(37)		(10)	
Situation *3b*. The district councillor, law enforcement, and secret societies and dance groups	6	94	77	23
Number of councillors	(51)		(13)	
Case 4. The clan head and the district head Situation *4a*. The district councillor and district head succession	97	3	86	14
Number of councillors	(30)		(7)	
Situation *4b*. The district councillor and clan head succession	59	41	50	50
Number of councillors	(41)		(10)	
Total [a]	30	70	67	33
	(227)		(61)	

Note
[a] See Table 9, note [a].

which it was the practice for one person to serve as clan head and district head.

Thus far, we have discerned a pattern of resolution of role conflict favouring the debureaucratic alternative. But contrasting patterns emerge when examining the data from another perspective, one focusing on the *type* of district councillor effecting resolution. As a group, the elected councillors were far more disposed than their appointed colleagues, the 'Native Authority councillors', to resolve role conflict debureaucratically. (See Table 13.) Whereas a majority of the elected councillors who perceived role conflict would resolve it debureaucratically in four of the six situations, the exceptions being *4a* and *4b*, such resolution was effected by a majority of the 'Native Authority councillors' in only one situation, *3a*. Among 288 perceptions of role conflict by the councillors, 227 involve elected officials, sixty-one their appointed colleagues. Differences between the two groups are significant here, the elected councillors effecting debureaucratic resolution in 70 per cent of the observations pertaining to them, the appointed councillors in only 33 per cent ($p < 0.001$). The contrasting patterns of resolution call attention to the popular view of the appointed councillors as, in the words of one Idoma elder, 'Native Authority men inside and out'.

Ambivalence and resolution

Having identified the extent to which the district councillors resolved role conflict either bureaucratically or debureaucratically in six situations, I have still briefly to analyse the relationship between two variables, ambivalence and resolution. Data relevant to the analysis are reported in Table 14. Reflected in Set 1 in the table is a tendency for the proportionate incidence of bureaucratic resolution to increase significantly with the degree of ambivalence; the *lowest* proportionate incidence of that resolution is associated with *no ambivalence*, the *highest* with *very much ambivalence*. The striking similarity in Set 1 between the reports for *some ambivalence* and *very much ambivalence* generated the analyses in Set 2 and Set 3. An insignificant relationship is found to obtain in Set 2 between the direction of resolution and the proportionate incidence of *some ambivalence* and *very much ambivalence*. Contrastingly, Set 3 reveals a significant relationship between the variable 'resolution' and reports either of no difficulty or only minimal (i.e., some) difficulty encountered in resolving role conflict.

The relationship between ambivalence and resolution of role conflict in the study can be summarised as follows. Overall, the greater the difficulty experienced by the district councillors in effecting resolution, the more inclined they were to settle on the bureaucratic alternative as the major role to be fulfilled (Set 1). Among the 156 perceived situations of conflict which were unaccompanied by ambivalence, relatively few (28 per cent) were resolved bureaucratically. Where the perception of role conflict was accompanied by ambivalence, in whatever degree, the tendency toward bureaucratic resolution increased markedly. However, the data also point up a more significant relationship between the degree of ambivalence and the tendency to resolve role conflict bureaucratically within the lower range of the three-point scale (Set 3) than within the upper range (Set 2).

Table 14. Relationship between ambivalence experienced by councillors and their resolutions (percentages)

Degree of ambivalence	Number of perceived role conflict situations	Direction of resolution Bureau-cratic	Debureau-cratic	Significance level
Set 1.				
None	156	28	72	
Some	95	56	44	
Very much	37	59	41	$p < 0.001$
Set 2.				
Some	95	56	44	
Very much	37	59	41	$p < 0.90$
Set 3.				
None	156	28	72	
Some	95	56	44	$p < 0.001$

Interestingly, among the 132 perceptions of role conflict which were accompanied either by *some ambivalence* or by *very much ambivalence*, eighty-six (65 per cent) involved the appointed district councillors. Of the eighty-six, seventy-two (84 per cent) were resolved bureaucratically by the 'Native Authority councillors'. 'Native Authority men', to be sure – but troubled 'Native Authority men'!

Early investigators of 'community power' in the United States have been sharply criticised for, among other things, tending to ignore the fact that an actor's political power is apt to vary with different issues

(Hunter 1953: 1 ff.; Wolfinger 1960: 636–44; Dahl: 1958 463–9). Rather than attempt to establish the distribution of power with regard to particular issues and policy spheres, they usually sought to assign to presumed community 'influentials' what Wolfinger (1960: 638) has termed ' "general power" rankings'. Granting the ambitiousness of their undertaking, and its novelty at the time, it still does appear that the research strategy employed by those investigators may have caused them to cast misleading light upon relationships of power among the 'influentials' and between that group and the citizenry at large.

A similar perspective, with attendant problems, is extant in the literature on role conflict in sub-Saharan Africa. Previous investigators have tended to 'generalise' the predicament confronting chiefs, village headmen, and other local functionaries by stressing the great difficulty which those actors allegedly experienced in coping with role conflict. The study of district councillorship in Idoma challenges that claim. We have seen that the difficulty which an actor experiences in resolving role conflict can vary considerably between situations and, moreover, that it can vary considerably even between actors who confront the same situation of role conflict. Taken together, the findings presented in this chapter highlight the danger of not distinguishing between the three elements in any situation of role conflict. They suggest that the failure to plumb the objective, perceptual, and subjective elements may have caused investigators to misrepresent the extent to which local functionaries in Africa were even aware of bureaucratic–debureaucratic role conflict as well as the extent to which those who were aware of such conflict experienced difficulty in resolving it.

Chapter Ten   Coping with role conflict: legitimacy, obligation, and resolution among the district councillors

Having ascertained how the district councillors resolve role conflict, our attention is drawn to another set of questions. Why do those officials effect resolution as they do? Why do they respond bureaucratically to some situations and debureaucratically to others? What determines their evaluation of a major role among contradictory expectations?

In Chapter Six, it will be recalled, various factors of social structure and personality were seen as likely to influence an actor's decision in a situation of conflict to fulfil one role-expectation and reject its opposite. It was hypothesised that an actor will fulfil the expectation of those whom he believes to be most concerned with his role behaviour (the involvement factor), most able to enforce his compliance (the power factor), and most able to oversee his performance (the observability factor); and that he will fulfil the expectation which is most compatible with the needs of his personality. Two dimensions of role conflict – legitimacy and obligation – were seen as potentially relevant to the relationship between resolution, personality, and social structure. It was hypothesised that an actor who perceives role conflict will have a personal need to fulfil the expectation which he evaluates as more legitimate and/or more obligatory. Moreover, I observed that the two dimensions of role conflict cut across the three factors of social structure. On the assumption that those who are perceived as holding legitimate and/or obligatory expectations for an actor will have some involvement in, power over, and observability of his role behaviour, it was surmised that an actor's evaluations of role legitimacy and role obligation should prove useful in predicting his resolutions. The importance of tapping both dimensions in analysis of role conflict will become evident below as I pursue these questions.

My inquiry in this chapter is organised in six sections. The first is an analysis of the relationship between the district councillors' evaluations of role legitimacy and role obligation in six objective situations of conflict. Analysed next is the relationship between those evaluations and the degree to which the councillors experienced difficulty in coping with role conflict. The various sanctions which those officials anticipated if they did not conform with particular role-expectations are examined in the third section. The relationship between role sanction and ambivalence is then analysed. In the fifth section, a predictive model is constructed to analyse the relationship between role legitimacy, role obligation, and the way role conflict was resolved by the councillors. Finally, the concept of 'role buffering' is introduced to highlight the consequences at interrelated personal and societal levels of the councillors' reliance on the major role procedure to resolve bureaucratic-debureaucratic role conflict.

Before proceeding with the analysis, it would be well to review for the reader some basic definitions and operations pertaining to three concepts – legitimacy, obligation, and sanction; their employment is illustrated here with Situation 2. The concept of legitimacy denotes belief in the rightness or propriety of specific role-expectations. Thus, the district councillor who perceived that the district head would expect him to act bureaucratically in Situation 2 was probed as follows for his evaluation of the legitimacy of that expectation: 'Do you think that the district head has a right to expect you as a councillor to campaign for the NPC in the next election?' The role-expectation was scored as legitimate if he responded affirmatively to the question; conversely, it was scored as illegitimate if he responded negatively. The councillor was then probed for his evaluation of the obligatoriness of the expectation: 'Would the district head insist that you campaign for the NPC in the next election? That is, would he punish you for not doing what he expected you to do?' If the councillor responded affirmatively to the second question, he was asked: 'How would the district head punish you if you did not behave as he expected?' Upon specifying at least one sanction, the councillor's evaluation of the role-expectation was scored as obligatory, i.e., as one which, when unfulfilled in actual behaviour, was expected to result in punitive sanctioning at the hands of the district head. Conversely, a councillor who did not expect to be punished by the district head for failing to fulfil the role-expectation, or who expected to be punished but could not specify at least one sanction, was considered to have evaluated the role-expectation as optional, i.e., as one which, regardless of conformity or nonconformity in actual behaviour, was not expected to result in punitive sanction.

Legitimacy and obligation

To analyse the relationship between role legitimacy and role obligation, seventy-one district councillors were probed in the manner described above for their evaluations of the legitimacy and obligatoriness of expectations perceived held by audiences in the six situations. The operation eventually yielded 2,332 analysable observations as follows. A total of 3,583 observations was theoretically obtainable (the number of councillors multiplied by the number of audiences in each situation).[1] Immediately excluded from the analysis, however, were the 488 perceptions by those officials that various audiences would hold no expectation(s) for their behaviour in particular situations – thereby reducing the total to 3,095. The 3,095 evaluations of role legitimacy and role obligation were subsumed in six classes:

(1) *Legitimate/obligatory*. Expectations perceived as rightful and accompanied by punitive sanction in the event of nonconformity.

(2) *Legitimate/optional*. Expectations perceived as rightful and unaccompanied by punitive sanction in the event of nonconformity.

(3) *Illegitimate/obligatory*. Expectations perceived as improper and accompanied by punitive sanction in the event of nonconformity.

(4) *Illegitimate/optional*. Expectations perceived as improper and unaccompanied by punitive sanction in the event of nonconformity.

(5) *Legitimate/obligatory/optional*. Expectations perceived as rightful and accompanied by punitive sanction at the hands of some, but not all, members of an audience in the event of nonconformity.

(6) *Illegitimate/obligatory/optional*. Expectations perceived as improper and accompanied by punitive sanction at the hands of some, but not all, members of an audience in the event of nonconformity.

To ascertain the extent of association between legitimacy and obligation, it was necessary to treat the councillors' evaluations in classes (5) and (6) as not susceptible to analysis. Classes (1) to (4), on which

[1]The total (3,583) relates to situations perceived as involving *role consensus* among audiences as well as those perceived as involving *role conflict*. A larger N is obtained for purposes of analysis by focusing on consensual and conflictual situations.

the analysis focuses, subsume 2,332 (75 per cent) of the 3,095 evaluations of role legitimacy and role obligation which were obtained from
the councillors.[2]

The phi-coefficient (Guilford 1956: 311ff.) is employed to measure
the association between role legitimacy and role obligation. Phi-
coefficients reported in Table 15 reflect relatively uniform, highly
significant correlations between the two variables in six situations.[3]
These indicate a persistent tendency by the district councillors to view
as obligatory (i.e., sanction-bearing) role-expectations which they
evaluated as legitimate; and to regard as optional (i.e., unaccompanied by punitive sanction) expectations which they deemed
illegitimate. Those officials were clearly more prone to anticipate
punishment in the event of nonconformity with role-expectations
which they evaluated as rightful than with expectations which they
regarded as improper.

Examining the data employed in computing the phi-coefficients, I
find that the district councillors were frequently disposed to evaluate
as legitimate the role-expectations which they attributed to audiences. Among the 2,332 observations analysed, fully 86 per cent
involved expectations which they viewed audiences as rightfully holding for their behaviour: 68 per cent are to be found in the first class
(*legitimate*/obligatory), 18 per cent in the second class (*legitimate*/optional). Only 14 per cent of the observations involve expectations which the councillors regarded as improper: 3 per cent of these
are in the third class (*illegitimate*/obligatory), 11 per cent in the fourth
class (*illegitimate*/optional). This is rather surprising, given, on the
one hand, the antipathy which is widely felt in rural Idoma toward
strong chieftaincy and Native Authority centralisation, and, on the
other, its consequences for bureaucratic–debureaucratic role conflict
surrounding the councillors. Under the circumstances, quite different
evaluations of role legitimacy might be anticipated. For example,
those officials might be expected to stress the illegitimacy of bureaucratic role-expectations which they attributed to the Native Authority
leadership and its subordinates and appointees outside Oturkpo
Town, viz. the district heads, 'Native Authority councillors', and tax

[2]Classes (5) and (6) were excluded because respondents who perceived division among
the elders and young men were often unable to assess how many in each audience
would sanction their deviant behaviour.

[3]Interpretation of the observed phi is relative to the maximal phi computed from
marginal sums in the contingency tables (see Table 15).

collectors. This might be anticipated especially in Situation *1a*, Situation *2*, and Situation *3b*, where those audiences were widely viewed by the councillors as expecting them to act bureaucratically – authorising the district head to sign the payment vouchers, campaigning for the governing party, and reporting the associations' transgressions to higher authorities – and where a majority of the councillors preferred to resolve role conflict debureaucratically.

Table 15. Relationship between councillors' evaluations of role legitimacy and role obligation

Case and conflict situation	N [a]	Observed phi	Maximal phi	Significance level
Case 1. The District Council fund Situation *1a*. The district councillor and the council hall	432	0·419	0·657	p < 0·001
Case 2. Political parties Situation *2*. The district councillor and party campaigning	401	0·471	0·657	p < 0·001
Case 3. Secret societies and dance groups Situation *3a*. The district councillor and activism in secret societies and dance groups	256	0·453	0·628	p < 0·001
Situation *3b*. The district councillor, law enforcement, and secret societies and dance groups	417	0·413	0·653	p < 0·001
Case 4. The clan head and the district head Situation *4a*. The district councillor and district head succession	410	0·372	0·507	p < 0·001
Situation *4b*. The district councillor and clan head succession	416	0·316	0·545	p < 0·001
Total	2,332	0·446	0·627	p < 0·001

Note
[a] See pp. 202–3.

Coping with role conflict

To shed light on their motives for evaluating role legitimacy as they did, every district councillor was asked: 'Why do you think that the (audience) (has a right) (does not have a right) to expect you to act this way?' The various considerations which dominated the councillors' responses (their tolerance of individual initiative, their appreciation of political interest and awareness of legal responsibility in particular situations, and their sense of resignation combined with fear of punishment) help explain the high incidence of legitimate expectations:

Tolerance of individual initiative:

Who will say that the district head must not expect me to work for his party? Because I do not trust parties, I will not do this thing. But who will say that he is not free to expect me to be a 'Native Authority man'?

Appreciation of political interest:

I do not blame the elders for expecting me not to take part in choosing the clan head. I am a 'boy' and they fear that the young men and the Native Authority will steal the *oche* from them. Perhaps I, too, will fear the young men and the Native Authority some day.

Awareness of legal responsibility:

I am a councillor in the Native Authority. Who will say that the *Och'Idoma* must not expect me to speak to the district head of the thieves in Odumu? I must uphold the law.

Resignation and fear of punishment:

I have seen the white man hang slavers and headhunters. And I know that the *Och'Idoma* and the district head will punish me if I do not campaign for the NPC. I have always believed that the powerful man is also a righteous man. I am too old and too timid to believe it is no longer so.

The observations of an 'old and timid man' direct our attention to yet another aspect of the data on role legitimacy and role obligation, viz. the fact that punitive sanction was seen by the district councillors as pervading their role relationships with audiences in both the locality and the Native Authority. Seventy-one per cent of the observations analysed involve role-expectations which the councillors evaluated as sanction-bearing in the event of nonconformity: 68 per cent of these are in the first class (legitimate/*obligatory*), 3 per cent in the third class (illegitimate/*obligatory*).

Throughout the field investigation, informants often drew attention to the district councillors' propensity to feel victimised by audiences disposed to punish their deviant behaviour. Comments such as these point up the problem.

An elder:

The elders will scorn Imalanyi [pseudonym] if he tells the district head to sign the vouchers [in the council hall case]. And he will incur the wrath of Omepa [pseudonym], the district head, if he warns him not to sign. Imalanyi will not serve again in the council. Only a fool or a beggar will suffer for five shillings a month.

A district councillor:

I cannot please everybody. If I campaign for the NPC, my people will rebuke me and refuse to re-elect me to the council. If I refuse to campaign, the Native Authority will destroy me. I will pay more tax, or go to jail on a trumped-up charge. It is the way in Idoma.

As I shall argue below, this preoccupation with punishment, reflected also in the councillors' evaluations of role obligation, bears directly upon 'role buffering' as practised in their relationships with various audiences.

Legitimacy, obligation and ambivalence

At the beginning of this chapter several questions were posed which drew attention to the 'why' in the resolution of conflict of roles. It was suggested that the central question – Why is such conflict resolved bureaucratically in some situations and debureaucratically in others? – might best be addressed by considering the district councillors' evaluations of role legitimacy and role obligation. With this in mind, the first step taken was to analyse the relationship between those two variables. I proceed now by inquiring of the relationship between legitimacy, obligation, and a third variable – ambivalence, i.e., the extent to which difficulty was experienced by the councillors in selecting either the bureaucratic or the debureaucratic expectation as the major role to be fulfilled.

In the previous section, the district councillors' evaluations for particular audiences of role legitimacy and role obligation were organised in six classes, four of which (legitimate/obligatory, legitimate/optional, illegitimate/obligatory, and illegitimate/optional) were then employed in analysing the relationship between the two variables. Excluded from that analysis were role-expectations which the councillors evaluated as legitimate and obligatory/optional or illegitimate and obligatory/optional, i.e., expectations which, whether deemed rightful or improper, were seen as involving punishment by some, but not all, members of an audience in the event of nonconformity. But the same strategy need not be employed in analysing the relationship between legitimacy, obligation, and ambivalence; because the analysis will be seen to involve a shift in focus from evaluations for particular audiences to evaluations aggregated for all audiences in particular situations, the data subsumed in the six classes are all easily assimilated. The shift can be illustrated as follows. Whereas previously the focus was upon whether a councillor regarded as legitimate/obligatory, legitimate/optional, illegitimate/obligatory, or illegitimate/optional the bureaucratic role-expectation which he attributed to the tax collectors in Situation *1a*, the emphasis is now upon the *profile* which emerges for conflicting bureaucratic and debureaucratic expectations from his evaluations for all audiences involved in that situation. Taken together, do those evaluations indicate: (1) that both expectations were viewed by the councillor as legitimate and obligatory? or (2) that one was viewed overall as legitimate and obligatory, the other as illegitimate and optional? or, perhaps, (3) that both expectations were viewed as legitimate and obligatory/optional, i.e., as rightful and accompanied

Table 16. Relationship between mean ambivalence and different profiles of legitimacy and obligation in perceived situations of role conflict

Profile [a]		Observations [b] N	%	Mean ambivalence [c]
1. L–Ob	L–Ob	29	10·0	1·62
2. L–Ob	L–Opt	6	2·0	1·50
3. L–Ob	I–Ob	29	10·0	2·13
4. L–Ob	I–Opt	28	9·6	1·21
5. L–Opt	L–Opt	2	0·6	1·00
6. L–Opt	I–Opt	14	4·8	1·35
7. L–Ob–Opt	L–Ob	45	15·5	1·84
8. L–Ob–Opt	L–Opt	30	10·3	1·66
9. L–Ob–Opt	I–Ob	26	8·9	1·92
10. L–Ob–Opt	I–Opt	34	11·7	1·08
11. I–Ob–Opt	L–Ob	9	3·0	1·88
12. I–Ob–Opt	L–Opt	5	1·6	1·00
13. L–Ob–Opt	L–Ob–Opt	8	2·7	2·00
14. L–Ob–Opt	I–Ob–Opt	23	8·9	2·13
Total		288	99·6	

Notes
[a] L signifies evaluation of role-expectation as legitimate; I as illegitimate; Ob as obligatory; Opt as optional.

[b] See Table 9, note [a].

[c] 1·00 = no ambivalence; 2·00 = some ambivalence; 3·00 = very much ambivalence.

by punitive sanction at the hands of some, but not all, members of audiences involved in Situation *1a* in the event of nonconformity with either role-expectation? These three profiles, among others, were reflected in the councillors' evaluations of role legitimacy and role obligation in situations which they perceived as conflictual.

Table 16 reports (1) the fourteen profiles based upon aggregated evaluations of role legitimacy and role obligation in 288 situations of conflict perceived by the district councillors; (2) the incidence of each profile among the total number of observations; and (3) the mean score of ambivalence obtained for each profile. It will be seen that no profile predominates among the evaluations, the range being less than 1 per cent where the bureaucratic and the debureaucratic role-expectations were both aggregated as legitimate and optional (number 5) to less than 16 per cent where one expectation was viewed overall as legitimate and obligatory/optional, the other as legitimate and obligatory (number 7). Also evident in the table is a tendency for mean scores of ambivalence to fall within or slightly beyond the lower range (1·00–2·00) of the three-point scale. Among the fourteen profiles, numbers 3, 13, and 14 alone attain or surpass the level (2·00) which indicates that 'some (i.e., minimal) ambivalence' was experienced by the councillors in resolving role conflict.

Examining Table 16 still further, our attention is drawn to a possible correlation between the district councillors' evaluations of role legitimacy and role obligation and the degree to which they experienced difficulty in effecting resolution. The profiles with the seven highest mean scores of ambivalence (numbers 14, 3, 13, 9, 11, 7, 8 in rank order) all involve perceptions of conflicting legitimate and/or obligatory expectations. However, among the profiles with the seven lowest scores (numbers 1, 2, 6, 4, 10, 5, 12 in rank order), only four are found to involve conflict between legitimate and/or obligatory role-expectations (numbers 1, 2, 5, 10). Three hypotheses are suggested by the contrast:

(1) that councillors' ambivalence in choosing among given role alternatives will be greater in situations of conflict which are viewed as involving two legitimate and/or obligatory expectations than in situations which are viewed as involving a single legitimate and/or obligatory expectation;

(2) that councillors' ambivalence in choosing among given role alternatives will be greater in situations of conflict which are viewed as

involving two legitimate expectations than in situations which are viewed as involving a single legitimate expectation; and

(3) that councillors' ambivalence in choosing among given role alternatives will be greater in situations of conflict which are viewed as involving two obligatory expectations than in situations which are viewed as involving a single obligatory expectation.[4]

Mean scores of ambivalence reported in Table 17 confirm all three hypotheses; but with a relatively small difference between single legitimacy and dual legitimacy (mean scores: 1·62 and 1·72 respectively). Comparing Set 2 and Set 3 in the table, we find that the district councillors are more troubled by having to choose between conflicting obligatory expectations (mean score: 1·91) than between conflicting expectations of a legitimate character (mean score: 1·72). The councillors' disposition to see their own victimisation as a corollary of the need to resolve role conflict either bureaucratically or debureaucratically has already been noted. As might be expected, the greater ambivalence which they experience in that circumstance reflects also their need somehow to mitigate the effects of seemingly inevitable punishment. Needless to say, knowing the source of the problem does not ensure a satisfactory response to it:

When I support the district head, I am rebuked and ostracised by the elders. And when I support the elders, I am rebuked by the district head and threatened with arrest. I suffer too much as a councillor. I do not yet know how to stop this suffering.

A similar lament could be heard from many councillors.

Sanction

Obligation is a corollary of social organisation. Accordingly, every society needs to instil in its members motives for regulating their behaviour in conformity with social usage. These motives are shaped for the most part by sanctions, viz. by

. . . reaction[s] on the part of a society or a considerable number of its members to . . . mode[s] of behaviour which . . . [are] thereby approved (positive sanctions) or disapproved (negative sanctions). (Radcliffe–Brown 1961: 205)

Social usages are not, of course, uniformly binding upon the individual. Whereas some of these may be regarded by the members of

[4] These hypotheses concentrate on the district councillors' report that audiences would or would not insist on fulfilment of role-expectations. While insistence predicates punishment of deviant behaviour, the analysis here does not deal with specific sanctions.

society as obligatory, involving 'rules of behaviour the failure to observe which entails a negative sanction of some sort' (*ibid.:* 205),[5] other usages may be widely construed as not obligatory. Moreover, some which are obligatory for one individual may not entail negative sanctioning of another in the event of deviant behaviour. Rankings based on prestige, wealth, and power, among other factors, may affect the obligatoriness of social usages for different individuals in society.

Table 17. Relationship between mean ambivalence, single/dual legitimacy, and single/dual obligation in perceived situations of role conflict

Profile	N [a]	Mean ambivalence [b]
Set 1.		
Single legitimacy and/or single obligation: numbers 4, 6, 10, 12	81	1·17
Dual legitimacy and/or dual obligation: numbers 1, 2, 3, 5, 7, 8, 9, 11, 13, 14	207	1·85
Set 2.		
Single legitimacy: numbers 3, 4, 6, 9, 10, 11, 12, 14	168	1·62
Dual legitimacy: numbers 1, 2, 5, 7, 8, 13	120	1·72
Set 3.		
Single obligation: numbers 2, 4, 8, 10, 12	103	1·31
Dual obligation: numbers 1, 3, 7, 9, 11, 13, 14	169	1·91

Notes
[a] Refers to 288 observations in Sets 1 and 2 (see Table 9, note [a]); and to 272 observations in Set 3, where profiles 5 and 6 (see Table 16), each with optional expectations alone, are excluded from analysis. These two profiles account for remaining sixteen observations.

[b] 1·00 = no ambivalence; 2·00 = some ambivalence; 3·00 = very much ambivalence.

I have adapted for purposes of analysis of role conflict the aforementioned distinctions – between positive (remunerative) and negative (punitive) sanctions, between obligatory role-expectations which are sanction-bearing in the event of nonconformity and optional expectations which are not, and, additionally, between sanctions which are personal (originating in and directed toward the individual) and those which are social (originating in others and directed

[5] Also see Nadel (1957: 45–62).

toward the individual). Thus far, role obligation has been analysed without referring systematically to its adjunct, role sanction. In this section, we shall focus upon the latter, specifying the content and scope of punitive-social sanctions in Idoma from the perspective of those district councillors who perceived conflict between bureaucratic and debureaucratic role-expectations.

In all, nineteen sanctions were identified by the district councillors. These are discussed here within the framework of a typology based on two criteria: *content* (referring to the substance of sanctions which the councillors anticipated in the event of nonconformity with role-expectations) and *origin* (referring to their source historically and culturally; eight sanctions are typed as 'traditional', antedating European rule in Idoma; eleven are 'modern', springing as they do from the colonial experience).

(a) Traditional sanctions

These sanctions comprise two sub-types, the first essentially supernatural, the second social. Both are rooted in a cosmology and in patterns of behaviour which antedate the colonial era.

(i) *Supernatural*

(a) 'would curse me'

This sanction was universally regarded by informants as the most powerful by far. Administered by the elders, either individually or as a group, the curse invokes the ancestors' wrath against an offending councillor (see pp. 34–5).

(b) 'would ask the elders to curse me'

An audience appeals to an elder or a group of elders to invoke the ancestors' wrath against a recalcitrant councillor.

(c) 'would levy a fine against me to appease the ancestors'

A group of elders levies the fine, in currency and/or in kind, to placate the *alekwu* which would otherwise punish a recalcitrant councillor. The fine is presented to the ancestors by ritually sacrificing some domestic animal.

(d) 'would warn me of the consequences'

A councillor who does not conform with a particular expectation is solemnly 'warned of the consequences' – an oblique reference to the fact that the ancestors will visit great misfortune upon him, perhaps by arranging his untimely death, by spreading illness among his progeny, or by rendering his wives barren.

(e) 'would make me swear an oath'

Acting on their own initiative or at the behest of another offended audience, the oath is administered by the elders as a group or by a single elder in their name. Usually sworn upon a stone or an amulet, it commits an oath-taking councillor to conform henceforth with some approved mode of behaviour. The god, *Owoicho*, or his medium, the *alekwu*, is expected to unleash malevolent forces against the councillor if ever he violates the oath.

(ii) *Social*
(a) 'would rebuke me'
This sanction is a time-honoured device now widely employed to effect conformity with an approved mode of behaviour. Rebuke is delivered in various forms, including derisive laughter, ridicule, and public telling of ancient parables which express disapprobation of some contemporary act; and either as a diffuse sanction (applied spontaneously by members of an audience as individuals) or very often as an organised sanction (applied by members of an audience in accordance with a procedure prescribed by tradition, as in an *ojira* assembly specially convened for that purpose).

(b) 'would ostracise me'
Ostracism took various forms traditionally, ranging from brief refusals to fraternise with an offending party to permanent rejection of the accursed and of other malefactors. Rejection sometimes involved exile among enemy peoples; and perhaps murder, torture, or enslavement at their hands. In contemporary Idoma, ostracism is permanent only on those infrequent occasions when the curse is invoked. It is more apt to involve refusal to fraternise with a malefactor, the duration of the sanction reflecting the gravity of the offence.

(c) 'would drive me away'
This sanction is employed in contemporary Idoma, as it was traditionally, to deny a voice in the *ojira* assembly to those deemed ineligible to participate (e.g., women, young boys, and, in the case of a secret society or dance group, non-members). The interloper is driven away by blows and/or by humiliating protests from the conferees. This need not precipitate ostracism by the community.

(b) Modern sanctions
These sanctions originate in the colonial era and reflect the development in Idoma of a centralised Native Authority organisation based on strong chieftaincy and, ostensibly, on 'council democracy'. They also comprise two sub-types, the first involving reprisals by Native Authority police and judicial authorities, the second political and administrative punishment.

(i) *Police and judicial*
(a) 'would be disciplined by Native Authority police'
The constabulary based in Oturkpo Town is widely regarded as an arm of the Native Authority leadership. Some Idoma expect it to intimidate and even physically abuse persons whose challenge to the leadership and its policies is feared or resented.

(b) 'would arrest and jail me'

The district head and the Native Authority leadership are sometimes expected to arrange the arrest of a recalcitrant councillor. The victim expects to be imprisoned in the Native Authority facility in Oturkpo Town, either without a trial or following trial on a trumped-up charge. The six Circuit Courts in Idoma are also widely regarded as an arm of the Native Authority leadership, as were the twenty-two District Courts which operated until 1961.

(ii) *Political and administrative*

(a) 'would not re-elect me'

The audience whose role-expectation is not fulfilled would inform a councillor of its intention to campaign against his re-election.

(b) 'would dismiss me from the council'

High officials in the Native Authority are sometimes expected to dismiss a recalcitrant councillor on such grounds as incompetence and poor attendance at council meetings.

(c) 'would not elect me to another office'

Various councillors aspire to the office of representative councillor, occupancy of which involves rotating membership on the General Purposes Committee. Members of the District Council, which designates that official, may refuse to support a colleague's candidacy for representative councillor.

(d) 'would not renominate me'

A 'Native Authority councillor' who opposes the district head expects the latter not to recommend his reappointment by the Native Authority leadership.

(e) 'would advise against my renomination'

Members of the District Council and others in the locality may advise the district head not to recommend the reappointment of a recalcitrant councillor.

(f) 'would report me to higher authorities for disciplining'

An audience may sanction a councillor who does not conform with a role-expectation by advising the district head or the Native Authority leadership to take disciplinary action against him. In the latter case, the representative councillor is usually requested to lay the matter before the General Purposes Committee in Oturkpo Town.

(g) 'would abandon me in the council'

District councillors may punish a colleague by refusing to support him in council deliberations.

(h) 'would hurt me in the pocket'

A councillor may expect Native Authority superiors to punish him by increasing his annual tax levy or by withholding payment of his monthly sitting fee (see p. 68, note 7, 128, note 2).

(i) 'would dismiss me from the Native Authority'

Lacking civil service protection and trade union support, a councillor may expect summary dismissal from a salaried position in the Native Authority as punishment for his recalcitrance.

Sanctions of the traditional social type are seen by the district councillors as dominating their role relationships. Thus, among the 2,983 sanctions reported by councillors who evaluated particular expectations of their audiences as obligatory in perceived situations of conflict, nearly three-quarters involve that type as follows: 'would rebuke me', 64 per cent; 'would ostracise me', 9 per cent; 'would drive me away', 1 per cent. 'Rebuke' has the widest application among the nineteen sanctions which were identified by those officials; it is attributed at least once to every audience, from rural base to Native Authority pinnacle, in all six situations of conflict. Interestingly, among its 1,913 attributions to particular audiences, fully 77 per cent are seen by the councillors as involving organised sanctions, i.e., administration of the rebuke by an *ojira* assembly convened in the locality for that purpose. 'Ostracism' is attributed at least once to every local audience – elders, young men, tax collectors, and secret society and dance group members – in five of the six situations of conflict. The third sanction in this group has a more limited scope. Various audiences are expected to 'drive away' a councillor who does not conform with the debureaucratic role alternative in Situation *4a* and Situation *4b* – where, it will be recalled, the *ojira* assembly meets to select a new district head and a new clan head, respectively, and where some audiences are viewed as expecting that official not to participate in the proceedings.

Among the modern sanctions, only one, 'would not re-elect me', has wide applicability; it is attributed at least once to every local audience in all six conflict situations.[6] But its relatively low incidence overall (only 14 per cent of the sanctions reported by the district councillors involve that punishment) underscores the councillors' recognition of a tendency in Idoma to downgrade issues in triennial

[6]Despite the high turnover among district councillors, reflecting personal frustrations and deference to the principle of rotation in the politics of succession, this sanction was widely regarded as an effective check on deviant behaviour. Even those who did not aspire to re-election were seen as wanting to avoid the humiliation of appearing unfit to serve again.

election campaigns for that office. While audiences may disapprove of an incumbent's stand on particular issues, they are not apt to stress that factor in evaluating his eligibility for re-election. The remaining modern sanctions each represent fewer than 3 per cent of the total.

A final comment is relevant here with respect to sanctions of the traditional supernatural type. These represent only 3 per cent of the total reported by the district councillors. Of the 102 sanctions in this group, sixty-one involve the expectation that the elders 'would curse' a councillor's failure to conform with a particular role alternative. As might be expected, fifty-one of the sixty-one appear where more traditional matters are in dispute: associational life in Situation *3a* and Situation *3b*, and succession to chieftaincy in Situation *4a* and Situation *4b*. The relatively low incidence of that sanction overall reflects its special character. Various councillors and informants stressed that most transgressions would not warrant so fearsome a punishment as the curse, and others noted the disruptive social consequences which would attend its invocation. The following remarks by an elder and a councillor convey these sentiments:

I will not curse Okwu [pseudonym] because he tells Abo [pseudonym] to sign the payment vouchers [in the council hall case]. My people will be angry if I do this in a small matter. I will curse the councillor only when he 'spoils the land'. Okwu will not 'spoil the land' when the people know what I must do.

My people fear the curse and the suffering it brings. The elders know that too much suffering is bad for my people. They will not curse me.

The restraint which most elders exercise with regard to the curse derives then from the awe in which it is universally held. The elders possess the authority to punish a transgressor by invoking the wrath of the ancestors. Fearing the consequences, however, few will be tempted to do so.

Sanction and ambivalence

The typology of sanctions outlined above draws attention once again to the tendency in Idoma to discriminate between 'traditional ways' and those associated with colonial rule. When discussing specific punishments, the district councillors and other informants were apt to dwell upon their Idoma ('traditional') or their European ('modern') character – stressing the origin of sanctions rather than their potency as such. More sympathetic to traditional than to modern ways of regulating social behaviour, [7] they tended to see traditional sanctions as more likely to encourage conformity with role-expectations. Even those modern sanctions whose contemplation caused the greatest anxiety among respondents – police and judicial reprisals by Native Authority superiors – were widely regarded as less likely to promote conformity than traditional punishments of either a supernatural or a social character. In view of the above, I decided to adapt the *typology of sanctions* for an analysis of the relationship between role sanction and ambivalence. I employed the following procedure.

Profiles of sanctions were constructed for the bureaucratic and the debureaucratic role-expectation in each perceived situation of conflict by aggregating the *type(s) of punitive sanction(s)* which the district councillors had attributed to various audiences. For example, Olo Itodo (pseudonym) had reported (1) that the elders would curse him (a sanction of the traditional supernatural type) for not refusing to authorise the district head to sign the payment vouchers in the council-hall case (i.e., for not fulfilling the debureaucratic expectation in Situation *1a*); (2) that both the young men and the elected councillors would rebuke him (a sanction of the traditional social type) for not acting debureaucratically in that situation; and (3) that the remaining audiences would rebuke him (a sanction of the traditional social type) for refusing to authorise the district head to sign the vouchers (i.e., for not fulfilling the bureaucratic expectation in Situation *1a*). This report by Itodo can be seen as involving *different profiles of sanctions*. First, there is a profile of sanctions of the *traditional supernatural and traditional social types* ('would curse me' and 'would rebuke me') for the debureaucratic expectation which Itodo perceived the elders, young men, and elected councillors as holding for his behaviour in Situation *1a*. Second, there is a profile of sanctions of the *traditional social type* ('would rebuke me') for the bureaucratic expectation which he perceived the remaining audiences as holding for his behaviour in that situation.

Another district councillor, Ija Edikwu (pseudonym), had reported (1) that both the elders and young men would ostracise him (a sanction of the traditional social type) and refuse to re-elect him (a sanction of the modern political and administrative type) for not acting debureaucratically in Situation *1a*; (2) that the district head would rebuke him (a sanction of the traditional social type) and increase his

[7]Many Idoma were especially critical of the modern police and judicial sanctions, regarding them as unjust props of the Native Authority's arbitrary power.

Table 18. Profiles of sanctions in perceived situations of role conflict

Profile		N [a]
(a) Two profiles: same [b] (each involving obligatory role-expectations)		
	2–2	58
	4–4	9
	9–9	30
(b) Two profiles: different [b] (each involving obligatory role-expectations)		
	2–5	7
	2–6	6
	2–7	2
	2–8	5
	2–9	28
	2–10	7
	2–11	2
	4–6	1
	4–9	1
	6–9	16
	7–9	2
	9–10	5
(c) One profile [c]		
	1–#	1
	2–#	25
	3–#	1
	5–#	3
	6–#	19
	7–#	3
	8–#	4
	9–#	32
	10–#	4
(d) No profiles [d]		17

Notes

[a] Refers to 288 observations in the analysis (see Table 9, note [a]).
[b] Numbers separated by hyphens reflect numbers employed on p. 218 to identify eleven basic profiles of sanctions.
[c] Refers to perceived situations of role conflict where only one expectation was evaluated as obligatory. Numbers preceding hyphens reflect profile numbers on p. 218.
[d] Refers to perceived situations of role conflict where both expectations were evaluated as optional.

annual tax levy (a sanction of the modern political and administrative type) for not acting bureaucratically in that situation; and (3) that the remaining audiences would hold no expectation for his behaviour in Situation *1a*. This report by Edikwu can be seen as involving the *same profile of sanctions*. A profile of sanctions of the *traditional social and modern political and administrative types* is formed here by two sanctions which he attributed to both the elders and young men ('would ostracise me' and 'would not re-elect me'). The same profile of sanctions of the *traditional social and modern political and administrative types* is formed by two other sanctions which he attributed to the district head ('would rebuke me' and 'would hurt me in the pocket'). By definition, the construction of these profiles is unaffected by audiences which Edikwu perceived as holding no expectation for his behaviour.

Profiles of sanctions were constructed in this way for each of the 288 situations of role conflict which were perceived by the district councillors. The councillors' evaluations of role sanction in these situations yielded eleven basic profiles organised around individual sanctions of:

(1)   the traditional supernatural type;

(2)   the traditional social type;

(3)   the modern police and judicial type;

(4)   the modern political and administrative type;

(5)   the traditional supernatural and traditional social types;

(6)   the traditional supernatural, traditional social, and modern political and administrative types;

(7)   the traditional supernatural, traditional social, modern police and judicial, and modern political and administrative types;

(8)   the traditional social and modern police and judicial types;

(9)   the traditional social and modern political and administrative types;

(10)   the traditional social, modern police and judicial, and modern political and administrative types; and

(11)   the modern police and judicial and modern political and administrative types.

By definition, perceived situations of role conflict involve: (*a*) the same profile of sanctions (denoting obligatory bureaucratic and debureaucratic expectations)[8]; (*b*) different profiles of sanctions

---

[8] I stress that profiles of sanctions are constructed from the typology of sanctions in the preceding section, *not* from individual sanctions as such. Consequently, the same profile constructed for a particular situation of conflicting obligatory expectations may or may not be organised around the same individual sanctions. Two possibilities are illustrated here. (1) A district councillor may perceive the bureaucratic role-expectation held by various audiences as supported by two sanctions of the *modern political and administrative type* ('would hurt me in the pocket' and 'would dismiss me from the Native Authority'), the debureaucratic role-expectation held by other audi-

(denoting obligatory bureaucratic and debureaucratic expectations)[9]; (c) one profile of sanctions (denoting one obligatory expectation, bureaucratic or debureaucratic, and one optional expectation); or (d) no profiles of sanctions (denoting optional bureaucratic and debureaucratic expectations). Table 18 reports in categories (a), (b), (c), and (d) the distribution of the eleven profiles. For example, fifty-eight perceptions of role conflict in category (a) involve two obligatory expectations associated with the same profile of sanctions of the traditional social type (represented in the table as 2–2); in category (b), six perceptions of role conflict involve two obligatory expectations, one associated with the profile of sanctions of the traditional social type, the other with the profile of sanctions of the traditional supernatural, traditional social, and modern political and administrative types (represented in the table as 2–6). Categories (c) and (d) in the table relate to situations of conflict which were perceived by the councillors as involving, in the former, only one obligatory expectation, and, in the latter, no obligatory expectations.

The data in Table 18 underscore the observation made on p. 214 that sanctions of the traditional social type are seen by the district councillors as dominating their role relationships. Thus, 166 of the 179 perceived situations of conflict in categories (a) and (b) involve obligatory expectations whose two profiles of sanctions include punishments of the traditional social type. (The thirteen exceptions are represented in the table as 4–4 in category (a), as 2–11, 4–6, and 4–9 in category (b).) The same pattern occurs in category (c), where perceived situations of conflict involve only one obligatory expectation: ninety of the ninety-two situations in that category involve a profile of sanctions which includes punishments of the traditional social type. (The two exceptions are represented in the table as 1–# and 3–#.) Overall, 256 of the 271 perceived situations of conflict in the three categories involve punishments of that type.

ences as supported by two other sanctions of the *modern political and administrative type* ('would not re-elect me' and 'would abandon me in the council'). *Different sanctions* of the *same type* can be seen here as yielding the *same profile of sanctions* for conflicting expectations: *modern political and administrative* versus *modern political and administrative*. (2) Another councillor may perceive both the bureaucratic and the debureaucratic role-expectations held by different audiences as supported by the same two sanctions of the *traditional supernatural type* ('would curse me' and 'would make me swear an oath'). The *same sanctions* of the *same type* can be seen here as yielding the *same profile of sanctions* for conflicting expectations: *traditional supernatural* versus *traditional supernatural*.

[9]See the example of Olo Itodo and the council hall case on p. 216.

Modern sanctions (police and judicial, political and administrative) are less widely distributed in Table 18 than are traditional sanctions. This is to be expected, given the fact that the district councillors and other informants had usually stressed the greater importance of traditional sanctions generally and of sanctions of the traditional social type in particular. Only sixty-four of the 179 perceived situations of conflict in categories (a) and (b) involve obligatory expectations whose two profiles of sanctions include modern punishments. (The sixty-four situations are represented in the table as 4–4 and 9–9 in category (a), as 4–6, 4–9, 6–9, 7–9, and 9–10 in category (b).) Sixty-three of the ninety-two situations in category (c) involve a profile of sanctions which includes modern punishments. (The exceptions are represented in the table as 1–#, 2–#, and 5–#.) Overall, 177 of the 271 perceived situations of conflict in the three categories involve such punishments.

Having constructed eleven basic profiles of sanctions, and having examined aspects of their distribution, we now turn to the relationship between role sanction and ambivalence. That relationship is

Table 19. Relationship between ambivalence and profiles of sanctions in perceived situations of role conflict

Degree of ambivalence	(a) Same [a]		(b) Different [a]	
	2–2, 9–9	4–4,	2–5, 2–6, 2–7, 2–8, 2–9, 2–10, 2–11, 4–6, 4–9, 6–9, 7–9, 9–10	
	N [b]	%	N [b]	%
None	15	15	41	50
Some	57	59	29	35
Very much	25	26	12	15
Total	97	100	82	100
Mean ambivalence [c]	2·10		1·74	

Notes
[a] See Table 18, note [b].
[b] Refers to perceived situations of role conflict in these two categories of profiles.
[c] 1·00 = no ambivalence; 2·00 = some ambivalence; 3·00 = very much ambivalence.

analysed here with categories (*a*) and (*b*), i.e., in perceived situations of conflict involving two profiles of sanctions. In view of the tendency in Idoma to stress the origin of individual sanctions when distinguishing between them ('traditional' Idoma or 'modern' European), it is reasonable to expect that the degree of ambivalence which the district councillors experience in resolving role conflict will be related to their ability to distinguish also between groups of sanctions. For example, it is anticipated that councillors who perceive conflict between two obligatory expectations associated with the same profile of sanctions of the modern political and administrative type will experience greater difficulty deciding which expectation to fulfil than councillors who perceive conflict between two obligatory expectations one of which is associated with the profile of sanctions of the modern political and administrative type, the other with the profile of sanctions of the traditional social type. Accordingly, it is hypothesised that the councillor will experience greater ambivalence when he perceives conflicting expectations to be supported by the same types (profiles) of sanctions than when he perceives them to be supported by different types (profiles) of sanctions. Mean scores of ambivalence reported in Table 19 lend support to the hypothesis, as do the data on ambivalence reported in the upper portion of the table.[10]

A final observation is pertinent here on the relationship between role sanction and ambivalence. Consistently with our reasoning above, viz. that decision-making is apt to be fuller of stress where the options are less clearly defined, we might also expect to encounter the following: that difficulty in resolving role conflict will be greater where the district councillors face expectations which they regard as optional (category *d*), viz. as indistinguishable by profiles of sanctions, than where different profiles of sanctions are associated with two obligatory expectations (category *b*) or where one expectation is evaluated overall as obligatory and sanction-bearing, the other as optional (category *c*). But the mean scores of ambivalence obtained in the four categories do not fully bear this out:

(*a*)   2·10 on the three-point scale ($N = 97$)

(*b*)   1·74 ($N = 82$)

---

[10] Not unexpectedly, mean scores of ambivalence for categories (*c*) and (*d*) in Table 18 are lower than those for categories (*a*) and (*b*) in Table 19: (*a*) 2·10; (*b*) 1·74; (*c*) 1·04; (*d*) 1·13. Greater ambivalence is anticipated in situations involving choice among two obligatory expectations (categories *a* and *b*) than in situations involving only one obligatory expectation (category *c*) or no obligatory expectations (category *d*).

(c) 1·04 (N = 92)
(d) 1·13 (N = 17)

(N, totalling 288, refers to the number of situations in each category which the councillors perceived as conflictual.) As expected, a (slightly) higher score is obtained in category (d) than in category (c). But the score in category (d) falls considerably short of that in category (b). How to explain the apparent anomaly? Our attention is drawn once again to the councillors' preoccupation with punishment. Operating in a social milieu which seemed to them harsh and threatening, those officials were understandably prone to regard the opportunity to choose between conflicting *optional* expectations not as anxiety-inducing, but as a boon. They were apt to experience little or no ambivalence on those infrequent occasions when they felt themselves able to resolve role conflict either bureaucratically or debureaucratically with impunity. As one councillor put it, 'Only a foolish man will say he is in trouble when there is no one to punish him. I have not met such foolish men.'

Predicting resolution of role conflict

Hypotheses and operational definitions

Our task now is to analyse the relationship between role legitimacy, role obligation, and the way the district councillors resolved role conflict – that is to say, to highlight the link between their evaluations of the legitimacy and obligatoriness of conflicting expectations in particular situations and their selection ultimately of the bureaucratic or the debureaucratic alternative as the major role to be fulfilled (Magid 1967: 331–5). Three hypotheses constitute the focus of the analysis:

(1) that a councillor who perceives role conflict will fulfil the expectation which he evaluates as more legitimate;

(2) that a councillor who perceives role conflict will fulfil the expectation which he evaluates as more obligatory; and

(3) that a councillor who perceives role conflict will fulfil the expectation which he evaluates as more legitimate and more obligatory.

The analysis of the relationship between legitimacy, obligation, and direction of resolution is based upon these operational definitions: the degree of legitimacy and/or obligation is represented by the total number of times in a perceived situation of conflict that a district councillor evaluates an audience's expectation as legitimate and/or obligatory. For example, the bureaucratic expectation is construed as *more legitimate* in Situation *1a* if the councillor indicates that *more audiences rightfully hold it* than the debureaucratic expectation, viz. that the number of audiences who rightfully expect the councillor to authorise the district head to sign the payment vouchers in the case of the council-hall exceeds the number who rightfully hold the opposite expectation. Analogously, the bureaucratic expectation is construed as *more obligatory* in that situation if the councillor indicates that *more audiences would insist on fulfilment of it* than the debureaucratic expectation. More legitimate and more obligatory expectations need not, of course, coincide.[11]

At this juncture, a caveat ought to be noted. The operational definitions predicate a distinction between audiences in the majority and those in the minority. The analysis does *not* encompass the number and/or size of audiences in either. Moreover, the degree of obligation is *not* synonymous with the number and/or type and/or potency of sanctions anticipated for deviant behaviour. For example, the audience consisting of the Chief of Idoma and his colleagues on the General Purposes Committee, to whom the district councillor attributes the bureaucratic expectation in Situation *1a*, may constitute a minority with respect to the remaining audiences to whom he attributes the debureaucratic expectation. The councillor may evaluate *both* expectations as *legitimate* (rightful) and *obligatory* (supported by punitive sanction). In that event, he may choose to fulfil the expectation of the more threatening audience, the Chief and the Committee.[12] Nevertheless, the predictive model which I am employing here assumes that the behaviour of an actor is related to his ability to discriminate between majority and minority audiences holding obligatory and/or optional expectations.

Analysis

The analysis involves ascertaining the proportionate incidence of correct predictions of resolution of role conflict from degree of legitimacy, obligation, and legitimacy and obligation combined; and the

[11]In this study the coincidence of more legitimate and more obligatory expectations is anticipated by the relatively high incidence of legitimate/obligatory and illegitimate/optional expectations (see pp. 203–4).

[12]Feelings of threat could be engendered by fear of particular sanctions, persistence of the audience, etc.

proportionate incidence of correct predictions expected by chance alone. The procedures utilised are again illustrated with Situation *1a*: 2 × 2 contingency tables were generated for predictions from legitimacy (Figure *2a*), obligation (Figure *2b*), and legitimacy and obligation combined (Figure *2c*). Each table includes two variables, the direction of resolution *predicted for* and *reported by* the district councillors. Sixty-two councillors (87 per cent of those interviewed) perceived bureaucratic-debureaucratic role conflict in Situation *1a*.

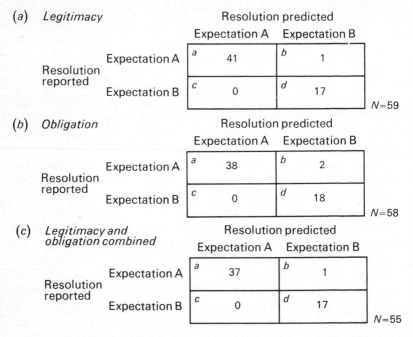

Fig. 2. Resolution reported by district councillors in Situation *1a*, and resolution predicted from legitimacy, obligation, and legitimacy and obligation combined. Cells are lettered to facilitate discussion in the text

Within that group, fifty-nine indicated that either A or B – for my purposes here, it is not necessary to specify whether these correspond to the bureaucratic or the debureaucratic role alternative – was the *more legitimate* expectation, fifty-eight that either *A* or *B* was the *more obligatory* expectation. Fifty-five councillors indicated that either *A* or *B* was the *more legitimate and more obligatory* expectation.

Excluded from the analysis are those district councillors who, while perceiving role conflict, did *not* evaluate expectation *A* or *B* as more legitimate (three councillors), more obligatory (four councillors), or more legitimate and more obligatory (seven councillors). (See pp. 249–51.) The number (*N*) used in the analysis was obtained by subtracting the number of councillors excluded from the number who perceived role conflict in Situation *1a*.

The proportion of correct predictions was obtained by computing $(a + d)/N$ in Figures *2a*, *2b*, and *2c*. The proportion of correct predictions expected by chance was obtained by computing

$$\frac{\dfrac{(a+b)\ (a+c)}{N} + \dfrac{(c+d)\ (b+d)}{N}}{N}$$

for each contingency table.

Results

Table 20 reports the results obtained from analysis of the six situations of conflict. It is evident from the table that there is a uniformly high proportion of correct predictions of resolution of role conflict from degree of legitimacy, obligation, and legitimacy and obligation combined, with the range for correct predictions in the six situations 0·842 to 1·000; the proportion of correct predictions exceeds 0·900 in every instance but three, Situation *2* (legitimacy, obligation) and Situation *4b* (legitimacy). Overall proportions (*Total* column) are 0·934 for legitimacy, 0·964 for obligation, and 0·978 for legitimacy and obligation combined. In all cases, the proportion of correct predictions is significantly beyond chance expectancy.[13]

The model based on two operationalised concepts – legitimacy and obligation – has thus facilitated predicting resolving behaviour. As hypothesised, when experiencing bureaucratic–debureaucratic cross-pressures, the district councillors are apt to respond by fulfilling the more legitimate and/or more obligatory role-expectation.

'Role buffering' in resolution of role conflict: a serendipitous finding

The district councillors' propensity to resolve role conflict by selecting either the bureaucratic or the debureaucratic expectation as the major role to be fulfilled has been examined both conceptually and

---

[13]Chi-squares and Fisher exact probabilities computed for the twenty-one contingency tables are all significant at the 0·003 level.

Table 20. Proportionate incidence of correct predictions of role conflict resolution and correct predictions expected by chance

Bases for prediction	Role conflict situation						
	1a	2	3a	3b	4a	4b	Total
Councillors perceiving role conflict[a]	62	27	47	64	51	37	288
Legitimacy							
N[b]	59	24	41	61	51	37	273
Correct predictions	0·983	0·875	0·975	0·934	0·902	0·892	0·934
Chance expectancy	0·583	0·516	0·556	0·597	0·506	0·800	0·506
Obligation							
N[b]	58	19	35	59	49	36	256
Correct predictions	0·965	0·842	1·000	0·949	0·979	1·000	0·964
Chance expectancy	0·558	0·631	0·558	0·565	0·510	0·894	0·503
Legitimacy and obligation combined							
N[b]	55	17	30	55	45	33	235
Correct predictions	0·982	0·941	1·000	0·963	0·978	1·000	0·978
Chance expectancy	0·502	0·670	0·606	0·602	0·502	0·885	0·505

Notes
[a] See Table 9, note [a].
[b] Refers to councillors in each situation whose evaluations indicated that A or B was the *more legitimate, more obligatory,* or *more legitimate and more obligatory* expectation, respectively. In the last column, 273 is 95 per cent of 288 perceived situations of role conflict; 256 is 89 per cent; and 235 is 82 per cent.

empirically. Still to be considered, however, are the consequences attending their reliance on that strategy.

The councillors' preference for the major role procedure in effecting resolution had important consequences at interrelated personal and societal levels. At the personal level, I have argued, those officials displayed a preoccupation with punishment at the hands of audiences. The following general comments by various councillors provide additional evidence of the widespread sensitivity to punitive sanction:

There are always differences over my actions. Elders and young men differ. Councillors and the *Och'Idoma* differ. But it is I who must suffer rebuke.

I will not be a councillor again. I suffer too much at the hands of my people.

Elected councillors call me a 'spy' when I support the *Och'Idoma*. They distrust me because I am a 'Native Authority councillor'.

Ironically, the district councillors bore some responsibility for the punishment which they fearfully anticipated. A relatively high incidence of obligatory expectations in situations of role conflict together with their reliance on a single procedure for resolution virtually ensured that fate. Apparently unwilling or unable to entertain more accommodating resolving behaviour (e.g., compromise, procrastination, or withdrawal in the form of resignation from office), they faced a common 'dilemma': choice between behavioural alternatives – the bureaucratic or the debureaucratic expectation – whose non-fulfilment, the councillors believed, would cause them to be punished.

At the same time, reliance on the major role procedure tended to exacerbate bureaucratic–debureaucratic tension in Idoma. The district councillors' decision to fulfil a role-expectation which promoted bureaucratisation involved their rejection of a role-expectation which favoured debureaucratisation, and *vice versa*. Resolution of role conflict on the basis of acceptance–rejection tended to encourage the movement of different social elements in opposite directions: tax collectors, 'Native Authority councillors', representative councillors, and district heads were pulled to a Native Authority leadership committed in fact to strong chieftaincy and centralised local government; and elected district councillors were drawn to elders and young men who generally preferred democratic rule along the lines of the traditional *ojira* assembly. That development intensified conflict in councillors' roles.

More accommodating behaviour by the 'men in the middle' might have helped to lessen the intensity of such conflict. But in post-independence Idoma, an accommodating outlook (especially willingness to compromise) was usually abandoned in contests between seemingly irreconcilable interests. The society was straining toward polarisation. Quick to 'join sides', as it were, the insufficiently flexible district councillors were at once contributors to, and victims of, polarisation.

Reliance on the major role procedure was a costly strategy for resolution.[14] Whether they acted bureaucratically or debureaucratically in particular situations of conflict, the district councillors were apt to foster polarisation in Idoma and, concomitantly, their own punishment by offended audiences. The process was depressingly

---

[14]Some 'payoffs' are examined on pp. 247–9.

circular: increasing polarisation between Native Authority pinnacle and rural base intensified councillors' role conflict; role conflict, where perceived, was resolved bureaucratically or debureaucratically, often precipitating punishment; and resolution of role conflict tended to promote polarisation. As I shall show presently, the circle was drawn still tighter by 'role buffering' in the councillors' role relationships.

'Role buffering'

Supported by a powerful regional government, and encountering no serious party opposition, the Native Authority leadership could reasonably hope to prevail over disaffected, albeit fragmented, local elements and their leaders on the District Councils. As those elements became increasingly aware of their own ineffectualness *vis-à-vis* Oturkpo Town and the district heads, and also that of the elected councillors, the popular mood turned bitter and despairing. That mood is perhaps best conveyed by contrasting developments in Idoma with those taking place contemporaneously among the neighbouring Tiv. Widespread dissatisfaction with the *status quo* in Tivland took a violent turn in 1960. A popular uprising against the Chief (known as the *Tor'Tiv*) and his supporters resulted in much bloodshed and destruction of property. Following suppression of the revolt, a substantial fine was levied collectively upon the Tiv and the District Officer was authorised by the Northern Region Government to act as Sole Native Authority in place of the *Tor'Tiv* and his administration (Dent 1966: 461–507; 1971: 448–62). That arrangement continued for several years and made a great impression upon the Idoma. In 1963, when the field investigation was in progress, few Idoma could be found contemplating or desiring a 'Tiv solution' – open rebellion – in their own province. As one informant put it, 'We know better than to be like the Tiv. Kaduna would punish us severely these days for such foolishness'.

As might be expected where violence and orderly change were regarded either as undesirable or infeasible, pent-up hostility eventually found its outlet. Frustration gave rise to aggression (Dollard *et al*. 1945: 1ff.). But unlike among the Tiv, the aggression was not directed mainly to the Native Authority leadership, the district heads, and their supporters, but instead was displaced primarily upon the 'men in the middle' whose leading stand against chiefly power and Native Authority centralisation helped to promote cleavage, but without altering the *status quo*. The district councillors were convenient scapegoats for disaffected elders and young men in the localities.[15] Significantly, neither the practitioners of such displacement nor its victims were confined to the rural base of Idoma society. Frustrated in its efforts to dispel a hostile popular mood; harassed by ambitious politicians both within and outside the division and by a regional government dissatisfied with certain Native Authority operations; and concerned lest a 'Tiv solution' be attempted some day by desperate elements in Idoma, the Native Authority leadership, too, had need of scapegoats. They were usually to be found among the district heads.

The practice of scapegoating as described briefly above is adapted here for analysis of role conflict by introducting a new concept, 'role buffering' – which refers to an audience's decision to punish not the individual(s) who fail(s) to conform with its role-expectation(s), but another individual (or group). The scapegoat acts as a 'buffer' by absorbing in some measure the impact of role conflict surrounding the nonconformist.[16] I describe first how that behaviour was first encountered.

Early in my field investigation I held discussions with numerous informants throughout Idoma mainly for two reasons: first, to begin building the mutual confidence and rapport on which the study had ultimately to depend, and second, to gather background material on bureaucratic–debureaucratic role conflict. These peripatetic discussions provided me with a 'feel', as it were, for the condition of the 'men in the middle', and also constituted an input when deciding which situations of conflict to analyse.

Many of the discussions revolved around the district councillors' preoccupation with punishment and their experience with scapegoating in the form of 'role buffering'. When detailing that practice, informants were apt also to draw attention to its wide scope and implications. District heads were portrayed as occasionally suffering similar distress. And it was reported, moreover, that the victims of 'role buffering' were neither local government officials exclusively nor, for that matter, necessarily 'living' Idoma. The ancestors were sometimes castigated by audiences on the grounds that they had

[15]Rowley (1965: 83) notes a similar situation in New Guinea.

[16]Notwithstanding the *inter-positional* structuring involved here, the term '*role* buffering' is preferred over '*position* buffering'. 'Buffering' emphasises *sanction*, which is a dimension of *role* rather than of *position* in the social structure.

withheld wise counsel from errant officials; scapegoating of this kind was said to occur in exceptional circumstances – where, for example, desperate men felt powerless to enforce conformity with their role-expectation(s). Finally, evidence was also gathered of 'role buffering' helping to shield or bolster some officials even as it was claiming its victims. Hoping to achieve that political objective, individuals sometimes volunteered to act as scapegoats.

Among elements outside the Native Authority, those most vulnerable to 'role buffering' were elders who had been instrumental in securing the election of candidates to the District Council. Embittered audiences might respond to a councillor's failure to conform with their role-expectation(s) by turning on his patrons. In this vein, one councillor observed that

my uncle, the senior elder, is always rebuked by the *ojira* when I must support the district head. But the *ojira* fears the district head's wrath and will do nothing to me. It will appeal to the elder, because the people still esteem his wisdom and his integrity. If I stand again for the council, the *ojira* will rebuke my uncle for supporting me, but it will not refuse to re-elect me. He is my patron.

In the case just mentioned, 'role buffering' was employed by the *ojira* assembly in the hope of turning the senior elder against his own protege. The strategy failed, leaving the offending councillor virtually free to disregard his constituents' views when dealing with the district head.

But offenders were not alone in capitalising on 'role buffering'. Recognising that it might also be manipulated to the victims' advantage, elders (and others) occasionally pursued some political interest by deliberately drawing hostile fire to themselves – as evidenced by the following case:

My people are pleased when Okwuli [pseudonym], the elected councillor, attacks the district head in the council. The 'Native Authority councillor', Agbada [pseudonym], will not denounce Okwuli's boldness because it will anger my people. Instead he comes to my compound to denounce me as a foolish old man because I do not rebuke Okwuli. He threatens to report me to the *Och'Idoma*. I ridicule Agbada for 'drinking Native Authority milk'. Agbada is the foolish man. He does not see that I encourage his insults. I speak to Okwuli of these insults and they anger Okwuli and embolden him. My people will resist the Native Authority and its lackeys. Okwuli will attack the district head in the council.

Thirty-eight cases of 'role buffering' in all were detailed by informants. Among these, the most intriguing by far were the half dozen which involved *dual conflict of roles*, i.e., conflict in two interrelated situations, each with a different focal actor. While 'role buffering' was said to take place usually where a single situation of role conflict obtained, i.e., where only one focal actor was involved, various informants also noted its occurrence where the district councillor and the district head each faced bureaucratic–debureaucratic cross-pressures in separate, albeit closely related, situations. A curious pattern of role interaction was reportedly organised around scapegoating in the latter circumstance. According to informants, the two officials unintentionally shielded each other from hostile audiences, the councillor by incurring the sanction of various constituents, the district head by receiving punishment from his superiors in Oturkpo Town. Despite this, 'role buffering' in the two situations was seen as redounding to the disadvantage of the councillor – the district head supposedly being encouraged by it to punish his subordinate's failure to conform with bureaucratic role-expectations. Unanticipated, this scenario appeared to me to merit further examination.

Among the six cases alluded to above of 'role buffering' involving dual role conflict, one drew attention to both those officials caught up in a bitter dispute over the construction of a District Council hall. The decision was taken, accordingly, to incorporate that dispute into the study as the backdrop to two situations of conflict in Case I – where, it will be recalled, the district councillor faced conflicting role-expectations with regard to his authorising the district head to sign payment vouchers accelerating completion of the facility (Situation *1a*) and where the district head confronted similar conflict with regard to his eventually signing those documents (Situation *1b*). The connection between 'role buffering' in the two situations, and its negative implications for the councillors, may both be illuminated by analysing the councillors' role perceptions in the council hall case and their evaluations of role obligation.

Role conflict was associated more frequently with the district councillor than with the district head. Whereas sixty-two councillors (87 per cent of those interviewed) perceived themselves as facing conflicting expectations in Situation *1a*, only forty-five (63 per cent) viewed the district head as experiencing role conflict in Situation *1b*. Moreover, the district head was regarded as more likely than the councillor to resolve role conflict bureaucratically. Among the forty-five councillors who perceived Situation *1b* as conflictual, 78 per cent opined that the district head would sign the vouchers; only 29 per cent of the sixty-two councillors who perceived role conflict in Situation *1a* said that they would resolve it by authorising him to take that action. In all five districts on which the study concentrates, a council majority expected the district head to ignore its mandate and comply instead with the General Purposes Committee's directive to sign the vouchers. Finally, the councillor was viewed as more likely than the district head to suffer punishment for deviant behaviour. (See Table 21.) Fully 70 per cent of the role-expectations which the councillors attributed to various audiences in Situation *1a* were regarded by those officials as sanction-bearing in the event of their not conforming. In Situation *1b*, however, only 33 per cent of the role-expectations which they attributed to audiences were regarded as sanction-bearing in the event of nonconformity by the district head.[17]

A common thread connects all these findings – one formed of powerlessness and despair. Together they underscore what had often been conveyed to me about the district councillors' condition and what first-hand observation had repeatedly affirmed: that those officials were indeed 'men in the middle'; that they were less efficacious, more frustrated, and more obsessed with punishment than the district head who, enjoying the support of Oturkpo Town, continued to dominate district affairs; that they were also ill-suited, despite their

Table 21. Incidence of combinations of role legitimacy and role obligation in Case 1 (percentages)

Conflict situation	N [a]	Combination [b]				Total %
		L-Ob	L-Opt	I-Ob	I-Opt	
1a. The district councillor and the council hall	432	67	19	3	11	100
1b. The district head and the council hall	343	23	11	10	55	99

Notes
[a] See pp. 202–3; and Table 15, Situation *1a*.
[b] *L* signifies evaluation of role-expectation as legitimate; *I* as illegitimate; *Ob* as obligatory; *Opt* as optional.

[17]The phi-coefficient was employed to measure the extent of association between the district councillors' evaluations of role legitimacy and role obligation in Situation *1b*: observed phi, 0·525; maximal phi, 0·968; $p < 0.001$. This finding is consistent with the highly significant correlations obtained in the other situations (see pp 203–6).

prestige as local leaders and their debureaucratic proclivities, to spearhead a popular drive against strong chieftaincy and centralised political authority.[18] And adding to the councillors' burden, as I shall show, was 'role buffering' in such cases as that involving the council hall.

Concerned as I am in Case 1 with 'role buffering' involving dual role conflict, I now draw attention to the forty-four district councillors (all but five elected to office) who perceived Situation *1a* and Situation *1b* as conflictual. Of particular interest here are the role-expectations which they attributed to various audiences in the two situations; and also their evaluations of role obligation. Fifteen councillors in that group (34 per cent) reported that all the elders and young men in the *ojira* assembly would expect the appropriate officials to act debureaucratically in the council hall case – the councillor by refusing to authorise signing of the payment vouchers, the district head by acceding to the council majority. Twenty-four councillors (55 per cent) saw a majority of the elders and young men as taking the same position. And five councillors (11 per cent) – all appointed to office – reported that the *ojira* would unanimously expect the councillor and the district head to act bureaucratically in the matter.

A quite different pattern obtains, however, for audiences at the middle and upper levels of the Native Authority – pointing up once again the strain between apex and base in Idoma. Forty-one of the forty-four district councillors (93 per cent) reported that the district head would expect them to act bureaucratically in Situation *1a*; and all forty-four councillors reported that the Native Authority leadership in Oturkpo Town would expect the councillor and the district head to act bureaucratically in Situation *1a* and Situation *1b* respectively.

Distinct patterns also obtain with regard to role obligation. Thirty-eight of the thirty-nine district councillors (97 per cent) who reported that all (or a majority of) the elders and young men would expect them to act debureaucratically in Situation *1a* observed that those elements would punish the councillor for authorising the dis-

---

[18]Most district councillors attributed their weak leadership to their rural isolation (which combined with the widespread aversion to party politics to preclude the organisation of dissent across district lines) and their limited official powers (which made them dependent on goodwill in Oturkpo Town).

trict head to sign the vouchers.[19] All five councillors who reported that those audiences would unanimously expect the councillor to act bureaucratically in the matter also construed the role-expectation as obligatory. Essentially the same evaluations were recorded for the district head audience. Thus, thirty-eight of the forty-one councillors (93 per cent) who reported that the district head would expect them to act bureaucratically in Situation 1a proceeded to evaluate the role-expectation as obligatory. Among the four audiences on which the discussion centres, the most striking finding involves the Chief of Idoma and his colleagues on the General Purposes Committee. Only two of the forty-four councillors (5 per cent) who perceived the Native Authority leadership as expecting them to act bureaucratically in Situation 1a reported that that audience would punish the councillor for refusing to authorise the district head to sign the vouchers.

But the pattern of evaluations was reversed for the four audiences in Situation 1b. Thus, thirty-six of the thirty-nine district councillors (92 per cent) who reported that all (or a majority of) the elders and young men would expect the district head to act debureaucratically in that situation observed that the two audiences would not punish the district head for signing the payment vouchers.[20] The five 'Native Authority councillors' who reported that the *ojira* assembly would unanimously expect the district head to act bureaucratically in Situation 1b also construed the role-expectation as optional. But all forty-four councillors who perceived the Native Authority leadership as expecting the district head to act bureaucratically reported that the former would punish its subordinate for refusing to sign the vouchers.

The contrasting patterns in Case 1 may be summarised as follows. (1) Whereas local audiences were widely seen as expecting the district councillor to act debureaucractically, the district head and the Native

[19]Interestingly, the twenty-four district councillors in that group who saw a small minority of the elders and young men as expecting them to act bureaucratically in Situation 1a all evaluated the role-expectation as optional – indicating that those elements were seen as not especially concerned with the councillors' failure to conform with the role alternative which signified support for the Native Authority leadership in Oturkpo Town (see pp. 141–2).

[20]The twenty-two district councillors in that group who saw a sizeable minority of the elders and young men as expecting the district head to act bureaucratically in Situation 1b – allegedly out of fear of the Native Authority leadership – all evaluated the role-expectation as optional – indicating that those elements were regarded as more concerned with not appearing to encourage the district head to defy his superiors than with actually enforcing his conformity with the role alternative which signified support for the Native Authority leadership (see pp. 144–5).

Authority leadership were generally regarded as expecting him to act bureaucratically. (2) Whereas local audiences were widely seen as expecting the district head to act debureaucratically,[21] the leadership was generally regarded as expecting him to act bureaucratically. (3) Whereas local audiences were widely expected to punish the councillor's deviant behaviour, not the district head's, Oturkpo Town was generally expected to punish the district head's role transgression, not the councillor's. (And the district head was also widely expected to punish the councillor's deviant behaviour.) These findings recall the 'role buffering' scenario which various informants had sketched early in the field investigation (see pp 230–1). It remains now to 'flesh out' the plot with some essential details.

To determine what part, if any, 'role buffering' did play in the district councillors' thinking about Case 1, these questions were asked of the thirty-eight councillors (all elected to office) whose role perceptions and evaluations of role obligation reflected *all three* viewpoints summarised above: 'Why do you think that the elders and young men would punish you for authorising the district head to sign the payment vouchers in the council hall case, but not the district head if he went ahead and signed them?' 'Why do you think that Oturkpo Town would punish the district head for refusing to sign the vouchers, but not you if you refused to authorise the district head to sign them?' 'And why do you think that the district head would punish you if you refused to authorise him to sign the vouchers?' In their responses, thirty-five of the thirty-eight councillors (92 per cent) stressed the importance of scapegoating in the form of 'role buffering'.

Without exception, those district councillors interpreted the council hall case as a 'tug-of-war', as it were, between the constituency, on

<hr />

[21]The reference here is only to the thirty-nine district councillors who observed that all (or a majority of) the elders and young men would expect the councillor and the district head to act debureaucratically in the council hall case. As we have seen (on p. 142ff.), more than a quarter of the seventy-one councillors interviewed reported that the elders and young men would expect the district head to act bureaucratically in Situation 1b; and approximately a third opined that a sizeable minority in each of those audiences would expect the district head to take that position. No matter that those elements would allegedly hold the bureaucratic expectation in Situation 1b out of fear of the Native Authority leadership, and that they were regarded by the councillors as not likely to punish the district head for refusing to conform with that role alternative. The councillors' perception of timidity among such elements was still an important source of their feelings of inefficacy and frustration *vis-à-vis* Native Authority pinnacle *and* rural base in Idoma.

the one hand, and a local government apparatus organised around strong chieftaincy and centralised political authority, on the other. The respondents' differing emphases were of minor import here. Whereas most underscored the essentially symbolic confrontation in Case I between apex and base in Idoma, a few did view the matter more narrowly as a contest over the administration of the District Council fund. In any event, the elders and young men were both regarded as expecting their elected representatives to stand firm against the Native Authority leadership and its subordinate, the district head. By authorising signing of the payment vouchers, the councillor would appear to the two local audiences to betray the constituency interest. Such behaviour could be expected, in and of itself, to produce punishment by the *ojira* assembly.[22]

But more was at stake here than conformity of district councillors with the debureaucratic role-expectation. According to the thirty-five respondents, the expectation that their deviant behaviour would be severely sanctioned by the *ojira* assembly in Situation *1a* was related also to the high probability that the district head would defy the council majority and sign the vouchers anyway. The councillors explained that the *ojira*, realising its own inefficacy *vis-à-vis* higher officialdom in the Native Authority and fearing reprisals, would be disinclined to sanction the district head's bureaucratic behaviour in Situation *1b*. The two local audiences were seen as apt to vent their bitterness and frustration by scapegoating the official who was expected to demonstrate his greater efficacy in the struggle against chiefly power and Native Authority centralisation and over whose behaviour they could, in the final analysis, exercise far greater control, viz. the councillor. Punishment of the latter's deviant behaviour in Situation *1a* was seen not merely as an expression of local dissatisfaction with his performance in that instance but also as a more general displacement of hostile affect upon the councillor caught between constituents powerless to alter the direction of local government affairs and an increasingly powerful Native Authority.

The Native Authority leadership's posture in Case I was seen by the thirty-five councillors as bearing a close resemblance to that of the elders and young men: the district head and the district councillor were both regarded as virtual hostages of their most proximate audi-

[22]For purposes of convenience, I have treated the *ojira* assembly as a single audience here. In fact, the assembly includes the two local audiences with which I have been mainly concerned in analysing 'role buffering' – the elders and young men.

ence, the leadership and the *ojira* assembly, respectively. Essentially a political operative serving on condition of 'good behaviour', the district head had ultimately to depend on the confidence of his superiors in Oturkpo Town. His refusal to sign the payment vouchers, the respondents explained, would produce punishment ranging from sharp rebuke to dismissal or judicial prosecution (perhaps on charges of extortion, bribery, or embezzlement of tax revenues). Aware of his dependent status, the district head could usually be counted on to treat his superiors' role-expectation as a directive and to act accordingly (see pp. 59, note 22, 260–5).

But role interaction between the Native Authority leadership and the district councillor was seen in a very different light. Most respondents opined that, while the leadership would undoubtedly prefer to have the councillors' support in Case 1 – 'to keep the books straight,' as one of those officials cynically remarked, 'not as a sign of our affection and loyalty' – Oturkpo Town was quite prepared, if necessary, to proceed without it. The district head would be instructed to press for authorisation by a council majority before signing the payment vouchers; but sign he must. In that event, punishment of the councillors' intransigence was seen by all the respondents as a futile and perhaps even a hazardous course for Oturkpo Town to pursue. Popular discontent might coalesce in its wake, threatening disruption and violence. As one councillor put it,

The *Och'Idoma* will seek our support in the matter of the council hall. But he will not punish our refusal to join the scheme [to defraud the District Council fund]. Why risk a bloody 'Tiv solution' here? It is safer to command the obedience of the district head. He will sign the vouchers. My people will be outraged, but they will understand the Native Authority is his father.

Thirty-two councillors observed that confidence in the district head's behaviour would combine with fear of provoking a 'Tiv solution' to restrain the Native Authority leadership from punishing their role transgression in Situation *1a*.

The leadership's posture in the council hall case was seen also as paralleling that of the elders and young men with regard to 'role buffering'. Dependent, in the final analysis, on the goodwill of the Northern Region Government, the leadership was particularly sensitive to its patron's shifting moods. By 1963, it will be recalled, the Native Treasury affair was straining relations between Kaduna and Oturkpo Town, and simultaneously galvanising political conspiracy against the centre in Idoma. On the defensive for the first time since the creation of an Idoma Chieftaincy more than a decade before, the Chief and his administration were having difficulty in putting down the challenge (see pp. 55–6). As part of their overall effort, they had increasingly to call upon the district heads to 'protect the flank', as it were. Unable to dispel a hostile popular mood on its own initiative, and preoccupied with a deteriorating situation at the centre, Oturkpo Town began to press their subordinates to enlarge its base of support in the districts.[23]

According to the thirty-five respondents, the harsh punishment which they expected the Native Authority leadership to mete out to the district head (should he refuse to sign the payment vouchers) reflected more than a negative response to the latter's behaviour in Situation 1b. The strong opposition which was foreseen among constituents and their elected representatives in the council hall case was expected to increase Oturkpo Town's pressure on the district head to rally popular support. Such an undertaking appeared doomed from the start, and all the respondents opined that that official would be held accountable for the debacle. Punishment of the district head's deviant behaviour in Situation 1b was thus seen both as an expression from above of dissatisfaction with his performance in that instance and, moreover, as scapegoating of yet another official caught between local interests opposing strong chieftaincy and Native Authority centralisation and a leadership frustrated in its efforts to mobilise broad rural support for the confrontation with political foes at the centre.

As might be expected in these circumstances, the district head was widely regarded as likely to punish the district councillor's refusal to authorise signing of the payment vouchers – both as a means of achieving the latter's concurrence in Situation 1a and as an earnest of his own continuing effort to mobilise rural support for the beleaguered Native Authority leadership in Oturkpo Town. Thirty-two of the thirty-five respondents (91 per cent) observed that a district head, usually self-confident and overbearing on these occasions – one was heard to address a belligerent council, 'I am *oche* [chief]. You who do not like me, take me to the Native Authority!' – would probably see the need to demonstrate his own loyalty and industry as

[23]Idoma Division was by now firmly tied to the NPC. Hence, the campaign to enlarge the base of rural support had little, if anything, to do with inter-party competition. It was initiated by the Native Authority leadership essentially to check a rival NPC faction. Rural dwellers correctly viewed the matter as an NPC family dispute, not as a challenge to chiefly power and Native Authority centralisation as such.

outweighing the risk of provoking a 'Tiv solution' in his province. As I shall show, herein lay the source of the disadvantage which ultimately redounded to the councillor.

To be sure, 'role buffering' did provide some immediate benefits to the two focal actors in Case 1. Thus each scapegoat was seen by all the respondents as 'buffering' the other from hostile audiences – the district head inadvertently insulating the district councillor from the Native Authority leadership, the councillor unintentionally shielding the district head from the elders and young men. In each instance, 'role buffering' absorbed in some measure the impact of bureaucratic–debureaucratic role conflict surrounding the two officials, freeing them to conform with the role-expectation of the most threatening audience(s) – the district head with that of his superiors in Oturkpo Town, the councillor with that of his constituents in the *ojira* assembly. But this structuring of role interaction, involving as it did responsiveness to proximate audiences,[24] also left the councillor vulnerable to the antagonistic district head. The former was now caught between audiences which he perceived as holding conflicting obligatory expectations for his behaviour– the district head on one side and the elders and young men on the other. Sharing their constituents' feelings of powerlessness and despair *vis-à-vis* higher authorities, and also fearing reprisals, the councillors were also reluctant to risk sanctioning the district head's behaviour. 'Role buffering' thus exposed the councillors to a hostile audience in Case 1 – the district head – but afforded them no real opportunity to redress the imbalance. Their situation is illuminated in this discussion by a councillor of a similar case evolving at the time of the study:

Recently when the *Och'Idoma* said that my people must soon work on the new grass airstrip [part of the Northern Region communications and transportation network], the district head told me that I must take them to the place. The *ojira* protested that it is not right for poor farmers to do this work without money. The people refused, and said I must not be a 'Native Authority lackey'. They said the district head must stand with the poor farmers. When the *Och'Idoma* heard of this stubbornness, he rebuked the district head and said the district head would be punished for angering the Sardauna [the Northern Premier]. The *Och'Idoma* said the district head must lead the people himself. The district head said I must do it, and he threatened to bring me to the Native Authority police if I refused to lead my people to the place. When I told this to the *ojira*, the elders protested that the district head is a

---

[24] An analogue of the *proximate audience* factor in role interaction can be found in Merton's discussion (1961: 374ff.) of observability.

'lackey'. They said I must stand with them, or be disgraced in the *ojira*. I pleaded with the district head to bring money or leave my people to do their farmwork. He ridiculed me. The matter is not settled yet. Because I will not lead my people to the airstrip, I cannot do this thing, the district head will take me to the Native Authority police in Oturkpo Town. The district head will suffer the *Och'Idoma*'s wrath because my people are stubborn. But because they are right, I will suffer even more.

From the elected councillors' viewpoint, then, the most important effect of 'role buffering' involving dual role conflict was its reaffirmation of the depressing circularity of their condition. As increasing polarisation between Native Authority pinnacle and rural base intensified role conflict for councillors, they felt compelled to resolve it either bureaucratically or debureaucratically, thereby inviting punishment from one quarter or another. 'Role buffering' in such cases as that involving the council hall – and the airstrip – strengthened their impulse to resolve role conflict debureaucratically. And resolution of role conflict fostered polarisation in Idoma.

Part V Conclusion

Chapter Eleven Glancing back and looking ahead: some reflections on the analysis of role conflict in Idoma

By now the reader may have discerned a paradox in the district councillors' condition as 'men in the middle', a paradox brought out by the juxtaposition of several key findings in the study. The first of these involves the councillors' preoccupation with punishment at the hands of audiences offended by their behaviour in their roles. Those officials generally regarded themselves as suffering far more than others in Idoma from role conflict rooted in the clash of interests between apex and base – a view shared, incidentally, by most informants. Subjected to role-expectations reflecting, on the one hand, support for, and on the other, opposition to, strong chieftaincy and Native Authority centralisation, they tended to anticipate more frequent and harsher punishment of their own deviant behaviour – whether bureaucratic or debureaucratic – than, for example, that of the district head. In the light of that finding, the councillors might reasonably be expected to manifest considerable ambivalence in choosing among alternative obligatory role demands. In fact, they usually experienced little or no difficulty in resolving role conflict.

Especially striking in this regard are the reports of ambivalent feelings by the thirty-five district councillors who complained of being victimised by 'role buffering' in the council hall case. Considerable ambivalence might be expected to obtain particularly where the councillors saw their resolutions as provoking either punishment by the vengeful district head (for not acting bureaucratically in Situation *1a*) or scapegoating by frustrated elders and young men (for not acting debureaucratically). But this expectation is not borne out by the data. Rather, thirty-one of the thirty-five councillors (88 per cent) who reported 'role buffering' in Case 1 said they would have no difficulty choosing among obligatory role alternatives in Situation *1a*.

And only two councillors observed that they would experience very much ambivalence resolving role conflict in that situation.

How is the paradox to be explained? And how is the ease with which the district councillors usually resolved role conflict – despite their professed concern with punishment in its wake – to be accounted for? The search for an answer here must begin by re-examining the conflict in Idoma over chiefly power and centralised political authority – with an eye to identifying its symbolic and its substantive aspects and their implications for the councillors caught in its midst.

The conflict surrounding chieftaincy in the Native Authority was less over ideology than over specifics. Indeed, it would have been difficult to find an Idoma – young or old, schooled or unschooled, Native Authority loyalist or political dissident[1] – who did not share in the traditional ideology of proud and vigorous chieftaincy. The Idoma were still deeply attached in the early independence period to the institution which symbolised for them the vitality of ritual and political life and which, moreover, legitimised their feelings of superiority *vis-à-vis* historic enemies – including, among others, the Egede in the division's south-east quadrant.

But the commitment to chieftaincy had always been tempered by fear of its autocratic potential. Lofty idealism and hard-headed realism had always suffused chieftaincy affairs, and shaped a popular attitude toward the institution which was a mixture of devotion and distrust – the latter element recognisable in the elaborate measures which were taken in pre-colonial times to prevent power from accruing to the clan head. As I have described, his behaviour was regulated then by three constitutional devices: by the countervailing authority of the *ojira* assembly; by certain rituals of office; and by the principles of rotation and seniority in succession to chieftaincy. More than any other factor perhaps, it was this ambivalence toward chieftaincy which caused the institution to exist sporadically before the European advent and to achieve only symbolic greatness.

As might be expected where rapid institutional change was the highest priority, officialdom representing the Crown's paramount authority misjudged (or ignored) the depth of that ambivalence.

[1]The dissidents included an NPC faction seeking control of the Native Authority organisation; opponents within the AG and the NCNC; and rural dwellers favouring a restoration in some form of the traditional constitutional equilibrium. The three groups were not mutually exclusive.

Through all its policy twists and turns, the colonial Administration stayed wedded to the single objective of constructing a disciplined and efficient Native Authority. To that end, it cultivated the institution of chieftaincy initially at the district level and eventually also at the divisional level. Its model was the political architecture in the Moslem North – the Fulani emirship atop a hierarchy of subordinate chieftaincies. Alert to the symbolism which still surrounded the clan headship – despite its apparent moribundity at the inception of colonial rule – European officials tried desperately to capitalise on it. Playing upon the commitment to the *idea* of chieftaincy, they rehabilitated and strengthened that institution in the person of the district head – a move which anticipated the establishment of a divisional paramountcy. The strategy was bold, seeking as it did to transplant Fulani chieftaincy in an Idoma soil made rich by European norms and popular devotion to an ancient institution. And it was costly. Sacrificing Idoma constitutionalism fuelled political instability in chieftaincy affairs – and exacerbated the deep-seated fear of autocratic rule. Numerous developments up to independence – by which time Ogiri Oko had manipulated post-war 'democratisation' to promote centralisation under his powerful Idoma Chieftaincy, and the district heads had to be content governing virtually unchecked in their own provinces – lent substance to that fear.

The essentially conservative Idoma had generally backed Ogiri Oko's defence of the institution of chieftaincy in the face of attacks by the IHRU upon traditionalist clan heads and district heads. They hoped all the while that this would promote restoration of the constitutional equilibrium rooted in principles of chieftaincy, gerontocracy, and democracy in the *ojira*. But their confidence had been misplaced, and by 1960, when Oko died, rural dwellers were already evincing impatience with his failure to eliminate autocratic district headships; they were beginning to speak more stridently among themselves of the need somehow to undo the *status quo*. Their mood was shortly fuelled by the appointment of Ajene Ukpabi, an Egede, to succeed his father-in-law as *Och'Idoma*, and by the political intrigue which was evolving at the centre in its wake. In the districts, the discussion largely revolved around the symbolic and substantive aspects of chieftaincy in the division, and its corollary, centralised political authority. Some favoured terminating the Idoma Chieftaincy and dismantling the Native Authority machinery in Oturkpo Town; they contended that Native Authority centralisation, organised around a powerful divisional chieftaincy, was at base incompatible with their constitutional traditions as people without instituted rulers. The argument was also pressed in this quarter with attention to Ukpabi's humiliating incumbency. Lacking Oko's political dexterity, the second *Och'Idoma* could not hope to emulate his predecessor's power and prestige. This pleased Ukpabi's detractors, but it hardly satisfied them. The profound resentment which they harboured toward him as a scion of the pariah Egede helped galvanise their opposition to the Idoma Chieftaincy as such. However, this was the minority viewpoint. Most Idoma stressed the practical need to retain the office; they argued for incorporating the Idoma Chieftaincy into a revitalised constitutional system after unseating the incumbent.

What of these stirrings? What was their essential character? Where were they channelled? And with what consequences for the district councillors? Popular disaffection was a deep-seated mood in Idoma in the aftermath of independence, a 'state of mind', as it were – and *not* an organised force. Several factors helped aggravate its amorphousness. Distrusting both the nationalist parties and the reformist IHRU – these were widely seen as promising more violence and instability and as furthering the erosion of traditional ways – and not wanting to antagonise unnecessarily the regional government and its NPC allies in the Native Authority, most rural dwellers were loath to channel their disaffection into the party arena. It seemed judicious at the time to eschew partisanship in local affairs and to ratify NPC power periodically in regional and federal elections. Recognising, too, that a popular uprising – organised or spontaneous – would be brutally suppressed by the authorities, they were understandably reluctant to seek change with a 'Tiv solution'. The prevailing attitude, then, was one of opposing the *status quo* in principle, but, wherever necessary, co-operating with it in fact.

Lest that attitude be mistaken for a conciliatory mood, however, it needs to be emphasised that co-operation implied neither compromise politics nor a desire therefor. On the contrary, most rural dwellers were apt to regard their prime interest – restoration of the constitutional equilibrium in some form – as irreconcilable with strong chieftaincy and centralisation in the Native Authority. As might be expected in that circumstance, many issues which arose day by day were seen in the localities – and also in Oturkpo Town – as evidence of the contest between seemingly polarised interests. Great strain was placed on the cohesiveness of Idoma society by this out-

I

look, and by its corollary, a restiveness which found its main expression in the refusal of most rural dwellers to co-operate with the Native Authority in all but essential matters.

But because the Idoma were hardly bold risk-takers in pursuing their political objectives, the movement toward polarisation was gradual and unspectacular. Cautious almost to a fault, they rarely put up resistance where it seemed destined to fail. When asked to evaluate that posture, one district councillor – himself a member of an opposition party – answered peremptorily:

The 'Tivvie' [Tiv man] refuses to pay tax! And he burns and pillages! The Idoma man will not be so bold and so foolish!

However, the Idoma man was disposed to stand firmly against the Native Authority leadership and its loyal subordinates where he felt that resistance could help check the erosion of traditional ways – as in the cases involving associational life (Situation *3b*) and succession to clan head (Situation *4b*); or that it could be mounted at low cost to symbolise their disaffection – as in the council hall case (Situation *1a*).

The struggle against the Native Authority *status quo* could thus be seen as essentially a rearguard action. Great battles were fought – rhetorically – to recover ground already lost to the 'enemy' at district headquarters and in Oturkpo Town. But unlike the Tiv, the Idoma never thought (or knew better than) to go on the offensive. As a relentless 'enemy' continued to push against their rampart, the sense of frustration and despair deepened in the rural areas.

As disillusionment with local government 'democratisation' grew in the decade before independence, and as violence and party politics came increasingly to be regarded as counterproductive, frustrated rural dwellers either abandoned the struggle altogether or resolved to carry it on by other means. But because the options seemed few at the time, most turned in desperation to the District Councils. In the period 1960–63 these bodies were widely acclaimed as the vanguard of popular resistance to chiefly power and Native Authority centralisation. Despite the councils' isolation and limited powers, as a rule the elected members were not averse to taking the lead. As rural dwellers, they shared the popular mood of disaffection, as well as their constituents' resolve somehow to alter the course of Native Authority affairs, in order to check further erosion of traditional ways and to restore the constitutional order. Their commitment to those political objectives had been affirmed during the campaign, and they, too, despaired of finding a better way to continue the struggle. Their primary task as local leaders, as they and their constituents saw it, was to stand firmly against a determined adversary. Onerous as that task was, they rarely sought to persuade their followers of its futility, or to operate as political brokers between apex and base in Idoma.

Appearances notwithstanding, the posture usually assumed by the elected district councillors was only occasionally in the heroic mould alone. While a few of those officials undoubtedly evinced great courage and selflessness in assailing Oturkpo Town and the district head at council meetings – and when resolving role conflict debureaucratically – most councillors usually acted with some caution and also out of particularistic motives. It will be recalled that rivalry between kin groups, endemic in Idoma, had been a key factor in the District Council elections in 1962 – and that even as they were seeking a wider forum in which to oppose the Native Authority *status quo*, nearly all the candidates were striving to enhance their sublineage's (and, coincidentally, their own) prestige and influence in the constituency. Significantly, these objectives were virtually indistinguishable in the popular mind, and the councillors were widely regarded as likely to benefit themselves and their kinsmen most in constituency affairs by promoting restoration of the constitutional equilibrium and by working to restrict the centre's impact on the locality. For example, the councillors and their kinsmen could expect to be hailed when, directly or indirectly, the former attacked chiefly power and Native Authority centralisation in the council. And the councillors' stature would be further enhanced (as would their kinsmen's) if they got the district head to be more responsive to the clan, lineage, or sublineage *ojira* on particular local government matters – including tax assessment and the appointment of tax collectors[2] – or if they managed to subvert efforts by Oturkpo Town to mobilise communal labour for projects outside the locality (see pp. 239–40). By the same token, the councillors could expect to lose prestige and influence in the constituency if their performance on these fronts was deemed weak or ineffectual. Rival kin groups were always poised to 'score points', as it were, at the expense of such officials and their sublineage mates.

---

[2] While these powers were formally lodged in the District Councils, they were apt to be exercised unilaterally by the district heads upon consultation with their friends and political allies in the localities.

The several considerations which were just seen as motivating the elected district councillors to accept leadership of an ebbing struggle against the Native Authority *status quo* (i.e., their absorption in the popular mood of disaffection, their conviction that no other means were available to carry the struggle forward, and finally, their disposition to exploit it for personal and group advantage), direct our attention once again to the paradox which initiated the discussion in this section: the ease with which the councillors usually resolved bureaucratic–debureaucratic role conflict, despite their concern with being punished in its wake. As with most of their constituents, those officials tended to see political life in the division as dominated by the conflict between Idoma constitutionalism and the Native Authority. In this view, politics was not the 'art of the possible', of compromise, but the ebb and flow of a struggle between interests presumed to be antithetical. Their lives having usually spanned the era of effective colonial rule in Idoma – from the end of World War I to independence in 1960 – the councillors easily absorbed that vision. They, too, had internalised the conflict's symbolic and substantive aspects – wanting, as they did, to sustain the traditional ideology of chieftaincy while opposing, as had their forebears, autocratic rule which flourished in its name. And they had also concluded that alien schemes for 'democratic' local government held no promise of thwarting such rule. As one councillor very forcefully put it, 'This is not your place, white man, your government offends the ancestors and it spoils the land!' Nearly half a century of European rule had assaulted this outlook, but had not managed to displace it. Nor had its by-product, nationalism. On the contrary, the constitutional equilibrium was still widely regarded in Idoma as the appropriate way to organise political life – with or without a divisional chieftaincy. Was this wish to make local government fit the traditional mould of chieftaincy, gerontocracy, and democracy in the *ojira*, fanciful? Undoubtedly, given the political realities of the early 1960s, in Idoma and elsewhere in Nigeria, it was. But fired by deep frustration and nostalgia, it still had a powerful grip on the imaginations of this rural people and their elected representatives.

As might be expected in that atmosphere, the elected councillors had little difficulty in choosing sides. Their concern with punishment notwithstanding, where role conflict appeared to them to originate in, and affect, the struggle against strong chieftaincy and centralised political authority, they were apt to resolve it with little or no difficulty – usually debureaucratically. While some of those officials took comfort in the knowledge that their punishment would end with a relatively short tenure in office – these were not careerists, after all, but farmers destined to remain on the land – many more were fortified by evidence that, for all its disutilities, joining the vanguard of the struggle also helped raise their stock (and their kinsmen's) in the council constituency.[3] For most, political leadership was a fusion of what they held to be high social purpose and particularistic interest.

This is the backdrop to bureaucratic–debureaucratic role conflict surrounding the district councillors in Idoma and their response thereto.

When assessing the utility of the case-study approach in analysis of role conflict (see p. 22–3), I observed that it can serve two important purposes, among others: to help generate insights and hypotheses which, when tested on the African continent, should deepen our understanding of a problem – role conflict – which is reportedly widespread among local leaders in independent Africa; and to help strengthen the link between African studies – a largely idiographic enterprise still – and the nomothetic social sciences. The two objectives were pursued by organising the study of bureaucratic–debureaucratic role conflict around the analytic variables and hypotheses outlined on pp. 124–6. In what remains of Chapter Eleven I shall draw attention to various aspects of the investigation in Idoma, with a view to undertaking cognate research in the future in Africa and elsewhere.

Predicting resolution of role conflict

The possibility of constructing social theory scientifically around the concept of 'role' has long attracted scholarly interest. Following that lodestar, if not a common research strategy, social scientists have managed to produce a substantial literature thus far under the rubric of 'role theory'. Withal it appears that 'role theory' has some way to go still before it can be considered a component of scientific theory. When finally it sheds conceptual ambiguity and includes a body of testable and tested generalisations which enhance explanation and

---

[3]An analogue can be found in Ward's report (1955: 180) on village officials in eastern and southern Asia. Often recruited by direct popular election, and lacking civil service status, they, too, were apt to favour particularistic village interests when resolving bureaucratic–debureaucratic role conflict.

prediction of social phenomena, then will it legitimately lay claim to that status. Until then, to cite Eckstein's words (1963: 393) out of context, 'it will call our attention to the "real forces" in [social life] and to the need for better definitions and operations for dealing with these forces'.

The construction of social theory around the concept of 'role' requires, among other things, great refinement in empirical research. Nowhere is this need more evident than in the design of predictive models for role behaviour. To that end, I proposed a model based on two operationalised concepts – legitimacy and obligation – and it was seen as facilitating prediction of the district councillors' resolving behaviour. As hypothesised, those officials were apt to resolve role conflict by fulfilling the more legitimate and/or more obligatory role-expectation.

A more definitive evaluation of the model's predictive utility must, however, await subsequent cross-validation.[4] Let it suffice here to note that its utility is limited by two assumptions: (1) of differences in the degree of legitimacy and/or obligation (it will be recalled that the existence of such differences was established by comparing the total number of times in a perceived situation of role conflict that the district councillor evaluated the bureaucratic and the debureaucratic expectation as legitimate and/or obligatory); and (2) of evaluation of the major role as the *exclusive* procedure for resolving role conflict. The model was not intended for situations of conflict involving legitimate and/or obligatory expectations associated with an *equal* number of audiences – for example, where the councillor perceived the elders, young men, tax collectors, and elected councillors as legitimately insisting that he not take part in the *ojira* assembly which chooses the clan head (Situation *4b*), and where he perceived four other audiences, the 'Native Authority councillors', representative councillors, district head, and Native Authority leadership, as legitimately insisting that he take part in the proceedings. Nor was it intended to treat resolution involving procedures other than evaluation and fulfilment of a major role among given behavioural alternatives. A more comprehensive model is needed for predictions, (1) from equal legitimacy and/or obligation to resolution involving the major role procedure; (2) from equal legitimacy and/or obligation to such resolving behaviour as withdrawal or compromise (Gross *et al.*

[4]Partial cross-validation of the model can be found in Ehrlich (1959: 53ff.).

1958: 281ff.; Miller and Shull 1962: 148ff.); and (3) from differences in the degree of legitimacy and/or obligation to a wider range of resolving behaviours.

Treating the two variables dichotomously (legitimate/illegitimate, obligatory/optional) has courted the dilemma of equal legitimacy and/or obligation. Can more refined models be constructed and the risk of that dilemma be lessened? A polychotomous approach commends itself. Auguring greater refinement and predictability are continuous variables built into the following questions: '*How much right do the elders have to expect you not to take part in the ojira assembly which chooses the clan head?*' and '*How much would the elders insist that you not take part?*' Other potentially useful models may be based on (1) punitive-social sanctions ranked for potency; (2) typologies of sanctions; and (3) audiences more frequently associated with behavioural alternatives selected by actors who perceive role conflict (Sutcliffe and Haberman 1956: 695–703; Miller and Shull 1962: 148ff.; Ehrlich *et al.* 1962: 95–6; Preiss and Ehrlich 1966: 118–20).

Whatever strategy is employed, social inquiry is apt to benefit in at least two ways from efforts to refine models for predicting resolution of role conflict. Investigators will become more sensitive to the 'real forces' in social life (including actors' evaluations of role legitimacy and role obligation) and to the need for their analysis cross-culturally. And, by undertaking such analysis, they will be better able to test the validity of 'role theory' as a component of scientific theory.

Role sanction

A community affirms what Radcliffe-Brown (1961: 210–11) has referred to as 'social sentiments' – its own definition of 'social health', as it were – by variously punishing its members' transgressions and also by rewarding their conformity with social usage. To apprehend fully those sentiments, and their consequences for the members' role behaviour, the investigator has necessarily to address, individually and by type, a whole range of sanctions operative in any community. But this immediately poses a problem. In virtually all societies, punitive sanctions are more specific than remunerative ones, and social sanctions (originating in others and directed toward the focal actor) are more readily identifiable than personal ones (originating in and directed toward that actor). It is hardly surprising, therefore, that studies of role conflict are characteristically asymmetric with regard to sanction, and usually concentrate on the punitive–social type alone. Probably moved more by practical than by theoretical considerations, investigators generally choose to ignore or de-emphasize other types.

While the present study reflects that 'tradition' in the analysis of role conflict, several of its findings do suggest that types of sanction other than the punitive–social may be sufficiently patent to permit of more systematic investigation. Thus, various district councillors drew attention as follows to punitive––personal, remunerative–personal, and remunerative–social sanction in the council hall case:

Could I sleep well if I disobeyed the elders and told the district head to sign the payment vouchers? (*punitive–personal*)

I know that I am a good man when I obey the *ojira* and not the *Och'Idoma*. (*remunerative–personal*)

My people will praise my boldness if I challenge the district head not to sign the vouchers. (*remunerative–social*)

The relative significance of these types of sanction cannot be assessed for Idoma, let alone for other societies, with the data now available to me, but their presence in the former does raise several intriguing questions. To what extent do remunerative sanctions account for conformity with the role-expectation of the most proximate audience(s) in situations involving 'role buffering'? Would the councillors act debureaucratically in Situation 1a for personal satisfaction and/or to gain their constituents' praise – and not merely to avoid being punished by the elders and young men? Are specific remunerative sanctions monopolised by particular audiences or more frequently invoked by them? Are symbolic and/or material rewards transmitted by the least proximate audiences in role interaction? If so, how? Directly? Or indirectly, as where the Native Authority leadership in Oturkpo Town invites the intercession of another audience – perhaps the district head, 'Native Authority councillor', or tax collector – to reward an elected councillor's sympathetic role behaviour? Do punitive–social and punitive–personal sanctions operate independently? Or do the former engender the latter? Answers to such questions as these await empirical investigation of the more inclusive typology of sanctions in diverse cultural settings, an exercise which requires more comprehensive analysis of role conflict, and concomitantly, greater understanding of the mechanisms which instil into the individual motives for regulating his behaviour in conformity with social usage.

Dual role conflict, 'role buffering', and situational analysis

The discovery of scapegoating behaviour in the form of 'role buffering' in two interrelated situations in the council hall case points up the need to avoid exaggerating the discreteness and autonomy of particular situations of role conflict. Put differently, the investigator should beware of 'locking' the focal actor into place situationally, along with the latter's various audiences, and then subjecting their relationship to analysis in that narrow context alone.[5] Historical and socio-cultural factors must also be weighed in situational analysis, along with the impact on institutions of diverse personalities involved in their workings (Gluckman, ed. 1964: 181; Gluckman 1968a: 1–77; Van Velsen 1964: xxvi). Moreover, the effect(s) which role interaction in one situation may have upon that in others should be examined – for example, where the same individual is the focal actor in different, albeit related situations, or, as in related situations in the council hall case, where two individuals each occupy a focal position (the district councillor in Situation *1a*, the district head in Situation *1b*) and an audience position (the councillor in Situation *1b*, the district head in Situation *1a*). To dismiss or underemphasise this cautionary note when analysing role conflict is to risk distorting social process by fastening onto a situational 'slice' of it.

Even as the analysis of 'role buffering' underscores the need to explore the possible link (1) between role interaction in diverse situations of conflict, and (2) between those situations, the personalities of individual participants, and overriding historical and socio-cultural factors, it also alerts us to some problems which may attend that effort. These were first encountered as several district councillors discussed scapegoating in Case 1. It will be recalled that thirty-five councillors had observed two things: firstly, that frustrated local audiences would vent their hostility to chiefly power and centralised political authority by scapegoating the councillor if he failed to act debureaucratically in Situation *1a*, i.e., if he went ahead and advised the district head to sign the payment vouchers; and secondly, that the harassed Native Authority leadership would scapegoat the district head if he failed to act bureaucratically in Situation *1b*, i.e., if he

---

[5]A similar problem has often been noted with regard to studies of organisational decision-making and 'community power structure'.

refused to sign the vouchers. Among those thirty-five officials, five (14 per cent) volunteered the opinion that they would be punished severely in the *council hall case*, along with the district head, regardless of their resolving behaviour in the *respective situations*. The five councillors proceeded to explain that they would be scapegoated by the elders and young men not for resolving role conflict debureaucratically in Situation *1a* – in accordance with their constituents' obligatory role-expectation – but rather, for failing to prevent the district head from acting bureaucratically in Situation *1b*; and that the district head would be scapegoated by Oturkpo Town not for resolving role conflict bureaucratically in the latter situation – in accordance with his superiors' obligatory role-expectation – but for having to act without the support of a council majority in the former. All five councillors had distinguished here between the council hall case as such and the particular situations which it subsumed.

Various reasons can be adduced as possibly explaining why those councillors could anticipate their own punishment as scapegoats, along with that of the district head, despite conformity with the obligatory role-expectation which the former had attributed to local audiences and the Native Authority leadership in Situation *1a* and Situation *1b* respectively. The councillors' responses may have been an artifact of specific questions put to them or of the decision to organise Case I around dual role conflict (i.e., two situations of conflict), or both. But several considerations cast doubt on the importance of those factors. To begin with, I took great care in discussions with councillors and other informants early in the field investigation to ensure that such cases as that involving the council hall did in fact revolve around two separable situations of conflict, each with a different focal actor. Because that case was adapted from another which could be observed first-hand in Idoma at the time, confirming its appropriateness for analysis in that form was a relatively simple task. Moreover, had specific questions or the two-situation format, or both, had an overriding influence, it would be reasonable to expect far more than that modest number of councillors – five, in all – to become 'ensnared' by their interlocutor. Finally, it should be noted that still another group of those officials had already managed to make the difficult distinction in the pre-test questionnaire between social role and personal role. Lacking conclusive – indeed, any – evidence to the contrary, it is not unreasonable to suggest that in both instances the distinctions rendered were born of an alternative set of factors – including the respondents' individual acuity, personal outlook, and political experiences.

Significantly, each of the five councillors insisted on distinguishing between the council hall case – as the symbol of a larger struggle in Idoma over the character of the Native Authority – and the two situations of conflict which they regarded together as only a concrete aspect of it. Those officials repeatedly admonished me that while the case – the struggle – shaped Situation *1a* and Situation *1b*, it was not wholly absorbed into them. The following comments by two of the councillors highlight this viewpoint, along with its implications for scapegoating even where there was conformity with an obligatory role-expectation:

The district councillor stands between his people and the 'big men' in the Native Authority. And the district head between the people and Oturkpo Town. But these two matters are only a part of the story which you have put to me. That is why I say that I would be punished in the council hall case even if I obeyed the *ojira* [in Situation *1a*]. And that the district head would also be punished even if he obeyed his master [in Situation *1b*].

I say that the struggle is bigger than the two matters of which we speak [in Situation *1a* and Situation *1b*]. They are part of the struggle in this case, but only a part. The war is always bigger than its battles, the struggle is always bigger than its parts. Do you see why in this case, the struggle, my people will still punish their obedient servant and the Native Authority will still punish its district head?

Intensive probing failed to elicit any evidence that the five councillors were alluding to some other conflict situation(s) which they might have regarded as implicit in Case 1. On the contrary, each stuck adamantly to the view that Situation *1a* and Situation *1b* had both materialised within a larger context – and that he and the district head would therefore be scapegoated not as a reaction to their conforming behaviour in the respective situations, but as punishment for their failure to produce a decisive breakthrough in the transcendent struggle that was, symbolically, the council hall case itself. In this conception, the case was of two elements, one substantive and endogenous to the particular situations which it embraced, the other essentially symbolic and exogenous to those particularities.

It is tempting to speculate here that the distinction rendered by the five councillors is not unique in Idoma thought, its corollary being that people's commitment to an institution – chieftaincy – which, while existing sporadically before the advent of European rule, still managed to achieve symbolic greatness as an ideological artifact. If

255

this line of speculation is warranted, then I may be entitled to conjecture as follows: that the struggle which was found gripping the popular imagination in the early independence period is destined to survive for some time to come – ebbing and flowing to be sure, but fed always by deep frustration and nostalgia, and by a fascination with the idea of proud and vigorous chieftaincy and a simultaneous profound distrust of it.

Its particularistic interest aside, the foregoing discussion of dual role conflict and endogenous (substantive) and exogenous (symbolic) elements in 'role buffering' in Idoma reminds us that social life, while subsuming individual situations, is not entirely constructed out of them (Turner 1966: 240). Accordingly, we should beware of laying too much stress upon the single analytic situation (or, indeed, any number of such situations) in studying role conflict. Excessive preoccupation with the discrete, autonomous situation risks intellectual sundering of the social fabric and its reconstruction in the mind's eye as a caricature of social life. On that note of caution and of challenge, I conclude my analysis of role conflict surrounding the district councillors in Idoma.[6]

---

[6]The district heads' perspectives on role conflict in the council hall case are examined, along with their social backgrounds, on pp 260–5.

Part VI
Appendices

Appendix A The interview schedule

Limitations of space prevent publication of a lengthy interview schedule constructed in English and Idoma. Its 241 items are summarised below. I shall be pleased to make the complete schedule available to readers upon request.

Interviews were conducted with each subject in two phases, on different occasions. They commenced in each phase with a discussion of my background as a university lecturer and my objectives in Idoma. The matter of confidentiality was also broached and underlined.

Phase I interviews focused on the district councillors' backgrounds. Data were obtained from those officials on personal, family, and extended kin matters; residence; education of self and kin and aspirations for children; language competence; travel experience; media exposure, political information, and political perspectives; religious affiliation and observance; subsistence production and employment; political party affiliation and political experience; associational activity (in secret societies, dance groups, and age groups); income and socio-economic status. Pertinent data are reported in Chapter Four.[1]

Phase II interviews of the district councillors were organised in three parts. The first dealt with the process of getting elected or appointed to the District Council in 1962 and, where appropriate, in 1958 and 1955. Data were obtained on candidate interests and motivations; campaign strategy (kinship considerations, alliance-building, corruption and generosity); and, in the case of 'Native Authority councillors', interests and motivations of district heads who largely controlled the appointment process. These are reported in Chapter Five.

---

[1]Five district heads were interviewed in Phase I as to their own backgrounds. In Phase II, they were questioned on accession politics surrounding the district councillorship, the councillors' party activities, and role behaviour in Situation *1a* and Situation *1b*. Pertinent data are reported in Appendix B.

Appendix A

The second part extended Phase I questioning of the district councillors with regard to their involvement in political party life.

The last part of the Phase II interview focused on role behaviour, viz. the district councillors' role perceptions for various audiences in six situations; the councillors' evaluations of role legitimacy, obligation, and sanction for audiences in each situation; the extent to which those officials experienced difficulty (ambivalence) resolving role conflict; and the way they resolved role conflict. The format for role perception questions in the six situations can be found in Chapter Seven and Chapter Eight along with pertinent data. Question format and data on role legitimacy, obligation, sanction, and resolution can be found in Chapter Ten, on ambivalence and resolution in Chapter Nine. Councillors were also probed on 'role buffering' – scapegoating – in the council hall case (Situation *1a* and Situation *1b*); the data are analysed in Chapter Ten.[2]

[2]See previous note.

Appendix B The district heads: their social backgrounds and their perspectives on role behaviour in Case 1

Among the district councillor's role relationships with various Native Authority officials, that involving the district head was the most important one by far. I have shown that the former's hostility to chiefly power and centralised political authority in Idoma was reinforced by the knowledge that the district head had benefited greatly under colonial rule and in its aftermath – to the detriment of most rural dwellers who preferred to restore the traditional constitutional equilibrium in some form. Because of the pivotal role interaction between those two officials, it is useful to highlight the social backgrounds of the five district heads involved in the study as well as their perspectives on role behaviour in the face of bureaucratic–debureaucratic tension. For the latter purpose, I shall focus on the two situations in the council hall case.

With the exception of five background factors, the district heads are hardly distinguishable as a group from the district councillors. Attention is drawn, therefore, to these factors: age, socio-economic status, working experiences, political background, and associational activity.

The district heads were older as a group than the district councillors, the former's ages ranging from 46 to 86 (mean, 63; median, 66), the latter's from 32 to 64 (mean, 50; median, 49).

Fifty-four (76 per cent) of the seventy-one district councillors were poor or modest farmers. The district heads were decidedly better off. Three were very prosperous farmers with bicycles, radios, and more than one tin-roofed house; two of the three also owned motor cars. Four district heads had between six and fourteen wives, most obtained with brideprice payments. While district head salaries were impressive by rural Idoma standards – ranging between £6 and more than £18 monthly – they were insufficient to account for the wide

Appendix B

disparity between the the two groups of officials. The district headship was lucrative – extralegally – for every incumbent.

Unlike most district councillors, all the district heads were Native
Authority careerists – their local government service averaging
twenty-three years. Three had served as district head for at least a
decade – one nearly twenty-nine years – and all had previously held
other posts. Clearly these were 'Native Authority men'.

All but one district head had employed family connections to
advance his position. Two had been appointed to office with the
strong backing of their close relative, Chief Ogiri Oko. They then
sought to improve their political fortunes by arranging marriages
between close relatives and two other district heads in the group.
Those four officials could anticipate a relatively secure and prosperous tenure in the administration of Oko's son-in-law and successor,
Ajene Ukpabi – unless they some day lost the goodwill in Oturkpo
Town on which they were ultimately dependent.

Predictably, the district heads were all strong supporters of the
NPC, acting as its patron in their districts. Contrastingly, NPC supporters among the district councillors were usually indifferent toward
the governing party.

Whereas most district councillors were active in associational life,
every district head had been constrained by age and/or official
responsibilities to cease involvement in various secret societies and
dance groups. They were strongly oriented, however, to other aspects
of traditional life. Thus, three district heads were also clan heads, and
the other two aspired to that office of great prestige.

Many parallels were encountered between the district heads' aggregate responses in the council hall case and the district councillors'.
These are summarised here, along with some dissimilarities.

That the two groups of officials held similar views as to the hostile
confrontation between apex and base in Idoma is borne out in Situation *1a*. Ninety-four per cent of the seventy-one councillors and all
five district heads viewed the Native Authority leadership in Oturkpo
Town as expecting the councillors to authorise signing of the payment
vouchers. Only 13 per cent of the councillors attributed the same
bureaucratic role expectation to the elders and young men, and all
the district heads reported that only a small minority of those two
audiences in their districts would expect the councillors to act
bureaucratically in Situation *1a*.

As with the district councillors, most district heads regarded the tax collectors and appointed councillors as essentially 'Native Authority men'.

The most striking disparities in Situation *1a* involve the representative councillor and district-head audiences. Slightly more than half of the district councillors (53 per cent) perceived the former audience as expecting them not to authorise signing of the payment vouchers. And nearly half of the councillors (45 per cent) regarded the district head as also expecting them to act debureaucratically in Situation *1a*. All five district heads reported, however, that they and the representative councillors would expect every district councillor to heed the Native Authority leadership and authorise signing of the vouchers.[1]

Parallels were also encountered in Situation *1b*. Twenty-eight per cent of the district councillors reported that the elders and young men would expect the district head to sign the payment vouchers, and two district heads (40 per cent) also perceived those audiences as expecting that official to act bureaucratically in the matter.[2] As with the district councillors who perceived role conflict among the elders, young men, and elected councillors, the district heads who reported such conflict also viewed a sizeable minority of the first two audiences and only a handful of the third as expecting the district head to act bureaucratically in Situation *1b*. Every councillor and district head who perceived role conflict among tax collectors and 'Native Authority councillors' estimated that nearly all the members of those two audiences would expect the district head to sign the vouchers. Predictably, all the councillors and district heads attributed that role-expectation to the Chief of Idoma and his colleagues on the General Purposes Committee.

Overall, sixty-two (87 per cent) of the seventy-one district councillors perceived Situation *1a* as conflictual. And forty-five councillors (63 per cent) perceived role conflict in Situation *1b*. All five district

---

[1]Six representative councillors were serving in the five districts under investigation. Three of those officials were also district councillors, and they were interviewed in the study (along with two of the three remaining representative councillors). All five indicated that they would indeed expect every district councillor to act bureaucratically in Situation *1a*. Overall, these interviews revealed that the representative councillors, expecting to sit periodically on the policy-making General Purposes Committee, were also 'Native Authority men'.

[2]The 28 per cent figure refers to twenty district councillors, twelve of whom were serving under the two district heads who reported that the elders and young men would expect the district head to act bureaucratically in Situation *1b*.

heads viewed both situations as conflictual. This last finding was probably exceptional, however. Other evidence, including informal conversations with the district heads, indicated that those officials generally experienced less role conflict than the councillors.

Among the sixty-two district councillors who perceived role conflict in Situation *1a*, twenty-five said that they would experience ambivalence in resolving it. Fourteen of the twenty-five were serving under three district heads who opined that a sizeable minority of the councillors in their administrative units would have difficulty deciding what to do in that situation. Those district heads presided over councils with thirteen, twelve, and ten members, respectively. Sizeable minorities in the three councils together would probably approximate the fourteen councillors above.

Sixteen of the forty-five district councillors who perceived Situation *1b* as conflictual opined that the district head would have difficulty deciding what to do. Eleven of the sixteen were serving under two district heads who reported that they would indeed experience ambivalence in that situation.

Among the sixty-two district councillors who perceived role conflict in Situation *1a*, 71 per cent said that they would resolve it debureaucratically, i.e., by refusing to authorise the district head to sign the payment vouchers. Thirty-five (78 per cent) of the forty-five councillors who perceived Situation *1b* as conflictual observed that the district head would resolve it by signing the vouchers. Of the fifty-three elected councillors who viewed Situation *1a* as conflictual, forty-eight said that they would resolve it debureaucratically. And seven of the nine 'Native Authority councillors' who perceived role conflict in that situation reported that they would fulfil the bureaucratic expectation. The district heads' responses were very similar here to the district councillors'. Thus, all five district heads reported that all or nearly all the elected councillors in their units would resolve role conflict debureaucratically in Situation *1a*; they reported, too, that all the 'Native Authority councillors' would resolve it bureaucratically. All five district heads vouchsafed that they themselves would act bureaucratically in Situation *1b*, resolving role conflict in favour of their superiors in Oturkpo Town.

Parallel responses were also obtained with respect to evaluations of role legitimacy and role obligation. Both the district councillors and district heads tended to view as obligatory (i.e., sanction-bearing) role-expectations which they evaluated as legitimate, and to regard as optional (i.e., unaccompanied by punitive sanction) expectations which they deemed illegitimate. The two groups of officials were more prone to anticipate punishment in the event of nonconformity with role-expectations which they evaluated as rightful than with expectations which they regarded as improper. Moreover, the district heads shared the councillors' view that the latter were more likely than the former to suffer punishment for deviant behaviour. Fully 70 per cent of the role-expectations which the councillors attributed to various audiences in Situation *1a* were viewed by those officials as sanction-bearing in the event of their own nonconformity. In Situation *1b*, however, only 33 per cent of the role-expectations which they attributed to various audiences were viewed as sanction-bearing in the event of nonconformity by the district head. Comparably, 73 per cent of the expectations which the district heads perceived audiences as holding in Situation *1a* were evaluated by those officials as obligatory, as were only 37 per cent of the expectations in Situation *1b*.

Finally, two district heads reported that they would be victimised by 'role buffering' – scapegoating – in the council hall case, along with many of the elected district councillors in their units – the former for failing to act bureaucratically in Situation *1b* (thereby offending harassed superiors in Oturkpo Town), the latter either for not acting debureaucratically in Situation *1a* (thereby offending frustrated local audiences) or for fulfilling that expectation (and consequently offending the district head). A similiar report had been made by thirty-five councillors. Twenty-four of the thirty-five were serving under those two district heads, and the eleven remaining councillors in two other districts. One of the two district heads volunteered the opinion that he would be scapegoated from above, and at least a few of the elected councillors from below, despite his conformity with the Native Authority leadership's obligatory role-expectation in Situation *1b* and the councillors' conformity with their constituents' obligatory expectation in Situation *1a*. As had five councillors, the district head went on to explain that that outcome would reflect the distinction in his own mind between the council hall case as such, symbolising the continuing struggle in Idoma over strong chieftaincy and Native Authority centralisation, and the two role conflict situations which it embraced. Three of the five councillors were serving under that district head, the two remaining councillors in two other districts.

The parallel findings reported above are hardly surprising. Interacting intensively within a relatively small and politically constricted arena, the district councillors and district heads could be expected to display great sensitivity to each other's role behaviour in the face of bureaucratic–debureaucratic tension.

Appendix C In the field in Idoma

Getting started

My decision to work in Idoma reflected a desire to relate interests in Nigeria's minority peoples and the Northern Region's local government scheme. Specifically, I hoped to learn how Native Authority 'democratisation' among that 'Middle Belt' people might affect, and be affected by, the modern Idoma Chieftaincy and a traditional chieftaincy institution organised around the clan headship.

The investigation began in Autumn 1962 with (1) archival work at the National Archives branches in Enugu and Kaduna and at the Divisional Office and Native Authority secretariat in Oturkpo Town; (2) conversations in Idoma Division with the District Officer (who represented the Northern Region Minister for Local Government), the Chief of Idoma and others in the Native Authority leadership, and various European missionaries; and (3) a trip to University College, Ibadan to confer with Professor Robert Armstrong, who helped sensitise me to Idoma's political landscape.

Professional identity

But for my interpreter-informant (see below), I did not reveal to anyone in Idoma that I was a political scientist – lest that fact arouse anxieties over my being there. Rather, I stressed my status as a university lecturer come to learn the ways of Idoma. I was usually referred to either as *ubeke* (white man) or, with far greater esteem, as *iticha* (the teacher). Many Idoma came to regard me positively as an anthropologist who would, like C. K. Meek, R. C. Abraham, and Robert Armstrong before me, publicise their ways. A few sceptics opined that I was either a white Superintendent of Nigeria Police or, as one put it, 'a damned tax collector!'.

The interpreter-informant

I could not hope to acquire a working knowledge of Idoma *and* execute the investigation during a year of fieldwork; I therefore had to settle for picking up bits and pieces of the language along the way. But there was yet another reason for my not wanting to invest heavily in language training. Competence in Idoma would undoubtedly be beneficial, but it could not reasonably be expected *ipso facto* to generate the rapport which was essential in fieldwork. Rapport-building could be better facilitated, I thought, if I could employ as an interpreter-informant a widely-respected Idoma who could lead me into a system of on-going social and political relationships and who would be sufficiently interested in the project and available to work closely with me on a full-time basis.[1] According to Robert Armstrong, Audu Entonu was such a person. (See pp. 79–80.) There was the matter of his political oppositionism, however, and his reliability. Armstrong was reassuring here, and I engaged Audu's services on settling into Idoma.

The decision to engage Audu Entonu affected my choice of research sites. Audu lived in Oturkpo Town (as I did) and his political antenna was especially sensitive in the administrative centre and in central and northern Idoma. He could be expected to operate there with maximum effectiveness. As logistical problems also conspired against my working in remote southern and western Idoma, I decided to concentrate on five districts in the central and northern sectors.[2]

Early on I was introduced by Audu Entonu to a wide range of political actors in Idoma, including Native Authority operatives throughout the division and leaders of the various party organisations and factions. These contacts were intensified between December 1962 and August 1963, with many informal meetings in Native Authority offices, private residences, and the Paradise Bar, a political haunt in Oturkpo Town. Free-wheeling discussions, frequently held in English without Audu's attendance, covered the spectrum of political issues and personalities in Idoma.

In that nine-month period Audu Entonu and I together attended all District Council meetings in the five units on which the investigation centred; the councils usually deliberated in Idoma, requiring translation.

[1] A similiar approach can be found in Whyte's study (1964: 13–21) of street-corner society in an American city.

[2] Interviewing was officially banned in strife-torn Adoka district in central Idoma (see p. 170). Isolated, malarial Agatu district on the Benue River was bypassed in the study to avoid health and logistical problems. (See Map 3, p. 20.)

Interviewing

A pre-test questionnaire was constructed in English and Idoma and administered in late January to six former district councillors who were chosen for their availability. Phase I interviews began immediately upon revision of the pre-test questionnaire. Conducted between mid-February and early May, they averaged two hours (without interruptions). Phase II interviews, averaging three hours, were conducted between mid-May and late August. Normally two interviews were held each day.

Phase I and Phase II interviews were both absorbed into a larger social experience, extending up to five hours each and including breaks for eating, drinking, bantering, and so forth. The pace was unhurried, permitting my host and his family and neighbours to express their customary sociability and hospitality. All but twenty-one interviews, in Phase II, were conducted in the district councillors' and district heads' village compounds or Oturkpo Town dwellings. A severe attack of malaria left me bedridden for two weeks in June, whereupon Audu Entonu transported twenty-one councillors to my town residence for interviews.

Archival work in Oturkpo Town and late evening meetings with notables and others in the administrative centre were organised around a rigorous schedule of six interview days per week between February and August.

The interview population in five districts was to have numbered ninety-four: eighty-nine district councillors and five district heads. All were interviewed in Phase I, eighty-two councillors and four district heads in Idoma through the interpreter-informant, six councillors and one district head in English (with Audu Entonu attending and occasionally intervening), and a Tiv councillor in his own language. (Audu was fluent in Tiv.) The Chief of Idoma had periodically expressed his dissatisfaction with my decision to engage a political foe as interpreter-informant. Finally, in late August, I was advised by him that Audu could no longer accompany me into the districts, and that the Native Authority would help me secure an equally qualified replacement. Fieldwork was nearly completed by then – seventy-one councillors and five district heads had already been interviewed in two phases, and the archival investigation had been concluded several weeks before in Oturkpo Town. It was soon clear to all that no suitable replacement could be found for Audu, with or without assistance from the Native Authority. Accordingly, I decided not to attempt to interview the remaining councillors in Phase II: sixteen Idoma-speakers and the Tiv from Ochekwu district, one Idoma-speaker from Oturkpo district. The empirical analysis in *Men in the Middle* focuses on the seventy-one councillors interviewed in *both* phases.

References

Abraham, R. C. (c. 1935), 'Reorganization report for Agala District' (unpublished).
— (1940), *The Tiv People*. London: Crown Agents for the Colonies on Behalf of the Government of Nigeria.
Ackerman, N. (1951), 'Social role and total personality', *American Journal of Orthopsychiatry* XXI.
Agboola, S. A. (1961), 'The Middle Belt of Nigeria – The basis of unity', *Nigerian Geographical Journal* 4.
Akpan, N. U. (1967), *Epitaph to Indirect Rule: A Discourse on Local Government in Africa*. London: Cass.
Apter, D. E. (1955), *The Gold Coast in Transition*. Princeton, N. J.: Princeton University Press.
Armstrong, R. G. (1954), 'A West African inquest', *American Anthropologist* 56.
— (1955), 'The Idoma-speaking peoples', in *Peoples of the Niger–Benue Confluence*, D. Forde, ed. London: International African Institute.
Baikie, W. B. (1856), *Narrative of an Exploring Voyage Up the Rivers Kw'ora and Bi'nue (Commonly Known as the Niger and Tshadda) in 1854*. London: Murray.
Barnes, J. A. (1967), *Politics in a Changing Society: A Political History of the Fort Jameson Ngoni*. Manchester: Manchester University Press.
Barth, H. (1857), *Travels and Discoveries in North and Central Africa: Being a Journal of an Expedition Undertaken Under the Auspices of H. B. M.'s Government in the Years 1849–1855*, vol. 2. London: Longman, Green, Longman, and Roberts.
Bassa Province (refers to Northern Nigeria. Bassa Province) (c. 1910), 'Note on general and political developments in the area of Bassa Province' (unpublished).
Beattie, J. (1960), *Bunyoro: An African Kingdom*. New York: Holt, Rinehart, and Winston.
Benue High Court (refers to Northern Nigeria. Benue Province. High

Court) (1962), Oko *vs*. Idoma Native Authority and Oko. Suit No. MD/15/1962.

Benue Province (refers to Northern Nigeria. Benue Province) (1927), 'Annual report for Idoma Division' (unpublished).

— (1930), 'Annual report for Idoma Division' (unpublished).

— (11 May 1934), 'Memorandum from Secretary, Northern Provinces, to Benue Province Resident and Idoma Senior District Officer' (unpublished).

— (18 January 1935), 'Pembleton's commentary on Shaw's reorganization report for Ochekwu District sent to Secretary, Northern Provinces' (unpublished).

— (22 August 1938), 'Memorandum from Idoma District Officer to Idoma Senior District Officer' (unpublished).

— (1939), 'Annual report for Idoma Division' (unpublished).

— (1948), 'Annual report for Idoma Division' (unpublished).

— (1950), 'Annual report for Idoma Division' (unpublished).

— (1952), 'Annual report for Idoma Division' (unpublished).

Biddle, B. J., and E. J. Thomas, eds. (1966), *Role Theory: Concepts and Research*. New York: Wiley.

Bidwell, C. E. (1965), 'The schools as a formal organization', in *Handbook of Organizations*, J. G. March, ed. Chicago: Rand McNally.

Blitz, L. F., ed. (1965), *The Politics and Administration of Nigerian Government*. New York: Praeger.

Bohannan, P. (1957), *Justice and Judgment Among the Tiv*. London: Oxford University Press.

Bowen, E. S. (1964), *Return to Laughter*. Garden City, N.Y.: Doubleday.

Brown, R. (1959), 'Indirect rule as a policy of adaptation', *The Thirteenth Conference Proceedings of the Rhodes–Livingstone Institute for Social Research, Lusaka, Northern Rhodesia*.

Burchard, W. W. (1954), 'Role conflicts in military chaplains', *American Sociological Review* XIX.

Burdo, A. (1880), *The Niger and the Benueh: Travels in Central Africa*. London: Bentley.

Burke, F. (1958), 'The role of the chief in Uganda', *Journal of African Administration* X.

— (1964), *Local Government and Politics in Uganda*. Syracuse: Syracuse University Press.

Burns, A. (1955), *History of Nigeria*. London: Allen & Unwin.

Busia, K. A. (1951), *The Position of the Chief in the Modern Political System of Ashanti*. London: Oxford University Press.

Cameron, D. (1934), *The Principles of Native Administration and Their Application*. Lagos, Nigeria: Government Printer.

Clignet, R. (1967), 'Environmental change, types of descent, and child-rearing practices', in *The City in Modern Africa*, H. Miner, ed. New York: Praeger.

Cohen, R. (1960), 'Structure of Kanuri Society', Ph.D. dissertation, Department of Sociology and Anthropology, University of Wisconsin (unpublished).

Coleman, J. S. (1958), *Nigeria: Background to Nationalism*. Berkeley: University of California Press.

Colson, E. (1948), 'Modern political organization of the Plateau Tonga', *African Studies* 7.

— (1960), *Social Organization of the Gwembe Tonga*. Manchester: Manchester University Press.

— (1962), *The Plateau Tonga: Social and Religious Studies*. Manchester: Manchester University Press.

— (1971), *The Social Consequences of Resettlement: The Impact of the Kariba Settlement Upon the Gwembe Tonga*. Manchester: Manchester University Press.

Cooley, C. H. (1909), *Social Organization*. New York: Scribner's Sons.

— (1918), *Social Process*. New York: Scribner's Sons.

Coser, L. (1966), *The Functions of Social Conflict*. New York: Free Press.

Cottrell, L. S., jr. (1942), 'The adjustment of the individual to his age and sex roles', *American Sociological Review* VII.

Cowan, L. G. (1958), *Local Government in West Africa*. New York: Columbia University Press.

Crocker, W. R. (1936), *Nigeria: Critique of British Colonial Administration*. London: Allen & Unwin.

Crowder, M., and O. Ikime, eds. (1970), *West African Chiefs: Their Changing Status Under Colonial Rule and Independence*. New York: Africana.

Crowther, S. (1855), *Journey of an Expedition up the Niger and Tshadda Rivers in 1854*. London: Church Missionary Society.

Cunnison, I. (1959), *The Luapula Peoples of Northern Rhodesia: Custom and History in Tribal Politics*. Manchester: Manchester University Press.

References

Dahl, R. A. (1956), *A Preface to Democratic Theory*. Chicago: University of Chicago Press.

— (1957), 'The concept of power', *Behavioral Science* II.

— (1958), 'A critique of the ruling elite model', *American Political Science Review* 52.

Denham, R. S. *et al.* (1831), *Travels and Discoveries in Northern and Central Africa, 1822, 1823, 1824*. vol. 4. London: Murray.

Dent, M. J. (1966), 'A minority party – the UMBC', in *Nigerian Government and Politics: Prelude to the Revolution*, J. P. Mackintosh, ed. Evanston, Ill.: Northwestern University Press.

— (1971), 'Tarka and the Tiv: a perspective on Nigerian federation', *Nigeria: Modernization and the Politics of Communalism*, R. Melson and H. Wolpe, eds. East Lansing: Michigan State University Press.

Dollard, J. *et al.* (1945), *Frustration and Aggression*. New Haven, Conn.: Yale University Press.

Dudley, B. J. (1968), *Parties and Politics in Northern Nigeria*. London: Cass.

Duverger, M. (1955), *Political Parties: Their Organization and Activity in the Modern State*. New York: Wiley.

Eaton, R. M. (1959), *General Logic*. New York: Scribner.

Eckstein, H. (1963), 'Group theory and the comparative study of pressure groups', in *Comparative Politics*, H. Eckstein and D. E. Apter, eds. Glencoe, Ill.: Free Press.

Ehrlich, H. J. (1959), 'The analysis of role conflicts in a complex organization: the police', Ph.D. dissertation, Department of Sociology and Anthropology, Michigan State University (unpublished).

Ehrlich, H. J. *et al.* (1962), 'The study of role conflict: explorations in methodology', *Sociometry* 25.

Eisenstadt, S. N. (1958), 'Bureaucracy and bureaucratization: a trend report', *Current Sociology* 7.

— (1959), 'Bureaucracy, bureaucratization, and debureaucratization', *Administrative Science Quarterly* IV.

— (1964), *From Generation to Generation: Age Groups and Social Structure*. Glencoe, Ill.: Free Press

Elliott, H. (1937a), 'Reorganization report for Agatu District' (unpublished).

— (1937b), 'Reorganization report for Boju District' (unpublished).

Epstein, A. L. (1958), *Politics in an Urban African Community*. Manchester: Manchester University Press.

Erasmus, C. J. (1952), 'The leader vs. tradition: a case study', *American Anthropologist* LIV.

Ezera, K. (1964), *Constitutional Developments in Nigeria*. Cambridge: Cambridge University Press.

Fallers, L. A. (1955), 'The predicament of the modern African chief: an instance from Uganda', *American Anthropologist* LVII.

— (1965), *Bantu Bureaucracy: A Century of Political Evolution Among the Basoga of Uganda*. Chicago: University of Chicago Press.

Fleming, W. G. (1966), 'Authority, efficiency, and role stress: problems in the development of East African bureaucracies', *Administrative Science Quarterly* II.

Fortes, M. (1945), *The Dynamics of Clanship Among the Tallensi: Being the First Part of an Analysis of the Social Structure of a Trans–Volta Tribe*. London: Oxford University Press.

— (1948), 'The Ashanti social survey: a preliminary report', *Rhodes–Livingstone Journal* 6.

Fortes, M., and E. E. Evans-Pritchard, eds. (1961), *African Political Systems*. London: Oxford University Press.

Frampton, A. (1935), 'Notes on Egede District' (unpublished).

Gerth, H. H., and C. W. Mills, eds. and trans. (1958), *From Max Weber: Essays in Sociology*. New York: Oxford University Press.

Getzels, J. W., and E. G. Guba (1954), 'Role, role conflict, and effectiveness', *American Sociological Review* XIX.

Gluckman, M. (1961), 'The kingdom of the Zulu of South Africa', in *African Political Systems*, M. Fortes and E. E. Evans-Pritchard, eds. London: Oxford University Press.

— (1964), *Custom and Conflict in Africa*. New York: Barnes & Noble.

— (1965), *Politics, Law, and Ritual in Tribal Society*. Chicago: Aldine.

— (1968a), *Analysis of a Social Situation in Modern Zululand*. Manchester: Manchester University Press (Republication from *Bantu Studies*, 1940, and *African Studies*, 1942).

— (1968b), 'Inter-hierarchical roles: professional and party ethics in tribal areas in South and Central Africa', in *Local-Level Politics: Social and Cultural Perspectives*, M. Swartz, ed. Chicago: Aldine.

References

— (1969) 'The tribal area in South and Central Africa', in *Pluralism in Africa*, L. Kuper and M. G. Smith, eds. Berkeley: University of California Press.

— (1971), 'Tribalism, ruralism, and urbanism in South and Central Africa', in *Profiles of Change: African Society and Colonial Rule*, V. Turner, ed. Cambridge: Cambridge University Press.

Gluckman, M., ed. (1964), *Closed Systems and Open Minds: The Limits of Naivety in Social Anthropology*. Chicago: Aldine.

Gluckman, M. *et al.* (1949), 'The village headman in British Central Africa', *Africa* XIX.

Goffman, E. (1956), *The Presentation of Self in Everyday Life*. Edinburgh: University of Edinburgh Social Sciences Research Centre.

Goode, W. (1960), 'A theory of role strain', *American Sociological Review* XXV.

Great Britain. Colonial Office (1934), *Annual Report on the Social and Economic Progress of the People of Nigeria, 1933*. London: H.M.S.O.

— (1958), *Report of the Commission Appointed to Inquire into the Fears of Minorities and the Means of Allaying Them*. London: H.M.S.O.

Great Britain. House of Commons (1906), Cmd. 3620, in *Accounts and Papers: Colonies and British Possessions: Africa* LVII.

— (1945), *Proposals for the Revision of the Constitution of Nigeria*, Cmd. 6599. London: H.M.S.O.

Gross, N. *et al.* (1958), *Explorations in Role Analysis: Studies of the School Superintendency Role*. New York: Wiley.

Guilford, J. P. (1956), *Fundamental Statistics in Psychology and Education*. New York: McGraw-Hill.

Hanna, W. J., and J. L. Hanna (1967), 'The political structure of urban-centered African communities', in *The City in Modern Africa*, H. Miner, ed. New York: Praeger.

Heath, D. F. (*c.* 1940), 'African secret societies' (unpublished).

— (1941), 'Notes on Idoma Division' (unpublished).

Heidenheimer, A. J., ed. (1970), *Political Corruption: Readings in Comparative Analysis*. New York: Holt, Rinehart, and Winston.

Henderson, A. M., and T. Parsons, eds. and trans. (1947), *Max Weber: The Theory of Economic and Social Organization*. New York: Oxford University Press.

Heussler, R. (1968), *The British in Northern Nigeria*. London: Oxford University Press.

Hodgkin, T. (1961), *African Political Parties*. Baltimore: Penguin.

Homans, G. C. (1961), *Social Behavior: Its Elementary Forms*. New York: Harcourt, Brace, and World.

Hunter, F. (1953), *Community Power Structure*. Chapel Hill: University of North Carolina Press.

Idoma AG (refers to Action Group. Idoma Branch) (22 June 1957), 'Letter from Secretary to Premier, Northern Region of Nigeria' (unpublished).

Idoma Division (refers to Northern Nigeria. Benue Province. Idoma Division) (1935–50), 'Northern Area notes' (unpublished).

— (1939), 'Annual report' (unpublished).

— (May 1955), 'Guide for District Councils'. Zaria: Gaskiya.

— (6 August 1957), 'Letter from Idoma District Officer to Benue Province Resident' (unpublished).

Idoma Native Authority (refers to Northern Nigeria. Benue Province. Idoma Native Authority) (*c.* 1930s), 'Northern Area old district notebooks: Yangedde' (unpublished).

— (31 August 1931), 'Memorandum from Idoma Divisional Officer to Benue Province Resident on Idoma tribal and social organization' (unpublished).

— (23 May 1933), 'Memorandum from District Officer A. Frampton to Idoma Senior District Officer' (unpublished).

— (11 November 1933), 'Memorandum from Idoma Senior District Officer to Benue Province Resident' (unpublished).

— (April–May 1940), 'Proceedings of the Idoma Central Council' (unpublished).

— (*c.* 1950), 'Memorandum from Chief of Idoma to Senior District Officer' ('Dance guild file') (unpublished).

— (6 June 1957), 'Minutes of the Executive Meeting' (unpublished).

— (22 January 1958), 'Minutes of the Executive Meeting' (unpublished).

— (20 August 1958), 'Minutes of the Executive Meeting' (unpublished).

— (5 September 1958), 'Memorandum from Idoma Senior District Officer to Benue Province Resident'. No. G/COU. 1/3 (unpublished).

References

— (22 October 1960), 'Minutes of a special meeting of the Native Authority Executive'. Divisional Office No. GJ. 29/S.1 (unpublished).

— (1962–3), 'Census and Tax Assessment' (unpublished).

IHRU (refers to Idoma Hope Rising Union) (2 June 1956), 'Letter from President-General and Acting Secretary-General to Premier, Northern Region of Nigeria' (unpublished).

— (15 August 1957), 'Letter from General Secretary of Kwararrafa (Wukari) Congress to Secretary-General of Idoma Hope Rising Union' (unpublished).

Jacobson, E. *et al.* (1951), 'The use of the role concept in the study of complex organizations', *Journal of Social Issues* VII.

Kahn, R. *et al.* (1964), *Organizational Stress*. New York: Wiley.

Katz, E., and S. N. Eisenstadt (1960–1), 'Some sociological observations on the response of Israeli organizations to new immigrants', *Administrative Science Quarterly* V.

Kirk-Greene, A. H. M. (1958), *Adamawa Past and Present: An Historical Approach to the Development of a Northern Cameroons Province*. New York: Oxford University Press.

Kirk-Greene, A. H. M., ed. (1962), *Barth's Travels in Nigeria: Extracts from the Journals of Heinrich Barth's Travels in Nigeria, 1850–1855*. London: Oxford University Press.

Kothari, S., and R. Roy (1969), *Relations Between Politicians and Administrators at the Local Level*. New Delhi: Indian Institute of Public Administration and Centre of Applied Politics.

Kuper, H. (1947), *The Uniform of Color: A Study of White–Black Relationships in Swaziland*. Johannesburg: Witwatersrand University Press.

Laird, M., and Oldfield, R. A. K. (1837), *Narrative of an Expedition into the Interior of Africa by the Niger River . . . 1832, 1833, 1834*, vol. 1. London: Bentley.

Lasswell, H. D. (1960), *Psychopathology and Politics*. New York: Viking.

Last, M. (1970), 'Aspects of administration and dissent in Hausaland, 1800–1968', *Africa* XL.

Lerner, D. (1965), *The Passing of Traditional Society: Modernizing the Middle East*. New York: Free Press.

Leslie, S. A. S. (1936) 'Reorganization report for Yangedde District' (unpublished).

Linton, R. (1936), *The Study of Man*. New York: Appleton-Century.

Little, K. (1965–6), 'The political function of the Poro', *Africa* XXXV–XXXVI.

Lloyd, P. C. (1956), 'The changing role of the Yoruba traditional rulers', *Proceedings of the Third Annual Conference of the West African Institute of Social and Economic Research, Ibadan, Nigeria.*

Lugard, F. D. (1920), *Report on the Amalgamation of Northern and Southern Nigeria, and Administration, 1912–1919.* London: H.M.S.O.

— (1923), *The Dual Mandate in British Tropical Africa.* London: Blackwood.

— (1970), *Political Memoranda, 1913–1918.* London: Cass.

Mackintosh, J. P., ed. (1966), *Nigerian Government and Politics: Prelude to the Revolution.* Evanston, Ill.: Northwestern University Press.

Macleod, T. M. (n.d.), 'Report on the western areas of Okwoga Division' (unpublished).

Maddocks, K. P., and D. A. Pott (1951), *Local Government in the Northern Provinces of Nigeria.* Kaduna: Government Printer.

Magid, A. (1967), 'Dimensions of administrative role and conflict resolution among local officials in Nigeria', *Administrative Science Quarterly* XII.

— (1968), 'British rule and indigenous organization in Nigeria: a case-study in normative–institutional change', *Journal of African History* 9.

— (1969), 'Political science priorities in local African research', in *Research in Rural Africa*, N. Miller, ed. East Lansing: Canadian Journal of African Studies and the African Studies Center, Michigan State University.

— (1970), 'Methodological considerations in the study of African political and administrative behavior: the case of role conflict analysis', *African Studies Review* XIII.

— (1971), 'Minority politics in Northern Nigeria: the case of the Idoma Hope Rising Union', in *Nigeria: Modernization and the Politics of Communalism*, R. Melson and H. Wolpe, eds. East Lansing: Michigan State University Press.

— (1972), 'Political traditionalism in Nigeria: a case-study of secret societies and dance groups in local government', *Africa* XLII.

Mannoni, O. (1964), *Prospero and Caliban: The Psychology of Colonization.* New York: Praeger.

References

Mathews, A. B. (1933a), 'Anthropological investigations in Boju District' (unpublished).
— (1933b), 'Anthropological investigations in Oturkpo District' (unpublished).
— (1933c), 'Report on Yangedde District' (unpublished).
McMullan, M. (1961), 'A theory of corruption: based on a consideration of corruption in the public services and governments of British colonies and ex-colonies in West Africa', *Sociological Review* IX.
Mead, G. H. (1947), *Mind, Self, and Society*. Chicago: University of Chicago Press.
Meek, C. K. (1925), 'Anthropological notes on the Idoma' (unpublished).
— (1931), *A Sudanese Kingdom: An Ethnographical Survey of the Jukun-Speaking Peoples of Nigeria*. New York: Humanities.
Merton, R. K. (1957), 'The role-set: problems in sociological theory', *British Journal of Sociology* 8.
— (1961), *Social Theory and Social Structure*. Glencoe, Ill.: Free Press.
Middleton, J. (1971), 'Some effects of colonial rule among the Lugbara', in *Profiles of Change: African Society and Colonial Rule*, V. Turner, ed. Cambridge: Cambridge University Press.
Miller, D., and F. Shull (1962), 'The prediction of administrative role conflict resolutions', *Administrative Science Quarterly* 7.
Mitchell, J. C. (1949), 'The political organization of the Yao of southern Nyasaland', *African Studies* 8.
— (1956), *'The Yao Village: A Study in the Social Structure of a Nyasaland Tribe*. Manchester: Manchester University Press.
Mockler-Ferryman, A. F. (n.d.), *British Africa*. London: Cassell.
— (1892), *Up the Niger: A Narrative of Major Claude Macdonald's Mission to the Niger and Benue Rivers, West Africa*. London: Philip.
Monckton, J. C. (1927–8), 'Burial ceremonies of the Attah of Igala', *Journal of the African Society* XXVII.
Money, G. D. C. (1935a), 'Notes on procedure in Idoma Division' (unpublished).
— (1935b), 'Reorganization report for Oturkpo District' (unpublished)
Morton-Williams, P. (1960), 'The Yoruba Ogboni cult in Oyo', *Africa* XXX.

279

Munshi Province (refers to Northern Nigeria. Munshi Province) (30 June 1919), 'Half-year report for Okwoga District' (unpublished).
— (31 December 1919), 'Half-year report for Okwoga District' (unpublished).
— (1920), 'Annual report for Okwoga District' (unpublished).
— (30 June 1922), 'Half-year report for Okwoga District' (unpublished).
— (31 December 1922), 'Half-year report for Okwoga District' (unpublished).
— (1923), 'Annual report for Okwoga District' (unpublished).
— (c. 1925), 'General and assessment report for Okwoga Division' (unpublished).
Nadel, S. F. (1954), *Nupe Religion*. London: Routledge & Kegan Paul.
— (1957), *The Theory of Social Structure*. Glencoe, Ill.: Free Press.
National Conference on Local Government (1969), *The Future of Local Government in Nigeria*. Ife, Nigeria: University of Ife Press.
Neiman, L. J., and J. W. Hughes (1951), 'The problem of the concept of role – a re-survey of the literature', *Social Forces* XXX.
Nigeria (1917), *Laws: Order-in-Council No. 11*. Lagos: Government Printer.
— (1962), *Report of the Coker Commission of Inquiry into the Affairs of Certain Statutory Corporations in Western Nigeria*, 4 vols. Lagos: Government Printer.
Nigerian Citizen (1956), 19, 25, 28 January; 4, 15, 22, 25 February; 3, 17, 28, 31 March.
Nisbet, R. (1969), *Social Change and History: Aspects of the Western Theory of Development*. London: Oxford University Press.
Northern House of Assembly (refers to Northern Nigeria. House of Assembly) (5 August 1958), *Debates*, vol. 5, No. 21.
— (10 December 1958), *Debates*, vol. 5, No. 23.
Northern MLG (refers to Northern Nigeria. Ministry for Local Government) (3 March 1958). *The Idoma Native Authority District Councils Instruments, 1958*. Kaduna: Government Printer.
— (1961), *Native Authority Law of 1954*. Kaduna: Government Printer.
— (19 April 1962), 'The Idoma Native Authority District Councils Instruments, 1962', *Gazette*, vol. XI, supplement E.

References

— (12 September 1962), *Duties of Councillors*. Circular No. MLG. 42/82.

Northern Nigeria (1954), *Report on the Exchange of Customary Presents*. Kaduna: Government Printer.

Park, R. E. (1928), 'Human migration and the marginal man', *American Journal of Sociology* XXXIII.

— (1941), 'The social function of war', *American Journal of Sociology* XLVI.

Parsons, T. (1959), *The Social System*. Glencoe, Ill.: Free Press.

Perham, M. (1931), 'The system of native administration in Tanganyika', *Africa* IV.

— (1934a), 'A restatement of indirect rule', *Africa* VII.

— (1934b), 'Problems of indirect rule', *East Africa*.

— (1956), *Lugard*, 2 vols. London: Collins.

— (1962), *Native Administration in Nigeria*. London: Oxford University Press.

Post, K. W. J. (1963), *The Nigerian Federal Election of 1959: Politics and Administration in a Developing Political System*. New York: Oxford University Press.

Preiss, J., and H. J. Ehrlich (1966), *An Examination of Role Theory: The Case of the State Police*. Lincoln: University of Nebraska Press.

Radcliffe-Brown, A. R. (1961), *Structure and Function in Primitive Society*. Glencoe, Ill.: Free Press.

Redfield, R. (1963), *The Little Community and Peasant Society and Culture*. Chicago, Ill.: University of Chicago Press.

Richards, A. I., ed. (1960), *East African Chiefs: A Study of Political Development in Some Uganda and Tanganyika Tribes*. New York: Praeger.

Richards, A. I., and A. Kuper, eds. (1971), *Councils in Action*. Cambridge: Cambridge University Press.

Riggs, F. W. (1964), 'The ambivalence of feudalism and bureaucracy in traditional societies', paper delivered at the Annual Meeting of the American Political Science Association, Chicago, Illinois.

Rowley, C. D. (1965), *The New Guinea Villager: A Retrospect from 1964*. Melbourne: Cheshire.

Rudolph, L. I., and S. H. Rudolph (1969), *The Modernity of Tradition: Political Development in India*. Chicago, Ill.: University of Chicago Press.

Ruel, M. (1969), *Leopards and Leaders: Constitutional Politics*

Among a Cross River People. London: Tavistock.

Sarbin, T. (1959), 'Role theory', in G. Lindzey, ed. *Handbook of Social Psychology*, vol. 1. Reading, Mass.: Addison-Wesley.

Seeman, M. (1953), 'Role conflict and ambivalence in leadership', *American Sociological Review* XVIII.

Selznick, P. (1957), *Leadership in Administration.* New York: Harper & Row.

Shaw, J. H. (1934), 'Reorganization report for Ochekwu District' (unpublished).

Shils, E. (1960), 'The intellectuals in the development of the new States', *World Politics* XII.

Siegel, S. (1956), *Non-parametric Statistics for the Behavioral Sciences.* New York: McGraw-Hill.

Simmel, G. (1964), 'Conflict', in *Conflict and the Web of Group-Affiliations*, K. Wolff and R. Bendix, eds. New York: Free Press.

Skinner, E. P. (1963), 'Strangers in West African societies', *Africa* XXXIII.

Sklar, R. L. (1963), *Nigerian Political Parties: Power in an Emergent African Nation.* Princeton, N.J.: Princeton University Press.

— (1966), 'Nigerian politics: the ordeal of Chief Awolowo, 1960–1965', in *Politics in Africa*, G. Carter, ed. New York: Harcourt, Brace, and World.

— (1971), 'Nigerian politics in perspective', in *Nigeria: Modernization and the Politics of Communalism*, R. Melson and H. Wolpe. eds. East Lansing: Michigan State University Press.

Smith, J. N. (1931), 'Idoma tribal and social organization' (unpublished).

Smith, M. G. (1956) 'On segmentary lineage systems', *Journal of the Royal Anthropological Institute of Great Britain and Ireland* LXXXVI.

— (1960), *Government in Zazzau.* London: Oxford University Press.

Southall, A. (1967), 'Kampala-Mengo', in *The City in Modern Africa*, H. Miner, ed. New York: Praeger.

Southwold, M. (1964), 'Leadership, authority and the village community', in *The King's Men: Leadership and Status in Buganda on the Eve of Independence*, L. Fallers, ed. London: Oxford University Press.

Spiegel, J. (1957), 'The resolution of conflict within the family', *Psychiatry* XX.

References

Steiner, K. (1955), 'The Japanese village and its government', *Far Eastern Quarterly* 15.

Stinchcombe, A. (1968), *Constructing Social Theories*. New York: Harcourt, Brace, and World.

Stonequist, E. V. (1935), 'The problem of the marginal man', *American Journal of Sociology* XLI.

Sutcliffe, J. P., and M. Haberman (1956), 'Factors influencing choice in role conflict situations', *American Sociological Review* XXI.

Talbot, P. A. (1926), *The Peoples of Southern Nigeria*, vol. 1. London: Oxford University Press.

Temple, O., and C. L. Temple (1922), *Tribes, Provinces, Emirates, and States of the Northern Provinces of Nigeria: Compiled from Official Reports*. Lagos, Nigeria: Church Missionary Society Bookshop.

Thibaut, J., and H. Kelley (1959), *The Social Psychology of Groups*. New York: Wiley.

Toby, J. (1952), 'Some variables in role conflict analysis', *Social Forces* XXX.

Turner, R. H. (1947), 'The navy disbursing officer as a bureaucrat', *American Sociological Review* XII.

— (1956), 'Role-taking, role standpoint, and reference-group behavior', *American Journal of Sociology* LXI.

Turner, V. W. (1966), 'Ritual aspects of conflict control in African micropolitics', in *Political Anthropology*, M. J. Swartz *et al.*, eds. Chicago: Aldine.

Uganda (1961), *Report of the Uganda Relationships Commission*. Entebbe: Government Printer.

UMBC (refers to United Middle Belt Congress. Idoma Branch) (12 May 1956), 'Letter from General Secretary to Minister for Local Government, Northern Region of Nigeria' (unpublished).

Van Velsen, J. (1964), *The Politics of Kinship: A Study in Social Manipulation Among the Lakeside Tonga of Nyasaland*. Manchester: Manchester University Press.

Wallace, J. G. (1958), 'The Tiv system of election', *Journal of African Administration* 10.

Ward, R. E. (1955), 'Village government in Eastern and Southern Asia: a symposium', *Far Eastern Quarterly* 15.

Wardwell, W. I. (1955), 'The reduction of strain in a marginal social role', *American Journal of Sociology* LXI.

Men in the middle

Watson, W. (1958), Tribal Cohesion in a Money Economy: A Study of the Mambwe People of Northern Rhodesia. Manchester: Manchester University Press.

West, F. J. (1961), Political Advancement in the South Pacific: A Comparative Study of Colonial Practice in Fiji, Tahiti and American Samoa. Melbourne: Oxford University Press.

Wheeldon, P. D. (1969), 'The operation of voluntary associations and personal networks in the political process of an inter-ethnic community', in Social Networks in Urban Situations: Analyses of Personal Relationships in Central African Towns. J. C. Mitchell, ed. Manchester: Manchester University Press.

Whitaker, C. S., jr. (1967), 'A dysrhythmic process of political change', World Politics 19.

— (1970), The Politics of Tradition: Continuity and Change in Northern Nigeria, 1946–1966. Princeton, N.J.: Princeton University Press.

Whyte, W. F. (1964), 'The slum: on the evolution of street-corner society', in Reflections on Community Studies, A. J. Vidich et al., eds. New York: Wiley.

Wilson, G., and M. Wilson (1945), The Analysis of Social Change: Based on Observations in Central Africa. Cambridge: Cambridge University Press.

Wolff, K., ed. and trans. (1967), The Sociology of Georg Simmel. Glencoe, Ill.: Free Press.

Wolfinger, R. (1960), 'Reputation and reality in the study of "Community Power" ', American Sociological Review XXV.

Wraith, R. E. (3 September 1955), 'Local government and democracy, I, Intention and achievement'. West Africa.

— (1964), Local Government in West Africa. New York: Praeger.

Wraith, R. E. (3 September 1955), 'Local government and democracy, I, Intention and achievement', West Africa.

Wright, D. B. (1934), 'Report on the Oglewu and Ochobu clans' (unpublished).

— (1936), 'Anthropological investigations in Oglewu District' (unpublished).

Young, M. W. (1966), 'The divine kingship of the Jukun: a re-evaluation of some theories', Africa XXXVI.

Index

Index

Communal labour 58, 129, 132, 239–40, 247

Cooley, C. H. 13 note 7

Corruption in District Council election campaigns, 101–11; and generosity, 101–10; in Idoma, 50 note 12, 56 note 20, 157 note 4, 168 note 7; in Western Region, 73

Coser, L. 17, 18

Cottrell, L. S., Jr. 115

Cowan, L. G. 2 note 1, 51, 97, 101

Crocker, W. R. 44, 46, 48 note 10

Crowder, M. 2 note 1

Crowther, S. 26, 29, 41

Cunnison, I. 2 note 1

Dahl, R. A. 121, 123 note 11, 199

Dance groups backdrop to situations of role conflict, 154–69; in local government and politics, 78, 154–5, 157–8; official ambivalence towards, 155–6; popular ambivalence towards, 158; in social and recreational life, 33, 77–8, 154, 156–7

Denham, R. S. 28

Dent, M. J. 228

District Council fund backdrop to situations of role conflict, 133–45

District councillors ages of, 63–4; appointment as, 110–11; associational activities and traditional offices of, 76–8; education and language competence of, 66–7; election of, 87–110; media exposure, political information and political perspectives of, 70–6; personal profiles of, 79–84; religion of, 65–6; residence of, 64–5; tenure in office of, 62–3; travel experience of, 69–70; work experience and economic status of, 67–9

District Councils functions of, 11, 21, 58–9, 129–31, 133–5; organisation of, 127–31; recruitment to, 62, 85–112, 260

District headship backdrop to situations of role conflict, 169–82

District Officer 41–8, 53, 55 note 17, 56, 118, 134, 155–6, 171 note 11

Dollard, J. 123, 228

Dudley, B. J. 77 note 18, 96, 97

Duverger, M. 77

Eaton, R. M. 119

Echi dance group 81, 162, 166

Eckstein, H. 250

Egede 20, 55, 67, 68 note 7, 83, 243, 244

Ehrlich, H. J. 119 note 7, 123, 250 note 4, 251

Eisenstadt, S. N. 10, 39 note 16

Elliott, H. 27, 34, 36, 37, 38

Epstein, A. L. 2 note 1

Erasmus, C. J. 172 note 13

Evans-Pritchard, E. E. 13, 37

Ezera, K. 49 note 11, 73 note 15

Fallers, L. A. 2 note 1, 4, 13, 14 note 8, 15, 121

Fisher exact probability test 225 note 13

Fleming, W. G. 2 note 1

Fortes, M. 2 note 1, 32 note 7, 37, 76 note 17, 94 note 7, 173 note 14

Frampton, A. 55 note 18

Generosity and corruption, 101–10, 112, 258; in District Council election campaigns, 91, 101–10

Gerth, H. H. 4

Getzels, J. W. 119, 120, 123, 124

Gluckman, M. 2 note 1, 3, 4, 9, 13, 16, 84, 119 note 7, 253

Goffman, E. 123

Goode, W. 18 note 10, 121

Gross, N. 12, 114, 115, 121, 250

Guba, E. G. 119, 120, 123, 124

Guilford, J. P. 203

Haberman, M. 251

Hanna, J. L. 2 note 1

Index

Hanna, W. J. 2 note 1
Hausa-Fulani 26-8, 32, 37, 40, 43, 45, 50 note 10, 53, 67, 70, 72, 79, 82, 138, 244
Headhunting 42, 43, 77, 83, 155
Heath, D. F. 44, 48, 156
Heidenheimer, A. J. 101
Henderson, A. M. 4
Heussler, R. 9
Hodgkin, T. 77
Homans, G. C. 114 note 1
Hughes, J. W. 12
Hunter, F. 199

Ibo 28 note 3, 50 note 11, 67, 70, 72, 79, 83 note 23, 135 note 9, 148, 151
Ichahoho dance group 162, 166
Idoma 7, 19, 20, 27; age groups in, 36, 78, 80; ancestral cult in, 31, 34-5, 211-12; chieftaincy disputes in, 21, 32, 35-9, 42, 169-82; clan head and clan spokesmen in, 37-8; under colonial rule, 6-8, 11-12, 15-19, 40-54, 85-112, 133-5, 145-8, 154-9, 169-71, 243-50; compound family in, 30-1; constitutional polity in, 21, 35-9; co-operative societies in, 76-7; culture, cosmology, and social structure in, 30-5; democratic assembly in, 21, 36; in early independence period, 6-8, 11-12, 15-19, 55-9, 85-112, 133-5, 145-8, 154-9, 169-71, 243-50; earth cult in, 31, 34; generational conflict in, 39, 189; gerontocracy in, 21, 31, 36; ideal of unity in, 19, 35-6, 76, 98-9, 131; ideology of chieftaincy in, 37, 173, 180-1, 244, 256-7; 'Idoma proper,' 19-20, 26; kinship factor in District Council affairs, 85-112, 248-50; land (clan) in, 32; language in, 29-30; market-master, hamlet heads and constabulary in, 38-9; marriage in, 31; natural

environment and economy of, 30; origins and early history of, 26-9; population of, 20; ritual sanction in, 33, 158, 211-12; rotation principle in, 38, 55; secret societies and dance groups in, 39, 154-9; seniority principle in, 31, 38; sublineage and lineage in, 31; supreme being in, 34, 212; totemism in, 28; traditional law in, 33, 37, 39; uterine 'strangers' in, 32, 64-5; women's role in, 33
Idoma constitutionalism versus strong chieftaincy and Native Authority centralisation, 8, 11, 16-19, 21, 56-9, 87ff., 242-9, 255-6
Idoma Division creation of, 41-2
Idoma Hope Rising Union (IHRU) 29, 50, 53-4, 57, 80, 81, 86, 95-8, 102 note 15, 139 note 13, 145-7, 170, 244-5
'Idoma Magazine' 72, 83
Idoma Native Authority administrative departments in, 48; Advisory Council in, 48-52; Central Council in, 44-5, 47, 48; Chief of Idoma in, 48-50; Circuit Courts in, 53; District Councils in, 52; district heads in, 43, 45; General Purposes Committee in, 52; police in, 130; portfolio councillors in, 52; Representative Council in, 52; tax collectors in, 58; treasury in, 56
Igala 20, 26 note 1, 28-9, 35-7, 67, 70
Ikime, O. 2 note 1
Indirect rule 9, 40-54
Inter-hierarchical positions or roles 3, 6 note 3
Interviewing 258-9, 268-9
Islam 65-7, 97

Jacobson, E. 115, 119
Jukun 26-9, 37, 135 note 8

Kahn, R. 120, 124 note 12

287

Index

Index

Role perception in situations of role conflict, 136–45, 149–53, 159–69, 172–82

Role sanction 22; definition, 120–2, 125; in hypotheses, 125, 221; profiles of, 215–22; and role ambivalence, 125, 215–22; in situations of role conflict, 137; typologies for, 121, 209–15, 251–2

Role theory xi, 249–50

Rowley, C. D. 21 note 13, 168 note 7, 229 note 15

Roy, R. 114

Rudolph, L. I. 84

Rudolph, S. H. 84

Ruel, M. 154

Sarbin, T. 12

Secret societies backdrop to situations of role conflict, 154–69; in local government and politics, 78, 154–5, 157–8; official ambivalence towards, 155–6; popular ambivalence towards, 158; in social and recreational life, 33, 77–8, 154, 156–7

Seeman, M. 120

Selznick, P. 10

Shaw, J. H. 27, 37, 38

Shils, E. 80

Shull, F. 251

Siegel, S. 184, 193

Simmel, G. 13 note 7

Simpkins, E. 101

Single-clan districts 43, 46–7, 170 note 10, 171 note 12, 176, 179, 180

Skinner, E. P. 32 note 8

Sklar, R. L. 23, 73 note 15, 74, 77 note 18, 81, 97

Smith, J. N. 36

Smith, M. G. 40

Social theory 22–3, 114, 168 note 6, 249–51

Southall, A. 2 note 1

Southwold, M. 2 note 1, 15

Spearman rank correlation coefficient 193

Spiegel, J. 119, 123

Steiner, K. 92 note 5

Stinchcombe, A. 114

Stonequist, E. V. 79

Sutcliffe, J. P. 251

Talbot, P. A. 26 note 1

Temple, C. L. 155

Temple, O. 155

Thibaut, J. 114 note 1, 120 note 8

Thomas, E. J. 12

Tiv 28, 41, 42 note 6, 67, 70, 93 note 6, 108 note 19, 172 note 13, 228–9, 237, 239, 245–6, 268–9

Toby, J. 123

Turner, R. H. 10, 116

Turner, V. W. 256

Ukpabi, Chief Ajene xi, 55–6, 74 note 16, 75, 83, 94, 118, 138, 169, 244–5, 261

United Middle Belt Congress (UMBC) 97, 102 note 15

United People's Party (UPP) 73–4

Van Velsen, J. 2 note 1, 253

Wallace, J. G. 108 note 19, 172 note 13

Ward, R. E. 249 note 3

Wardwell, W. I. 123

Watson, W. 2 note 1

West, F. J. 21 note 13

Western Region emergency 73, 83

Wheeldon, P. D. 123

Whitaker, C. S., Jr. 2 note 1, 84

Whyte, W. F. 267 note 1

Wilson, G. 2 note 1

Wilson, M. 2 note 1

Wolff, K. 17, 168 note 6

Wolfinger, R. 199

Wraith, R. E. 51, 97, 101

Wright, D. B. 27, 34, 156

Yangedde district xi, 20, 32, 38, 62, 70

Fig. 1. Structure of role relationships between district councillor and audiences

Fig. 2. Resolution reported by district councillors in Situation *1a*, and resolution predicted from legitimacy, obligation, and legitimacy and obligation combined. Cells are lettered to facilitate discussion in the text

Map 1. The Federal Republic of Nigeria. Idoma Division in Benue-Plateau State is shaded

Map 2. Area occupied by Idoma-speaking peoples. Solid lines indicate boundaries of Nigeria States; broken lines indicate crescent-shaped area occupied by Idoma-speaking peoples

Map 3. Administrative districts in Idoma Division, showing the administrative centre of Idoma Division at Oturkpo Town (after Armstrong (1955))

Map 4. The Jukun (or Kororofa) Empire, late fifteenth to early seventeenth century. Centres of Kororofa power were at Wukari and Kororofa Town in Jukun territory. The arrows indicate the extent of the Empire at the height of its power